PRACTICAL DIVINITY

PRACTICAL DIVINITY

Theology
in the
Wesleyan
Tradition

THOMAS A. LANGFORD

ABINGDON PRESS o NASHVILLE

PRACTICAL DIVINITY: Theology in the Wesleyan Tradition

Copyright © 1983 by Abingdon Press

Library of Congress Cataloging in Publication Data

LANGFORD, THOMAS A.
  Practical divinity.
  Includes bibliographcal references and index.
  1. Theology, Methodist—History. I. Title.
  BX8331.2.L36   1983   230'.7'09   82-20653

ISBN 0-687-33326-1

MANUFACTURED BY THE PARTHENON PRESS AT
NASHVILLE, TENNESSEE, UNITED STATES OF AMERICA

PREFACE

THIS BOOK is an introduction and an invitation. Introducing a theological tradition that is seldom considered in its entire breadth and continuing vitality, it issues an invitation for interested persons to go beyond this initial presentation to more detailed study.

The title, *Practical Divinity*, originated with John Wesley. The words describe his understanding of the nature and purpose of theology. The use of *Wesleyan Tradition* is the result of much discussion and serious consideration. This phrase was chosen in an attempt to indicate the inner life of the tradition and emphasize the theological core of this movement. The term does not refer to specific ecclesiastical structures within Methodism, such as Wesleyan Methodism in Great Britain or the Wesleyan Church in the United States, nor is it intended to exclude important parts of the movement, such as the Evangelical United Brethren. The word *Methodist* was not used because of its denominational denotations, although this is not an altogether happy decision, since *Methodist* may be a synonym for *Wesleyan*. The decision was made principally in order to root the tradition in John Wesley and to trace his influence among those who are his heirs.

The primary effort of this study is to present the thought of persons and of theological trends with accuracy and fairness. The connections drawn among these thinkers represent one way to depict diverse and often unconscious relationships. The chief goal is to be as inclusive as a reasonable structure will allow and as specific as space and movement will permit. One basic decision needs to be made clear: Only those theologians who have written enough to provide adequate material for general characterization have been discussed.

This volume is an effort to bring the sweep and dynamics of the Wesleyan tradition to the attention of a wide audience. Description, not criticism, has been the primary intention. Thorough assessments of many of the theologians discussed, of the multiple trends in Wesleyan theology, and of the relation of this tradition to developments in other traditions are necessary and ongoing tasks, which, it is hoped, this introduction will help to stimulate.

All scholarship is indebted to various predecessors and contemporaries. A wide-ranging survey such as this is especially dependent upon many focused studies and monographs to provide detailed investigation of specific individuals, eras, and themes. I am conscious of indebtedness to many creative theologians and historical interpreters.

I wish to thank two individuals—Paul M. Bassett and Grant Wacker—who have generously reviewed the entire text. I especially thank my son, Thomas A. Langford, III, who has contributed to the research, discussed ideas, and made stylistic suggestions. Other persons have helpfully commented on parts of the text: Charles W. Brockwell, Jr., Dennis M. Campbell, Robert E. Cushman, Richard P. Heitzenrater, Creighton Lacy, Helmut Nausner, and McMurry S. Richey. To all these, I am indebted.

CONTENTS

CHAPTER 1

A LIVING TRADITION

A TRADITION is a stream through history. A stream may have neat clear banks, or it may flow across boundaries and be difficult to trace. Some streams seem to remain pure and carry their original water from source to estuary; others continually acquire new content and become mixtures from many springs. The headwaters of some streams are easy to locate, but others are almost impossible to discover. As with streams, so with traditions.

A historical stream is a tradition insofar as it possesses dominant characteristics and conveys an enduring sense of meaning. Tradition releases an inner pulsation that is felt, known by, and shapes those related to it, even if the basic awareness is not fully explicable. Tradition is organic. Staccato-paced sequential events do not, as such, make a cohesive, persisting movement. Traditions, connections of sense and sensibility, tie the past to the present and point, with tentative possibility, to the future. The effort of this book is to explore organic structure, distinctive characteristics, and

11

continuing vitality of the stream of Christian witness to which John Wesley gave impetus.

The Wesleyan movement is one stream in Christian history. Its point of origin is clear and its dominant current can be traced rather well. But the stream does not have neat boundaries. It divides and sometimes flows together again; it often takes on the coloration of the terrain through which it has passed; it experiences expansion and contraction. But through its many changes there have persisted qualities derived from its original source.

There is a tradition through which the spirit of John Wesley continues. Wesley could not have guessed the issue of his work; and he probably would react with surprise, satisfaction, or chagrin at the resulting currents. But he gave propulsion to a stream that has continued to the present.

Within the Holy, Catholic, Apostolic Church

John Wesley was keenly aware of his heritage in the whole Christian tradition. He was rooted in Scripture as the primary witness to the Creatorship of God, the Lordship of Jesus, and the sustaining presence of the Holy Spirit. Wesley's *Christian Library*, a collection of sources in Christian thought extending from the early church to his own time, partially indicates the range of his interests and the literature he believed was important for his followers. In this collection, as well as in his extensive editing, he included writings from widely different eras and areas of Christendom, indicating his indebtedness to an impressive array of predecessors. He prized the earliest church; he read Eastern preachers and theologians; he cared for the Roman Catholic spiritual tradition; and he was receptive to the example of the saints.

Wesley's own history was set in England in the western tradition of the Christian church, refracted through the Reformation and given specific form by the Church of

England. But he always retained extended sympathies. To place his movement within the context of the Universal Church is both historically and theologically correct. This is the necessary point of beginning.

A new tradition began with John Wesley; a specific history grew from English origins to spread across the British world and then around the globe. This was an evangelizing movement that regarded the proclamation of the gospel as its primary task. This was an ordering movement that set goals of spiritual maturity for its followers. This was a serving movement that brought new claims of moral responsibility and new visions of hope.

Tradition does matter, because tradition deals with human history concretely formed and distinctively shaped. Tradition is the formation of the Body of Christ in a specific history; tradition is the actual development of institution and persons, with their beauty and blemishes, their faith and failure, their bricks and blood. So the Wesleyan tradition is important, in its concrete actuality, for those who have been influenced by it.

The Wesleyan tradition has been built upon the foundation of John Wesley's sermons and biblical commentaries, "our doctrines"; has given moral shape to Christian life, "our discipline"; has sung the hymns of Charles Wesley, "our hymns"; and has studied Wesley's other writings and edited works, "our literature." These resources have given rise to dynamic life. Through continuity and change, the Wesleyan tradition has represented an ongoing reality as a part of the "Holy, Catholic, Apostolic Church."

Beginnings

The Wesleyan tradition had its beginnings in John Wesley (1703-1791). The genius of Wesley was expressed in his spirit; he was indomitable in his desire to love God first of all and to love his neighbor through Christlike service. This spirit propelled Wesley's revival movement and has been a sustaining power for his followers.

From his early life in Epworth through his school years, Wesley was devout and studious. He was a natural leader with firm commitments. At Oxford a group was gathered, and distinctive characteristics developed: exact discipline, liturgical rigorousness, and visitation of prisons. The members of this small, covenantal community supported, criticized, and encouraged one another in spiritual development. Generally ridiculed, the group was derided as The Holy Club, the Bible Moths, and the Methodists. The last name finally became fixed upon Wesley and his colleagues as a reproach. Nevertheless, from this beginning the Wesleyan, or Methodist, tradition began to grow. Many members of the original student group were transient, but one remained faithful—John's younger brother Charles (1707–1788). These brothers in the flesh became brothers in faith and common mission.

The early period of John Wesley's life was marked by unusual moral seriousness and disciplined piety. In 1725 he found new depth in the "holy living" tradition of Jeremy Taylor, a seventeenth-century English theologian, and placed great stress on moral achievement and personal religious endeavor. Then with the question of vocation pressing, the brothers volunteered for mission work among the Anglicans in Georgia: John served as a minister; Charles, also ordained, as private secretary to General James Oglethorpe. But their time in the New World was disappointing, and the growth that did take place was thoroughly agonizing. The brothers did not understand themselves well, and they understood the people they served almost not at all. They lacked sensitivity to common modes of life; they were overly wrought in their spiritual searching; they worked ineffectively with the settlers; they were unable to evangelize the Indians. Frustration brought retreat. Charles quickly returned to England and John soon followed.

On the voyage to America, a group of Moravians had impressed John with their possession of an assurance of their salvation. As they interrogated him about his own religious convictions, especially about his personal knowledge of Jesus Christ as his Savior, Wesley became distressed. He was uncertain whether he had had an experience such as they described. This concern, once created, continued while he was in Georgia, and upon his return to London he sought out the Moravian community. There Peter Böhler questioned and advised Wesley about his personal faith, further exciting the seeker's troubled spirit.

Wesley studied the doctrine of justification by grace through faith. This doctrine, he became convinced, was a faithful explication of scriptural teaching and was, as a matter of fact, being realized in the lives of others. On May 21, 1738, Charles underwent a "conversion." John's experience soon followed. The climactic moment came on May 24. Wesley described the occasion in his *Journal:*

> In the evening I went very unwillingly to a society in Aldersgate Street, where one was reading Luther's preface to the Romans. About a quarter before nine, while he was describing a change which God works in the heart through faith in Christ, I felt my heart strangely warmed. I felt I did trust in Christ, Christ alone for salvation; and an assurance was given me that He had taken away *my* sin, even *mine*, and saved *me* from the law of sin and death.[1]

With a group of friends, John went to Charles' lodgings, and together they rejoiced and sang a hymn Charles may have written the day before.

> Where shall my wondering soul begin?
> How shall I all to heaven aspire?
> A slave redeemed from death and sin,

15

A brand plucked from eternal fire,
How shall I equal triumphs raise,
Or sing my great deliverer's praise?

What John Wesley had experienced, he felt compelled to share: He was to proclaim this good news to everyone in every place; he was to "spread scriptural holiness over the land." Experimenting, adapting, risking failure, and meeting opposition, Wesley undertook his ministry afresh.

Strong leaders are seldom easy companions. Driven by a special sense of mission, such people move toward their goals with consuming intensity. John Wesley was such a leader. Surprisingly unconcerned about himself, he marked a path discovered only by tenacious and dangerous exploration. He was willing—indeed he desired—to expend himself and others for his mission. Everything was ordered for the sake of that enterprise. Personal life was arranged by its demands; corporate life was structured to serve its goals. Christian people were a community in mission, people on the way; and Wesley was compulsive in his drive, utterly disciplined by his task, disregarding smaller matters. He was never a relaxed companion; his affection and attention were beyond personal interest. His eye scanned large horizons. He traveled his own way, and others could follow . . . or not.

The goal was clear: to evangelize his nation. Compelled to share the gospel, he did so with immense energy. The impact of the renewal movement was extraordinary. John Wesley's career was, according to a Victorian writer, one of "unsefulness and locomotion."[2] He crisscrossed the country as he moved from Bristol to London to Oxford, then to Bath and Leicester, to Nottingham and Newcastle, and later to the reaches of Cornwall, Scotland, Wales, and Ireland. Traveling and preaching, he aroused the nation. "What Wesley did," one writer commented, "was to blow up the still living sparks into flame, to make all England glow as a furnace."[3]

16

The movement gained momentum as persons from all walks of life were captured by its fervor. Leadership came from priests of the Church of England—William Grimshaw of Haworth and Vincent Perronet of Shoreham. And it came also from a rich variety of others: John Nelson, a stonemason from Birstall; George Story, a printer and publisher; Alexander Mather, a baker; Thomas Oliver, a cobbler; John Cennick, a schoolmaster.

There were also opponents. From the beginning, detractors challenged the movement. By the mid-1740s some spoke of the "world against Methodism," and the force of the rejection was potent. With written ridicule and mob violence, the opposition attacked. Even a brief description is shocking: "In 1749 William Steward was first blinded, and then killed by a Welsh mob, the first but not the last Methodist martyr. Many of the preachers were pelted, beaten, stamped on, kicked, stripped, thrown into ponds, dragged along the ground by their hair, drenched with water from fire-hoses, gored by bulls, tarred and feathered."[4]

Theological controversy arose also with the revival movement. Disputes over such doctrines as predestination and human freedom separated evangelical compatriots. Wesley and George Whitefield, a friend from Oxford days and a premier evangelist of the era, moved apart. John Cennick and Lady Huntingdon affirmed Calvinist positions and not only parted from the Wesleys but soon broke with the established church.

In spite of opposition and internal conflict, the Wesleyan movement soon took distinctive shape. Newly formed mission life and a characteristic message developed. Organization of ways to share the gospel and nurture persons in Christian life was directed by concrete experience. "Societies" were formed—large groups that assembled regularly for preaching and spiritual instruction; "classes" were organized—small gatherings of about twelve persons who met for counsel, collection of weekly contributions, and personal testimony; even smaller "bands" of four or five were encouraged for closer spiritual direction. The intention of these arrangements was to introduce the participants to saving faith and, through discipline, to bring faith to fruition.

Wesley sensed a mandate to reach the mass of people who were unchurched and had not heard the gospel. From Oxford days he had ministered to those who were beyond the pale of the church, and when George Whitefield pressed him to begin preaching outside church buildings, he agreed, although with some trepidation. On Monday, April 2, 1739, Wesley undertook his first field preaching. The text for this occasion was "The Spirit of the Lord is upon me, because he hath anointed me to preach the gospel to the poor." The first step felt firm and one new possibility led to others. It was as though Wesley had crossed a ridge beyond which a fresh panorama appeared. He became an inveterate preacher, and resolute opposition could not prevent him from reaching the people and talking of God.

At that time, England was going through a period of population displacement from rural communities to manufacturing centers, cities where life was debased by "ignorance, squalor, and the habits of gin-drinking."[5] The work of John Wesley, Sir Herbert Butterfield remarks, was an important factor for the people in the cities, "the most brutalized section of the population."[6] In politics and economics, as well as in social conditions, England was undergoing rapid change, and John Wesley was a part of and influenced that change.

The relationship of any single movement to the total society, especially in a time of momentous change, is exceedingly complex. Wesley himself was aware of the tragic maladjustments that accompanied the Industrial Revolution. He was disturbed by bleak poverty, and he attempted personal and institutional reforms to help the poor and

imprisoned. He instituted educational and economic oppor-
tunities. He defended widows and opposed slavery. Though
he was never a revolutionary, John Wesley's concern was for
the people who were most maligned by the established
order.[7] He felt the poor had a special right to hear the gospel
and, for the most part, did not seek out or attempt to
evangelize the upper classes. For instance, Wesley did not
establish a single Methodist preaching post in any of the five
most privileged boroughs of London. He worked with those
in special need, and among the people he sought to serve, the
movement developed rapidly.

The Wesleyan revival became a wave that would move
across England, sweep over borders into Wales, Scotland,
and Ireland, extend across the Atlantic into Nova Scotia, the
other North American colonies, and to the Caribbean islands.
Dominated by a sense of evangelistic mission, both under
Wesley's direction and moving beyond his control, men and
women carried the message, organized classes, engaged in
works of charity, and withal, continued the Wesleyan
mission. "The life of John Wesley," George C. Cell, an
American interpreter, states, "spans the eighteenth century;
his constructive influence, the modern world."[8]

The cause had content. There was a message to be
proclaimed, a word to be heard. Wesley preached a theology
of grace—and he intended to interpret grace faithfully. He
was adamant about central truths. Yet he also exhibited an
unusual graciousness of spirit toward theological rivals and
attempted to establish unity among the diverse groups
involved in the evangelical revival. Through his last decades
he continued to lead; and his leadership was effective. He
picked up a light and illumined a hemisphere. He continued
to preach a clear and comprehensive message, a message that
became the fountainhead of the Wesleyan theological
tradition.

The Formation of Wesley's Theology

Wesley's theological views were not easily achieved, and they never became static. There were changes in emphasis and periods of recasting basic motifs—in 1725, in 1738, and in the period after 1760. Yet there is continuity in the development of persistent themes. The dominant characteristics of his theological perspective, characteristics that were formative of a tradition, should be delineated.

John Wesley appreciated his rich theological legacy and explored its resources. Samuel Wesley, his father, had indicated a study program in his "Advice to a Young Clergyman," prescribing a general education in logic, history, law, pharmacy, natural and experimental philosophy, chronology, geography, mathematics, poetry, and music—all constituting background. Then for the first three and one-half years in the parish, the young clergyman should study the Bible and the early Fathers; for the next three and one-half years, the writings of the English Carolines and Puritans.[9] John Wesley underwent a similar discipline, and to understand Wesley, one must know something of his sources.

One clue to Wesley's sense of important streams in the preceding tradition is found in his selection of materials for the *Christian Library*, the fifty-volume theological resource published from 1749 through 1755. The most immediately obvious fact is that the *Christian Library* is exactly what Wesley said it should be: "Extracts From the Abridgements of the Choicest Pieces of Practical Divinity." Intended to nurture Christian living, these writings reveal Wesley's theological sensitivity. Theology is important as it serves the interest of Christian formation. Theology is never an end, but is always a means for understanding and developing transformed living. There was little speculative interest involved in Wesley's theological investigations. He consistently turned theological reflection to practical service. Theology, in his understanding, was to be preached, sung, and lived. Consequently, volumes of the *Christian Library* are given over to actual life stories of people who embodied Christian truth: Philip Melancthon, a Lutheran theologian; John Calvin; Gregory Lopez, a Roman Catholic Spanish missionary to Mexico; Robert Bruce, an Edinburgh minister.

It is important that the Wesleyan movement came into existence during the Enlightenment and therefore, from the beginning, has carried a modern sensibility. The Enlightenment ushered in the modern period in western culture. Philosophically, this perspective began with René Descartes (1596–1650) and on the English scene was propounded by Herbert of Cherbury (1581–1648) and John Locke (1632–1704). More revolutionary for the West than the Reformation, which continued to accept the dominant assumptions of medieval life, the Enlightenment challenged inherited convictions about God and affirmed the radical independence and competent rationality of human beings. Hence autonomous rational people came to be the chief assured reality. For Wesley, this meant that the basic struggle was not an intramural battle between churches for political status or correct doctrinal interpretation; the struggle was rather with a God-denying world, a world that did not believe. To this world a radical challenge must be issued through proclamation of the gospel by Christian preaching and action.

Theologically, the critical issue for Wesley—and this has been recognized from the time of John Fletcher and Alexander Knox to that of George Croft Cell and Albert C. Outler—is the tension that exists between salvation by holy living and salvation by faith alone. That is, if salvation is granted as a free gift of grace, apart from our works (and perhaps even in spite of them), then of what value are good works and a disciplined life? Wesley, as a persistently practical theologian, sought to hold these two dimensions

21

together. Holy living had been a dominant preoccupation, but at Aldersgate, Wesley set priorities once and for all: Redemption is by grace through faith. But faith is embodied in love. Regeneration—spiritual rebirth—is given by God, and the resulting new life is expressed in love of God and neighbor. Wesley, Outler argues, made a significant contribution to the history of Christian thought when he recognized that the older Reformation tendency to polarize "faith alone" and "holy living" truncated the full Christian message. Wesley was convinced that the two must be held together and he attempted to speak for this larger vision. Outler states that Wesley constructed a new theory of salvation,

> based in part on classical Augustinian foundations (Christology, original sin, etc.) but that evangelized the Christian ethic and moralized the Christian evangel, that linked justification and regeneration, that affirmed both the imputation and impartation of righteousness, that repudiated both human self-assertion and passivity. He turned out "rules" by the dozen—but also with warnings that even the most scrupulous rule-keeping will get you only to the state of being an "almost Christian." He developed intensive small group nurture and therapy for Christian maturation. . . . But all of these were elements in his larger project: to describe and promote the Christian life as rooted in faith and fruiting in love.[10]

These themes will be explored in the next chapter. At the moment, the question is: From what sources did Wesley derive his position?

Wesley was most indebted to his immediate heritage. He was the son of Samuel and Susanna—who were originally dissenters, but had returned to the Church of England—and he was nurtured by their interests. He read the work of a variety of theologians, ranging from Puritans to Anglican high-church divines—Thomas Cranmer and John Preston, Ralph Cudworth, William Law, and Thomas Goad, among others.[11] In their writings he found positions that both formed and confirmed his views.

But Wesley's indebtedness was even broader. In the Protestant Reformation, as it was transmitted by German Pietism, he found the foundation of "faith alone," on which all else was built. The early church Fathers and Eastern Orthodoxy enriched his notion of holiness. From Roman Catholicism he gained challenging examples of holy living and a literature on mysticism.[12] The panorama was wide and deep. His Epworth home taught him to read widely and critically, but it was his own creativity that achieved a dynamic complementarity of diverse themes. The richly textured fabric that Wesley wove from this broad background is his most distinctive theological accomplishment.[13]

From John Wesley's life and thought, a tradition was born. By him, a past was reshaped. From him, a stream still flows, seeking to express, in changing contexts, his concern for practical divinity.

CHAPTER 2

SCRIPTURAL CHRISTIANITY:
John Wesley's Theology of Grace

T HEOLOGY, for John Wesley, was intended to transform life. Always in the service of presenting the gospel, theology was to underwrite the proclamation of the grace of God given in Jesus Christ for the redemption of all people.

The grace of God, as the redeeming activity of divine love, is the center of Wesley's theology. The themes Wesley emphasized came from his conviction that God's gracious love is the dominant reality in human life. Grace is God's active and continuous presence. Definitively expressed in Jesus Christ, grace covers the entirety of life: It creates, redeems, sustains, sanctifies, and glorifies. The Bible and Christian experience witness to grace: Justification is by grace; regeneration is the work of grace; grace preveniently takes initiative and may convey assurance of God's actual presence; grace leads to maturity in sanctification; undergirding the church's mission, grace is conveyed through preaching and ethical service and through the means God has established for relationship. Christian life is rooted and fulfilled in loving grace.

How is the grace of God in Jesus Christ known? What is the source of our knowledge? John Wesley believed that the Bible conveys this knowledge as its words are transported to experience by the Holy Spirit. Consequently, Wesley intended to be a biblical theologian. Scripture was the fundamental source of his theological expression; every doctrine must be measured against the standard presented in Scripture. What is said about God, about the world, about human beings must be said because the Scripture speaks. This principle was basic for Wesley and was contained in his theological bequest. Hence the two principal resources Wesley left his followers for their theological guidance were his sermons and his *Notes on the New Testament*.

The sermons are primarily a string of biblical quotations. He asserted, "I allow no other rule, whether of faith or practice, than the Holy Scriptures." And again, "My ground is the Bible. . . . I follow it in all things, both great and small."[1] Wesley preached the message of the Bible and would claim to do no more. His New Testament notes followed the lead of such scholars of his time as Hugo Grotius (1583–1645), a humanist, and especially Johann Albrecht Bengel (1687–1752), a Pietist. His intention was not so much to make any interpretation final, as to make the biblical source central. He reflected this openness in all his work as he attempted to join genuine piety with sound learning.

The Scriptures are the prime source of Wesley's theology, but the Scriptures become God's Word only by the lively power of the Holy Spirit. As early as 1735 on his trip to Georgia, Wesley claimed that he could be God's messenger only as God, by the Holy Spirit, invigorated the scriptural message. The internal witness of the Spirit is a necessary companion to the objective word of the Bible.

Wesley took Christian experience to be a medium of

25

theology, for scriptural teaching is confirmed in evangelical experience. A major characteristic of Wesley's theology is that importance is placed on empirical data as well as on direct immediate experience.[2] Not primarily a speculative thinker, Wesley's interest in abstract exploration was limited. He was, however, acutely aware of personal appropriation of God's grace and was careful in his observations, especially since he believed the Holy Spirit to be directly influential in human experience. Christian experience is a gift; it is the point of intersection of God and persons. Such a conviction underlay Wesley's interest in Christian biography as a rich resource for understanding the possibility of human experience of God.

Biblical interpretation always stands in relation to a specific culture, and Wesley reflected his own history. He came to the Bible as an Anglican, and he read and put the Scriptures together in ways that interrelated the themes from that inheritance. John Wesley gained a standpoint from forebears in the faith and developed his thought upon that foundation. But inheritance is to be tested by the Bible. When Wesley reclaimed an emphasis, such as the doctrine of sanctification, he did so because he believed it to be a biblical mandate.

For Wesley, the Christian tradition also played a crucial role in theological understanding. The experience of preceding witnesses and their contributions were of basic importance. Learned as a classicist, knowledgeable of Eastern Christianity, indebted to the Reformation tradition, and especially grounded in the Church of England, Wesley utilized all these traditions in interpreting the faith. He was remarkable in the breadth of his learning, in his willingness to accept from many sources, and in the ability to construct his work by studying that of others.

Theology should also make sense, Wesley believed, and he had confidence in human reason: common sense and clear thinking. Neither idolizing reason, as contemporary Deists

26

tended to do, nor suspecting it to be perverse, as Luther in his zeal sometimes claimed, Wesley accepted reason as being useful for theology. The truth of Scripture, attested by experience, is ordered by reason. While he did not possess a particularly subtle mind, it was quick, clear, retentive, and agile, and he believed that clear statements are persuasive. His commitment to service preempted long delay in reasoning or acting. Wesley's intellect was a part of his total character: direct, disciplined, and decisive.

Theology, he reasoned, has a practical goal: Christian truth must be applied to both personal and social life. Doctrine is for the purpose of Christian nurture and service. Wesley insisted that theology must carry practical import. Undergirding preaching, worship, and love of neighbor, Christian doctrine helps effect a thorough transformation of life.

When these matters are combined, the results are clearly framed: Truth is expressed in God's definitive self-presentation in Jesus Christ as this is conveyed by the Holy Spirit. The holy Scriptures are the primary source, and experience is the medium through which the historical and living Christ is made known to believers. Tradition, as the transmitter of the vital life of Christian community over time, instructs in the interpretation of that event as, again, the Holy Spirit brings the past to the present. In sum, the task of theology is to interpret the gracious presence of God rightly and to apply it effectively.

The following selection of theological themes is guided by Wesley's sense of God's grace. The constructive form of his thought is presented through the themes of justification, prevenient grace, assurance, sanctification, the church, and the means of grace.

Justification

Justification by grace through faith was a central motif in John Wesley's thought. He was emphatic: Salvation is the work of God. Salvation is a gracious gift of God and it must not be confused with human achievement, with the exercise of human will, or with the faithful pursuit of a Christian style of life. Salvation is the work of God and of no other; justification is by grace.[3] Charles Wesley emphasized this theme in many hymns.

> At last I own it cannot be
> That I should fit myself for thee:
> Here, then, to thee I all resign;
> Thine is the work, and only Thine.

It is significant that in Wesley's arrangement of his sermons, the very first is "Salvation by Faith." In this homily he stressed that a person's salvation is totally dependent upon God's free unmerited grace. He wrote, "Grace is the source; faith is the condition of salvation."[4] And, "It is this doctrine, which our Church justly calls *the strong rock and foundation of the Christian religion*."[5]

Wesley had to struggle to come to a clear understanding of the nature of justification. He grew up in an Anglican tradition which viewed moral achievement as a means to salvation, and he continued along this path through his time at Charterhouse and Christ Church, Oxford. The year 1725 was important, since it was then that the young, newly ordained Wesley began the study of Jeremy Taylor and became convinced of the centrality of "holy living" as taught by Taylor, Thomas a Kempis, and William Law. This study carried Wesley's moralism to new depths of commitment, and he was never to lose this commanding concern. He was, however, to change the foundation upon which it was built.

In 1738 at Aldersgate Street, he was converted to and subscribed to the chief doctrine of the Reformation: justification by faith. He had now found the base for true holiness. It was after this experience that he turned to an earnest examination of his own Anglican tradition. "I began," he wrote, "more narrowly to inquire what the doctrine of the Church of England is, concerning the much controverted point of justification by faith; and the sum of what I found in the *Homilies* I extracted and printed for the use of others."[6] Wesley thought of himself as faithful to his own church (although he clearly selected his stream within that tradition) and to the central tenet of historic Christianity as renewed by the Reformation.

In the sermon "Salvation by Faith," he presented the meaning of justification.

> This then is the salvation which is through faith, even in the present world: a salvation from sin, and the consequences of sin, both often expressed in the word *justification;* which, taken in the largest sense, implies a deliverance from guilt and punishment, by the atonement of Christ actually applied to the soul of the sinner now believing on him, and a deliverance from the whole body of sin, through Christ formed in his heart. So that he who is thus justified, or saved by faith, is *indeed* born again.[7]

The key phrases in this statement are "the present world," "deliverance," and "born again." So justification is actual deliverance from sin in present life; it issues into a new birth which begins maturation into the fullness of Christian living. Wesley's consistent central theme was salvation by faith—beginning in repentance and developing into a new life of holy living.

In his sermon "Justification by Faith," Wesley made his meaning clear: "The plain scriptural notion of justification is pardon, the forgiveness of sins."[8] This definition was set against other interpretations of justification: "being made actually righteous" (which recalls sanctification); or clearing from Satan's accusations, clearing from the accusation of the law; or God's judgment of persons contrary to the real nature of things—that is, that God believes us righteous when we are not. In contrast to these positions, Wesley stated simply, "Justification is pardon, the forgiveness of sins."

Justification is necessary because all people are sinners. Wesley viewed the fallen nature of humankind with fundamental seriousness. Although created in the image of God and in righteous relationship with God, human beings have fallen. The image of God is distorted through the disobedience and fall of Adam. In freedom, Adam disobeyed the divine command and brought upon himself "death, sickness, and pain, and folly, and vice, and slavery."[9] Wesley did not attempt to explain fully why Adam misused his freedom, but he did refer to "idolatrous self love" as the root of evil.[10] All people, as children of Adam, are participants in this Fall. Wesley understood Adam as the "federal head" or "representative" of the whole human race. As a result, fallen people are spiritually dead to God; they no longer possess the capacity for saving knowledge or love of God.

This theme pervades Wesley's writings. From his earliest extant sermon through his later development, he stressed this flawed condition of humanity. Reason, will, and liberty are not wholly destroyed, but they are drastically impaired and there is no resource for self-salvation. Corruption is ever present in human understanding, will, and affection. This debilitated condition necessitates grace to set human life right. Wesley could look with clear eyes at this fallen condition because he also knew that even the fallen are recipients of God's redemptive action. Human life, in its estrangement, is set within the context of grace; the atonement of Jesus Christ is the recreating power of God's love.

Justification is by grace through faith; grace makes faith a possibility, for faith is a graciously enabled response to grace. In this sense, "Faith, therefore, is the *necessary* condition of justification; yes, the *only necessary* condition thereof."[11] Now the issue tightens—What is faith? Wesley wrote,

I cannot describe the nature of this faith better than in the words of our own Church: "The only instrument of salvation" (whereof justification is one branch) "is faith; that is, a sure trust and confidence that God both hath and will forgive our sins, that He hath accepted us again into His favour, for the merits of Christ's death and passion."[12]

Faith, as Wesley defined it, is trust and confidence. It is response to the initiative of God. Human beings who were estranged from God are now, by forgiveness, drawn into positive relationship, a relationship with fulfilled meaning. Faith is knowledge of God, as God has prepared the way for and now prompts human response. Again Charles Wesley put this understanding into a hymn.

> Author of faith, to thee I lift
> My weary, longing eyes:
> O let me now receive that gift!
> My soul without it dies.

The source of faith is God. Wesley spoke of faith as "a divine supernatural ἔλεγκος, *evidence or conviction*, 'of things not seen,' not discoverable by our bodily senses, as being either past, future, or spiritual."[13] There is no self-salvation. Justification is a free gift, the gift of God in Jesus Christ; and faith, the condition of justification, also is a gift given to fallen persons.

Now we move to more difficult territory, for Wesley explained that while faith is a divine gift, it also involves human concurrence. Faith is a human act conforming to God's prior and initiating act. To say that faith is a condition of the relationship of persons with God is not the same as saying that faith, of itself, produces the relationship. Faith is so integral to the relationship that it is a redundancy to say "faith" and also "relationship." One of Wesley's contributions was the movement from legal to personal modes for interpreting the relation of God to persons.[14] To "have faith" is to be already in relationship with God and to acknowledge the existence of that relationship. Hence "human concurrence" does not mean that God and persons should be separated in such a way that the activity of each upon the other is an external event that allows no interpenetration; God and human beings do not meet as solid balls which collide and then ricochet. They meet in the most intimate and mutually involving ways. There is integrity on the part of each, but there is also involvement, so that integrity is found in interdependence. There is no neat traceable line between God's activity and human response, yet the reality of God's initiating grace and human response to it are both present. Faith is a double affirmation: It is an affirmation of the integrity of God and individuals, each by the other, each with the other. The priorities are clear: God is first in action and supreme in value; human acknowledgment is responsive.

Prevenient Grace

The issue of God's grace and human freedom comes to sharp focus in Wesley's doctrine of prevenient, or preceding, grace. He wrote:

> For, allowing that all souls of men are dead in sin by *nature*, this excuses none, seeing there is no man that is in a state of mere nature. There is no man, unless he has quenched the Spirit, that is wholly void of the grace of God. No man living is entirely destitute of what is vulgarly called "natural conscience." But this is not natural: it is more properly termed "preventing grace." Every man has a greater or less measure of this, which waiteth not for the call of man.[15]

Again, he noted, "A naturally free will, in the present state of mankind I do not understand. I only assert that there is a measure of free will supernaturally restored to every man, together with that supernatural light which enlightens every man that cometh into the world."[16] Human will, because of the Fall, is not free, but through Christ's atoning work there is a universal prevenient grace which restores human freedom.

For Wesley, prevenient grace was most fundamentally revealed in moral conscience: But what does this imply for moral action or faithful response? There has been diversity of interpretation. On one end of a spectrum, one can find an understanding of prevenient grace as a power given to human beings, an endowment of ability to take initiative and act righteously. There is no longer a "natural man," but only a graciously capable person. The emphasis in this case is on the power of humans to initiate movement toward God.[17] In the middle position, prevenient grace is interpreted as a conscience that can evoke repentance; people are, by grace, aware of their fallen condition and may or may not respond to God's gracious overture. Response, rather than initiative, is emphasized.[18] At the other end of the spectrum, prevenient grace has been interpreted in a more restrictive manner. Faith is altogether a gracious gift of God. The freedom of sinful humanity is only the liberty of rebellion; it is wholly negative. This freedom leads to despair; human inability is recognized, thanks to prevenient grace; and also, thanks to prevenient grace, humans cease to resist, and God's causality is able to operate.[19]

Wesley was rooted in the Bible. In Scripture he found the theme of divine sovereignty and also that of human moral responsibility, which implies freedom. He seemed to recognize that the only way to give place to both is not to release one to the other, but to put them into tension. Both themes are in the Bible, so both must be held in full integrity by theology. The theme of prevenient grace allowed Wesley to relate divine sovereignty and human freedom, but to maintain the tension was difficult. He refused to cut the gordian knot and so turned from both Augustine and Pelagius, and also from the early Reformers. This is one of the best illustrations of Wesley's intention to be faithful to Scripture.

Prevenient grace is an effect of the atonement of Jesus Christ. The grace of God in Christ creates a new possibility for human life, and to every human life God is antecedently and enablingly present. Charles Wesley expressed this:

> Long my imprisoned spirit lay,
>   Fast bound in sin and nature's night;
> Thine eye diffused a quickening ray,
>   I woke, the dungeon flamed with light:
> My chains fell off, my heart was free,
>   I rose, went forth, and followed thee.

To draw God's sovereignty and human freedom together is difficult, but Wesley was determined to bring the two into dynamic relationship. To follow his thought, we must move with careful steps. Wesley insisted, with the Reformers, that justification and faith are gifts of God. They are established by grace. But how does grace operate? Wesley could not accept predestination as unconditional election, and he catalogued his reasons. Unconditional election carries the consequence of unconditional reprobation; this consequence was Wesley's main opposition, because he believed that unconditional reprobation is unscriptural. He also added that such a doctrine makes preaching vain, tends to destroy holiness, fosters pride, tends to antinomianism (i.e., lawlessness, which was probably Wesley's second most serious concern), creates a disregard for those considered reprobate, undermines acts of charity, and dishonors the loving God of Christian revelation. Wesley was uneasy with an exclusive emphasis upon omnipotence; he believed the attributes of God should be kept in careful balance, so that justice, mercy, and truth are in complementary relationship with omnipotence. Of basic importance was his desire to understand the divine/human relationship as set forth in the Incarnation. God's sovereignty is expressed in Jesus Christ. In Christ, God addresses individuals in a manner that allows and solicits response.

Wesley's opposition to predestination also must be set into the cultural development of the time. As an Enlightenment man, he saw an atheistic world as the object of the principal struggle, with the attack focused on scientific interpretations of human life. Wesley was fighting to escape the use of natural-science models to account for human character. In that battle he opposed the Deists, who affirmed God as creator but who saw him as detached from the world; the influence of Isaac Newton, who interpreted the world with mechanistic models; and David Hartley, who argued that God had created the world as a system of inexorable necessity. Wesley explicitly mentioned these persons in his treatise "Thoughts on Necessity." He identified predestination with a mechanistic view of the world and a necessitarian view of human nature. In opposition, he intended to hold nature and grace together—not on the model of natural science or mechanical philosophy, but by affirming the distinctive character of human reason, action, and responsibility. In spite of his efforts, Wesley was unable to provide a completely adequate intellectual schema, but his sense was profoundly right as he attempted to protect an understanding of human nature as arising from the distinctiveness of personhood as graciously reconstituted by God.

There was for Wesley an "order of salvation," a dynamic movement of the Christian life from its inception to its fulfillment. Moving from conscience to conviction of sin, to repentance, to justification, to regeneration, to sanctification, to glorification, there is a pattern of gracious development. This development is built upon the active presence of the Holy Spirit as it encounters, wins assent, and transforms life. Hence justification results in regeneration. Forgiveness brings a changed condition of life. The old nature is set aside as new creation occurs. Those who are redeemed have been given a new nature, for they have had restored in them the image of God. Wesley was emphatic about the change that God's grace effects in human life; it is characteristic of his thought that he placed great emphasis upon the new life in Christ. This altered status is the most important fact of human existence; grace has changed the affections, the mind, and the will. Christians are new creatures, set once more in proper relationship with God and their neighbors.

Assurance

How does the believer experience justification by faith? Can a person be assured of justification? Through the middle period of his development, John Wesley was especially interested in the issue of assurance. Prior to his Aldersgate experience, he tenaciously sought personal certainty of his salvation in terms of the sincerity of his faith; after Aldersgate, he preached assurance of God's justification as a necessary aspect of Christian experience. Later he relaxed this position and spoke of assurance as a privilege, but not a necessity of Christian experience.

What, more exactly, is meant by *assurance*? It is clear that Wesley was attempting to interpret actual experience as resulting from God's grace, but how did he develop his understanding? One scriptural reference was consistently used in stating his position—Romans 8:16: "The Spirit itself beareth witness with our Spirit, that we are the children of God." Wesley saw this verse in the larger context of its section of the chapter, which stresses that if we live by the Spirit, we have received the spirit of sonship and may cry, "Abba, Father." That is, assurance is given within the setting of vital and lively relationship and is the fruit of and witness of this relationship.[20]

36

"We love him, because he first loved us" (I John 4:19). This was the focus of Wesley's emphasis on Christian experience. He was not attempting to express a novel view; rather, he was referring to the gracious covenantal relationship that runs through Scripture.[21] Wesley's use of assurance was an alternative to the Calvinist doctrine of election. Emphasizing the initiative of God and human response, he described assurance as the assurance of love, the assurance of present pardon, the certitude of God's presence as sustaining positive relationship. Again, we hear Charles Wesley singing:

> Arise, my soul, arise,
>   Shake off thy guilty fears;
> The bleeding Sacrifice
>   In my behalf appears;
> Before the throne my Surety stands,
> My name is written on his hands. . . .
>
> My God is reconciled;
>   His pardoning voice I hear;
> He owns me for his child,
>   I can no longer fear:
> With confidence I now draw nigh,
> And, "Father, Abba, Father," cry.

One key to Wesley's thought is the distinction he drew, in his mature thought, between *servant* and *son* in the divine/human relationship.[22] There is a servant relationship to God which is clearly ordered. But there is also the more complete life of the child of God. The relationship of a child to a parent is more complex, involves more freedom as well as responsibility, and offers more possibilities than that of a servant to a master. In the child/parent relationship assurance has a different basis; in place of legal order and social force, there is a developed trust and a knowledge gained from faithfulness.

37

Wesley thought in dynamic terms. Relationships are not static or finally set—there is interaction and constant renewal. It is clear that, although the basic stress was upon the assurance of God's justification, Wesley attempted to hold God's action in tension with human response, an arena in which he found fluctuation and change. He earnestly considered the actual character of relationships, which are at once both affirmation and question, assurance and doubt. At times one may be certain of a relationship—both of the love offered and the response made; at other times one may be certain of the love offered but uncertain of the ability to accept. Such variables contribute to the dynamics of actual relationships.

Over time, Wesley's understanding of the place of assurance in Christian life changed. Early in his career he stated that assurance is necessary for a complete relationship; where assurance is absent, relationship is incomplete. But, as he learned, this emphasis can be overplayed. In a letter to Richard Thompson, he remarked,

> I agree with you, that justifying faith cannot be a conviction that I am justified; and that a man who is not assured that his sins are forgiven may yet have a kind or degree of faith, which distinguishes him not only from a devil, but also from a Heathen; and on which I may admit him to the Lord's Supper. But still I believe the proper Christian faith, which purifies the heart, implies such a conviction.[23]

Two points in this quotation are important. First, Wesley allowed for some disjunction between the positive relationship established by God's activity, and the variability of human response. God's love is firm, but human decision may waver or be misunderstood. Second, Wesley felt that "proper Christian faith" includes the conviction of assurance, a point he supported from church history, mentioning the early church—explicitly, Origen, Chrysostom, Augustine—and the Reformers, especially Luther.[24] To know God is to know God as Savior. To know God savingly is to be consciously aware of God's redemptive presence. Wesley claimed that assurance, the inspiration of the Holy Spirit, and the revelation of Christ are all integrally related.[25] With a cry of discovery, he affirmed, "I know that I am accepted."[26]

Thus justification and assurance of justification were related in John Wesley's thought; both were based on the gracious initiative of God; both were descriptive of the nature of the relationship that God has established with human-kind. Faith is the antidote to human sin and opens the way to love. In these doctrines is laid a groundwork for the fullness of Christian life.

Christian Perfection

John Wesley always regarded himself as a biblical thinker; above all, he intended to be loyal to scriptural teaching. "When I began to make the Scripture my study (about seven-and-twenty years ago), I began to see that Christians are called to *love God with all their heart and to serve Him with all their strength:* which is precisely what I apprehended to be meant by the scriptural term perfection."[27] In some thirty New Testament passages, especially in the John letters, he found statements with which he had to come to terms. In I John 3:9, we read, "Whosoever is born of God doth not commit sin, for his seed remaineth in him: and he cannot sin, because he is born of God." This theme became the goal of John Wesley's life and his ministry. Love for God is the central theme. Wesley had long prayed the Anglican collect for purity at Matins, at Evensong, and at the Eucharist: "Cleanse the thoughts of our hearts by the inspiration of Thy Holy Spirit that we may perfectly love Thee. . . ."

To these influences must be added a rich lode mined from Eastern Orthodoxy and Roman Catholicism. Christian perfection, for Wesley, was the practical dimension of Christian faith; it is there that belief takes its concrete character. This interest was always present in his thought. It had directed his earliest spiritual striving, was given a new foundation at Aldersgate, and gained strength in his later years. The idea of Christian perfection, was the most distinctive aspect of Wesley's theology.

The founder of Methodism was a serious man; he was serious about his faith and about the commitment it represented. From the depth of his commitment he set before himself and his followers the ultimate goal of discipleship: the perfect love of God and of neighbor. Charles Wesley put the prayer for holiness into his hymns.

> Refining fire, go through my heart;
>   Illuminate my soul;
> Scatter thy life through every part,
>   And sanctify the whole.
>
> Give me a new, a perfect heart,
>   From doubt, and fear, and sorrow free;
> The mind which was in Christ impart,
>   And let my spirit cleave to thee.

The claim of Christian perfection was astonishing. Most traditional Protestants could not accept such a notion, for while Christ does save people in their sin, this is not salvation from sin, they said; full salvation is at the final time, not in this life. Wesley argued that such a notion limits God's ability to affect human life. He could not escape the theoretical possibility of God's redeeming power, for surely the Holy Spirit can convey such transformative power. But where was the proof? Where were the examples to which he could point? Wesley looked among his own followers and discovered some whom he felt were examples of Christian perfection. His chief evidence, however, was found in the biographies of saintly people: Gregory Lopez, Gaston Jean Baptiste de Renty, and especially Brother Lawrence. These were lives graced by God and brought to the white heat of divine love.

The perfect love for God! This ideal has a venerable history in Christian spirituality. The ultimate goal of the spiritual life is the simple, single-minded love for God; it is the worship of God with the whole heart. To love God carries with it a love for and a commitment to neighbor. Sanctification is two-dimensional; it is a response to the Great Commandments.

Sanctification is built upon justification and constitutes the goal, or true end, of human life. Justification opens the way to a new life; sanctification is the heart of religion and the goal of Christian living.[28] Love for God is the actual fruiting of mature Christian life. Justification, wrote Wesley,

> is not the being made actually just and righteous. This is *sanctification:* which is indeed, in some degree, the immediate fruit of justification, but, nevertheless is a distinct gift of God, and of a totally different nature. The one [justification] implies what God does for us through his Son; the other [sanctification] what he works in us by his Spirit.[29]

Theology cannot be separated from ethics; gracious ordering is continuous, from the point of beginning to the consummate realization of human life.

Christian holiness is first a gospel, and only then a quality of Christian life. George Croft Cell has spoken of the "Wesleyan reconstruction of the Christian ethic of life in an original and unique synthesis of the Protestant ethic of grace and the Catholic ethic of holiness."[30] Wesley was clear: God's grace is the ground of beatitude. Holiness is a gift of grace, not an achievement; it is the active work of the Holy Spirit to which the human spirit is called to respond, evoking love as the dominating motive of life. The fruition of sanctification is conformity to the mind of Christ; always, for Wesley, the

41

Holy Spirit reinforces our life in Christ. Christian perfection is progressive, a continual renewal of love and growth in love. Both realized and being realized, it is a love that matures into greater love.

Wesley was not content to speak only of possibility, nor was he satisfied with partial realization of the goal of human life. There was, consequently, a strong emphasis on entire sanctification. Entire sanctification is one stage in the process of Christian life. New birth, which occurs instantaneously, is followed by a gradual sanctification, which may lead to an instantaneous event of entire sanctification. A subsequent gradual development should also follow this event. By grace, human beings cooperate with God in gradual sanctification, but, Wesley stressed, instantaneous sanctification is exclusively God's work. Perfect deliverance from sin culminates in a positive perfection in love and obedience. Human life is fulfilled in holiness.

To love God necessarily carries with it a love for neighbor; sanctification implies, or more exactly, includes, the moral life. Sanctification is neither a personal spiritual cosmetic nor a gathering of moral merits. Sanctification, as having the mind of Christ, implies servanthood; it is expressed as an unrestrained caring for peoples. The new life is ethical in content. In his Covenant Service prayer, Wesley phrased his commitment this way: "Put me to what Thou wilt, rank me with whom Thou wilt—put me to doing, put me to suffering."

The experience of sanctification is the restoring of the defaced image of our creation. As fallen, persons have forfeited their authentic humanity; as sanctified, they are restored to and mature in the life that God intends. Human life is graced and reaches its goal of true joy.[31] Wesley was aware that new birth into Christ can degenerate into sentimental emotionalism, ineffective religiosity, or irrelevant piety. The new person still lives in the flesh and in the world, so the necessary corollary to liberation is discipline; the sanctified life is shaped by God's demands and human faithfulness.

It has been said that Charles Wesley's hymns always begin on earth and end in heaven. So it is with John Wesley's theology. He was firmly convinced of the coming day of Christ, which is not yet, but toward which humankind, with the whole creation, is moving. For Wesley, it was necessary to stress God's ultimate victory; but it was also important to affirm the penultimate reality of God's presence, now experienced as life that is drawn to God in increasingly focused love. John Wesley had a doctrine of final things, an eschatology, in which God's kingdom is being presently realized even as it points toward a consummating future. The Christian lives with the lively hope that God, who has begun a good thing, will fulfill it in the day of Jesus Christ.

The Church

The Holy Spirit challenges believers to full maturity in Jesus Christ; and the Holy Spirit gathers believers into worshiping and serving communities. The church is the community of the Holy Spirit. In his revision of the Thirty-nine Articles of the Church of England for Methodists in America, Wesley retained this article: "The visible Church is a congregation of faithful men in which the pure word of God is preached and the sacraments are duly administered according to Christ's ordinance in all those things that of necessity are requisite to the same." Wesley emphasized three qualities which the article indicates are essential to a visible church: living faith, preaching, and due administration of the sacraments.[32] For Wesley, preaching, as faithful witness to the Word, is the inaugurating reality of the life of the church, and the holiness of the church is a holiness that God graciously bestows. Further, Christ is present in unbroken continuity in the sacraments; and the gathered community is drawn together by the Holy Spirit, which then disperses the community in mission.[33] It was Wesley's effort to be comprehensive, and to insist upon emphases drawn from various church traditions, that was distinctive of his understanding of the church.

While Wesley did not include the three orders of the ministry—bishops, elders, and deacons—as part of his basic interpretation, legitimate ministry remained important, and he viewed validly ordained ministers as crucial. Wesley honored the established order; the right to administer the sacraments was a privilege conferred by the Holy Spirit and by the church. Yet he appointed lay people to the explicit task of preaching. As late as 1789 he argued that there were both prophetic and priestly roles in the ministry. His lay preachers were prophets and were to preach the Word; but they were not priests and therefore were not authorized to administer the sacraments.[34]

What about ordained priests? Wesley rejected the claim that there had been an unbroken succession of bishops as a third order of ministry; but just what Wesley meant has been the subject of much research and debate.[35] He believed there has been a succession—that is, a continuous stream of ordination. But this continuity had not always been effected by bishops of a third order, since elders (presbyters) had, at times of necessity, discharged this episcopal function. Such action, for Wesley, constituted a valid ordination.

The church, Wesley believed, was primarily a continuation of the apostolic witness. Christ alone is the foundation of the church and witness to the Word is witness to Christ, to his total work and benefits. Witness to Christ creates a community centered in the worship of God and extended through faithful mission. Undergirding the church, there is the persisting presence of Christ in Word and Sacrament.

There is a continuous dependence upon God's grace and a flowering of faith in the love for God and neighbor.

Means of Grace

For John Wesley, regular observance and utilization of the means of grace were requisite for growth in Christian life. The necessary presupposition of his discussion of the means of grace was the atonement of Jesus Christ, in which the guilt brought upon all people by Adam is cancelled by the righteousness of Christ.[36] Means of grace are provided for the enrichment of Christian life. Consequently, prayer, fasting, Christian conference, and Bible reading are conveyors of God's active presence; among more ordinary means are the preached Word of God and the Lord's Supper. All these means are "ordinary" in the sense that they are the usual ways in which God works to help people recover what was lost in the Fall. But none of these means is absolutely essential. The freedom of God is maintained; God may, in divine wisdom, work through extraordinary means. But in Scripture, Christians are commanded to utilize the ordinary means; therefore the Christian should pray, fast, study the Bible, hear the preached Word, and partake of the Lord's Supper.

In the atonement, Jesus Christ expressed the redeeming grace of God. The presence of the Holy Spirit applies redemption to human life by convicting, justifying, and sanctifying human beings. The sacraments of baptism and the Lord's Supper also convey grace. While baptism is not, in an absolute sense, necessary for salvation, it is the ordinary means of justification, a way to wash away guilt.[37] Through baptism, justification is conveyed and new birth is given. Baptism draws persons into the body of Christ.

A tension ran through Wesley's thought. The work begun in baptism should result in repentance, faith, and obedience.

Through these steps a person should grow steadily in grace and holiness. Nevertheless, it is evident that baptismal grace often is not utilized and the covenant is broken. And because people violate the relationship established in baptism, remedial action is necessary. Hence Wesley preached for a new sense of sinful alienation, for repentance, and for a new affirmation of God's redemptive love in Jesus Christ. The issue, Wesley insisted, is not baptism, but actual Christian experience.[38]

Baptism is the initiating representation of God's redeeming grace, but it is efficacious only when it is followed by actual repentance and conversion. Consonant with his emphasis upon evangelical experience, Wesley insisted that the redemptive work of Christ must be appropriated by persons. There is no mechanical transportation of grace; the decisive moment occurs when the Holy Spirit encounters the human spirit and evokes belief and continuing spiritual maturation. From his tradition, Wesley had learned to regard baptism as the washing away of original sin; from his observation of life, he was convinced of the necessity for bringing all people, even those who had fallen again after baptism, to an experience of faith.

The Lord's Supper is basic to spiritual nurture and is the supreme rite for conveying the grace of God. Typically, Wesley drew from many sources in an effort to comprehend the meaning of this sacrament. The eucharistic meal has three time-dimensions: (1) It represents the suffering of Christ, which is past, and therefore is a memorial meal; (2) it conveys the fruits of those sufferings in present graces; and (3) it assures believers of glory to come.[39] The kingdom's coming, presence, and ultimate fulfillment are held together.

The once-and-for-all act of Jesus Christ is continuously evoked by the Holy Spirit. And the Spirit leads into the future: The past issues into the present and persists into the future. The sacrament of the Lord's Supper is "A Pledge of

Heaven"; it is a foretaste of the communion of the saints, an anticipation of participation in the heavenly feast. The Eucharist prepares us for and assures us of our final destiny, for in this meal we are partakers in Christ, in his death and resurrection.

Participation in the Lord's Supper is twofold: a physical taking of the bread and wine, and a spiritual appropriation of the true body and blood of the Lord. These two dimensions are distinct aspects of a single unity. The bread and wine are the physical symbols that Jesus used and that continue to be used, but it is the presence and power of the Holy Spirit that conveys the vital and genuine empowerment of this sacrament in human life.

Wesley was careful to indicate that the presence is in the bread and wine, but not in a substantial or physical manner—Christ is actually present through the Holy Spirit. The hymns of Charles Wesley concentrated on the great objectivities of the faith:

> Come, Holy Ghost, Thine influence shed,
>   And realize the sign;
> Thy life infuse into the bread,
>   Thy power into the wine.
>
> Effectual let the tokens be,
>   And made by heavenly act.
> Fit channels to convey Thy love,
>   To every faithful heart.

Here we come to a distinctive point in Wesley's position— that the Lord's Supper can be a converting sacrament. This meal is not reserved for established believers, nor is it an act that is open only to the established Christian community. It is, obviously, a sacrament for believers—as a remembrance, a present vivification, and a future hope—but it also may be a means of conversion. The only invitation offered is to those "who do truly and earnestly repent" of their "sins . . . and intend to lead a new life, following the commandments of God." Participation in the eucharistic meal can be the inaugurating event in Christian faith. But though this sacrament may serve as a converting ordinance, it continues to be a confirming ordinance as well. Holy Communion may be the point of the beginning of Christian life; it is certainly the medium for growth in and enrichment of Christian living.

Conclusion

For Wesley, the gracious love of God found its definitive expression in Jesus Christ. In a basic sense, grace is Jesus Christ. Grace is the specific expression of God's nature and will, an incarnate and continuing presence. From the center in Jesus Christ, implications radiate, ranging from the prevenience of God to justification, regeneration, assurance, sanctification, means of grace, and final glorification. The grace of God, expressed in and defined by Jesus Christ, becomes inclusive of life.

John Wesley presented a comprehensive, biblically responsible theology of grace. Fidelity to the Scriptures leads along distinctive paths. Indebted to many, he also made his own emphases. Wesley did not intend uniqueness; rather, his great desire was to be faithful to the canonical Scriptures and the rich Christian tradition, to be attentive to the data of Christian experience, and to use his mind responsibly. These intentions were fused by a passionate love for Christ and an indomitable will to serve as a faithful disciple. In his own time, and since, his theological work has challenged people to respond and to follow.

CHAPTER 3

INTERPRETERS AND SUCCESSORS:
Wesleyan Theology in Great Britain in the Nineteenth Century

The subject [Methodist Doctrine] takes us back to the beginnings of the movement. There are two errors which we have at once to confront: that of assigning a doctrinal origin to the system, and that of making its origin entirely independent of doctrine.[1]

—William Burt Pope

THROUGH its first century several persons played important roles in the theological development that was an essential part of the Wesleyan tradition. To provide a sense of this development in Britain, we shall look at John Fletcher, Adam Clarke, Richard Watson, W. B. Pope, and Hugh Price Hughes. The historical sweep and range of positions are wide, but these theologians represent some of the characteristic formations of the tradition: They hold together piety and learning, intense love of God and of neighbor, biblical authority and ethical living.

49

John Fletcher

Time does not divide neatly in human history, and one major figure does not necessarily succeed another. John Fletcher was Wesley's contemporary and was invited to become Wesley's successor; he was also the most important early interpreter of Wesleyan themes in theology. But Fletcher died before Wesley. In order to describe the importance of Fletcher and his work in the developing tradition, it is necessary to review his distinctive qualities and theological interests. Of French Huguenot stock, John William Fletcher (Jean Guillaume de la Flechere) (1729–1785) was an example of Christian holiness. Generous with his life and possessions, he impressed those who knew him with his saintliness. Once asked by a government official whether there was any preferment he desired, Fletcher responded, "Thank you . . . but I want nothing except more grace."² In the Methodist Conference minutes of 1786, upon the usual question, "Who have died this year?" the answer was: "John Fletcher, a pattern of holiness, scarce to be paralleled in a century."

As a theologian, Fletcher was gifted. In the controversy between Wesley and some Calvinist evangelicals, which came to a climax between 1770 and 1778, Fletcher produced almost everything he ever wrote and in this conflict provided Wesley with strong theological support. The chief issue centered around whether Wesley had endorsed "works righteousness" at the 1770 conference. Fletcher claimed that Wesley was emphasizing particular truths drawn from the context of his total position in order to refute those who espoused antinomianism (the doctrine that the moral law is not applicable to Christians). Hence the title to Fletcher's series of letters—*Checks to Antinomianism* (there were five sections of "checks" in the completed work). To these statements Wesley gave his approval and thereby endorsed the first exposition of a distinctively Wesleyan theological position (though both men believed the position to be deeply rooted in historic Christian thought). So important was Fletcher in the movement that he has been called the Theologian of Methodism.[3]

The controversy with the Calvinists was the most basic struggle of the evangelical revival. Whitefield's adoption of Calvinistic positions initiated the dispute in 1739, and soon Wesley joined in the debate with "election" the issue. Wesley and Fletcher, rejected Calvinistic positions on predestination to damnation, irresistible grace, and final perseverance. But Wesley continued to believe in original sin and justification by grace through faith. The variances were profound, and after efforts to bridge the chasm were unsuccessful, the battle was bitterly fought. At the practical level, Wesley was convinced that the Calvinist position would result in antinomianism and hence undercut the drive for Christian holiness.

In 1770 the Methodist Conference met and discussed the issues. Again, Wesley's great fear was that people would be apathetic toward seeking and demonstrating salvation. In the conference statements, Wesley insisted that people could, by grace, put themselves in a position to receive grace and maintain the results of justification. A static condition of salvation was set aside in favor of a dynamic, moment-by-moment relationship with God. The conference minutes provoked immediate reaction from some of Calvinistic persuasion.

Through his writings, Fletcher became the spokesman for and the systematizer of the positions Wesley had taken. In order to set the issues of God's sovereignty and human freedom in perspective, Fletcher developed an understanding of history by which he explicated the more controversial matters. This view espoused a series of dispensations, or specific time periods, in each of which God works in ways special to that time. The scheme of history, as Fletcher saw it, was divided into three stages: that of the Father, that of the Son, and that of the Holy Spirit. The dispensation of the Father began with the revelation of God to Israel and therefore refers especially to the Old Testament. The dispensation of the Son was inaugurated by the coming of Christ and has to do with people who came to a knowledge of God through him. The dispensation of the Holy Spirit began at Pentecost and refers to the knowledge of God gained by those who have been made aware of God's presence as engaging Spirit.

Each of these periods of revelation refers both to God's activity in history and to human response to God's revelation. This background is important, for in his argument against predestination, Fletcher maintained that historical time—earthly history—must retain its significance, since historical decisions are an essential part of the divine/human mode of relationship. Human decision is important, but to make human choice primary, he claimed, deprives history of its divine dimension and its transcendent purpose.[4] Consequently, Fletcher maintained a dialectical relationship between God and human beings, but with a clear sense that ultimate sovereignty belongs to God. For Fletcher, that sovereignty was not so much an unquestioned power as an unfathomable love.

Throughout, Fletcher, almost alone, attempted to keep the controversy on a high plane. He wrote in a felicitous style, sometimes witty or satirical, but always conveying a strong sense of the argument. The issues were the character of God (in terms of the way God relates to humans) and the practical matters of Christian living. God is consistently depicted in terms of "moral" qualities, for Wesley had argued that predestination and reprobation defame the character of God. Fletcher's purpose was to restore the proper dialectical relationship between God and individuals. David C. Shipley has brought Fletcher's position into sharp focus:

1. Man is utterly dependent upon God's free gift of salvation, which cannot be earned but only received; and

2. The Christian religion is of a personal and moral character involving ethical demands on man and implying both human ability and human responsibility.[5]

Fletcher stated his own position in a later writing:

The error of rigid Calvinists centers in the denial of that evangelical liberty, whereby all men, under various dispensations of grace, may *without necessity* choose life. . . . And the error of rigid Arminians consists in not paying a cheerful homage to redeeming grace, for all the liberty and power which we have to choose life, and to work righteousness since the fall. . . .

To avoid equally these two extremes, we need only follow the Scripture-doctrine of free-will restored and assisted by *free-grace*.[6]

Wesley accepted Fletcher's presentation on grace and free will and commended it to his preachers. These "checks" undergirded the preaching of salvation as being available to all people through Christ's redemption; in addition, they expounded the privileges and obligations of Christian living.

Fletcher's contribution clarified Wesley's position by careful statement and clear presentation. There were some new suggestions, such as the relation of sanctification to the experience of Jesus' disciples at Pentecost (in the fifth check), the emphasis on the instantaneous event of sanctification, and the use of dispensational categories. In these ways Fletcher both reinforced and went beyond Wesley's theological work.

The Nineteenth Century

After Wesley's death his theology found new spokesmen. The earliest theologians in the ensuing tradition had known

Wesley personally, and they were influenced by the spirit of this theology that acknowledged the centrality of Jesus Christ and the authority of the Bible. John Wesley had attempted to revive scriptural Christianity, and he worked from this base in the construction of his own thoughts. A substantial part of Wesley's influence can be ascribed to his mediation of the biblical foundation upon which Christian life and thought must be built. It was in faithfulness to his witness that those who succeeded him in intellectual leadership followed his lead even as they undertook new interpretation.

Adam Clarke

As the Wesleyan tradition moved into the nineteenth century, new voices spoke to the changing situation. Adam Clarke (1760?–1832) continued the basic direction of Methodist theology in his development of biblical interpretation. In many ways Clarke was the epitome of all Wesley might have hoped for from his preachers: He combined biblical scholarship and practical concern in uncommon ways. Possessor of deep religious sense from early childhood, Clarke was drawn into the Methodist orbit in his teens. After becoming an itinerant preacher, he continued his studies and joined the first rank of scholars in England.

Clarke faced a changing institutional life and worked in arenas that would have been foreign to Wesley. A transitional figure, his ministry began under Wesley and his thought matured within the movement. Outliving Wesley by some forty years, he carried Methodist emphases into a new era. Though he bridged the time of change, his main buttress was always on the earlier side.

The energy of Adam Clarke was remarkable. In one eleven-month period he preached 568 sermons, in addition to "numerous exhortations," and traveled "some hundreds of miles" to accomplish these tasks.[7] During his active ministry he built schools, planned a retirement home for Methodist preachers and their widows, led missionary efforts, served three times as president of the Methodist Conference, organized drives to feed the hungry, and encouraged education for women in Northern Ireland. But preaching was his chief interest, and this he continued, always with warm evangelical fervor.

As a scholar he was equally impressive. A linguist of unusual ability, he worked with the British and Foreign Bible Society to translate the Scriptures into numerous foreign languages, translated the New Testament into the English of the day, wrote a commentary on the Old and New Testaments—giving some forty years to this one enterprise—wrote a number of notes on individual biblical words and concepts, translated the Coptic symbols on the Rosetta Stone which had baffled other scholars, and worked as archivist for the British government on its official records—to mention only some of his activities.

Any one of these vocations would represent a remarkable achievement, yet Clarke combined great learning with simple exposition. He stated his hope on the title page of his *Commentary*—that it might be "a help to a better understanding of the Sacred Writings." And in a letter, he rejoiced that his work "had been a means of doing good to the simple of heart, and the wise man."[8] Yet it was typical of his self-understanding that he wanted to be remembered primarily as a preacher of God's love for sinful persons.

Adam Clarke reinforced Wesley's interests. Typical of the orthodoxy of his time in his understanding of biblical authority, he assumed that the Scriptures provide a complete interpretation of the nature and will of God. He stated his position in his sermon on Romans 15:4. The biblical passage reads "Whatsoever things were written aforetime were written for our learning, that we through patience and comfort of the scriptures might have hope." Clarke's first two summary points were pertinent:

> 1. We must ever consider these Scriptures as coming from *God*, as divinely inspired, and as containing His infallible truth.
> 2. We should consider that it is by His grace and blessing that even His own Word becomes useful to us, for it is His grace alone that takes away the *veil of darkness and ignorance* from the mind, without which the pure, plain word of life cannot enter into our hearts, or become the power of God to our salvation.[9]

It is the task of the biblical theologian, under the guidance of the Holy Spirit, to render with care the meaning of Scripture and to present its application. Clarke was always, in intention, such a biblical theologian. Although in many of his sermons he developed systematic statements regarding Christian teaching—at times with extensive arguments, "Some Observations on the Being and Providence of God" (sermon 39)—he remained uneasy about systematic approaches. Consequently he spoke against those "who injudiciously, or incautiously *amass every text of Scripture,* which they think bears upon the subject they defend."[10]

Throughout his exposition Clarke followed Wesley's rule of using the best biblical scholarship of his day, and he remained close to Wesley on a number of cardinal points: the interpretation of God's grace, the nature of God's sovereignty, the offer of salvation to all persons, the basic importance of personal salvation, the teaching of justification and sanctification, and the meaning of assurance.

He differed from Wesley in one important view—the eternal Sonship of Jesus Christ—and this became a cause of concern and controversy. By his early twenties he was convinced that it was impossible to affirm the eternal Sonship of Jesus; that is, he maintained that before the Incarnation, Jesus was fully God and therefore of an *"eternal and unoriginated nature."* If this were not so, he argued, if Jesus were eternally derived from God and therefore subordinate to God, then his true eternity and his Godhead were destroyed, and if these were destroyed, then the atonement was annulled.[11] The issue for Clarke was the authenticity of the atonement—whether Jesus was able to offer the redemption of the Triune God to human life.

This became a crucial matter for some other Methodists, especially Richard Treffry, Jr., and Richard Watson. The integrity of the Trinity was believed to be at stake, and consequently the issue was immediately joined. Clarke's position was strongly opposed by most of his peers (although he never yielded) and the resulting refutation was viewed by some later interpreters as a singular victory for the orthodoxy of Methodist theology. As late as 1881, William Burt Pope could speak of the outcome of that debate as having preserved the doctrine of the Trinity, since "Methodism has had the high honor of indicating the eternal Sonship in a very marked manner."[12]

The style of theological scholarship which Clarke represented, however, was of basic importance for the Wesleyan tradition, for, like Wesley, he pointed to the Scriptures as the basis of theology and insisted upon testing every doctrine by reference to the Bible. Styles of interpretation and understandings of the role of Scripture will change, but throughout its history, Methodist theology has been characterized by a serious effort to understand the Bible thoroughly and to interpret it faithfully.

Richard Watson

The pursuit of theological development within the Wesleyan movement leads us quickly to Richard Watson

(1781–1833), who was the most influential theologian within Methodism on both sides of the Atlantic during the second and third quarters of the nineteenth century.

A precocious child, Watson had read some sixteen to eighteen volumes of a universal history before he was six. His education, however, was informal, and he was largely self-taught. At age seventeen he was received into the Methodist Conference on trial. Dominated by a principal interest in missions, he pursued this interest within Wesleyan Methodism, then moved to the Methodist New Connection, and finally returned to the Wesleyan Methodists.

Watson was the systematizer of Wesley's thought. Covering an unusual range of interests—from classical studies and world religions to previous theologians—he was intense, serious, and diligent, a writer whose life and thought were as sharply chiseled as his bodily features. His intellectual strong point was the organization of ideas, and his dominant quality was persistence. Orderly of mind, his major work, *Theological Institutes*, is clearly drawn and tenaciously carried through with a logical development of content.

Watson intended his work to be a theology for the Wesleyan movement; he served as missionary secretary of the church for four years and the dedication of the volumes to Jabez Bunting, the administrative leader of the Wesleyan church, was symbolic of his desire to work in relation to the church and its institutional life. His theology was practical, a theology to underwrite the life of a believing and witnessing community.

But the worlds of Wesley and Watson were in clear contrast. Wesley's world had been open; one feels the chill of the early morning air, the push of crowds and the rigor of rutted roads; there were rioting mobs and contagious religious conversions. Wesley had been at the center of a religious storm; there was danger and excitement, fear and hope. A new movement was underway, too powerful to be contained.

The world of Richard Watson was both more restricted and differently challenged. Methodism continued to expand—even more than in Wesley's day—but it had moved inside. The walls of the chapels became clearer boundaries; enthusiasm was channeled into ritual; and living together as a concrete community was found to be most difficult. The Wesleyan movement also experienced some of its most bitter attacks even as it was gaining acceptance by the larger society. Many persons regarded the movement with uncertainty and perhaps amusement, and not a few with disdain, but Methodism was vitally alive, even as it was under pressure to define its identity. Increasingly, Methodism was typified by the tradesman and greengrocer, the schoolmaster and the baker, rather than by the embattled witness or the fearless hymn-singer.

Richard Watson was of a different temper and assumed a different role than had Wesley. He was also a preacher, but as a theologian he understood his task as being a defender of the faith; he would argue for the validity of inherited Christian truth; he was an apologist. His chief external opponents were those who aligned themselves with Deist thought. English Deists were intellectually descended from Lord Herbert of Cherbury (1583–1648) and continued in strength through such seventeenth-century figures as Thomas Morgan, Thomas Chubb, Thomas Woolston, down to Matthew Tindal in the eighteenth century. The principal theological conviction of these thinkers was that the native rational capacity of human beings is sufficient for the discovery of religious truth. God was understood as the creator of the universe, but the Creator was detached from the created order, offering no direct or personal revelation. The light of "nature" was the foundation of all knowledge. This conviction, combined with the exploratory spirit of the Deists—often advanced against popular persuasion—refused to allow theological assumptions or conclusions to stand unchallenged. They confronted traditional Christian theology with claims that those who affirmed revelation would be forced to counter. Richard Watson gathered together a reasoned response for the Methodists. He aligned the Wesleyan tradition with a wide community of Christian theologians and argued for human reliance upon God's sovereignty as Creator, Sustainer, and Revealer. He particularly stressed the deductive use of Scripture and vigorously defended a high doctrine of scriptural inerrancy. With these emphases, he ignored the inductive style and exploring spirit that had characterized Wesley's use of Scripture.

Watson was also a defender of a particular stream within Christian theology against what might be called internal opponents. He was, he insisted, neither a Calvinist nor a Pelagian; he intended to conform to Wesleyanism, which, he believed, continued a major stream from the Reformation through English traditions. He advocated this mediating position extensively in *Theological Institutes,* exhibiting in these arguments more independence than he had shown against external adversaries.

Once again, Watson relied on a broad range of sources, especially the leaders and creeds of the Reformation, and English theologians, both Anglicans and Dissenters. Strikingly, he quoted only meagerly from Wesley in the *Theological Institutes,* and almost always from the sermons. But it is clear that he intended to be faithful to Wesley's positions. He would, in 1831, with deep appreciation, write a biography of John Wesley. It is obvious that his commitment to the Wesleyan tradition was firm.[13]

In the biography, Watson said of Wesley's theological position, "Although somewhat similar doctrines are found in many Arminian writers, yet in the theology of the Wesleys they derive life and vigor from the stronger views of the grace of God which were taught them by Moravian and Calvinistic brethren."[14] Watson contended most strongly against the Calvinists; one often battles most ardently those with whom one is most closely identified, for it is here that the distinctions become most crucial.

Nevertheless, it is the case that in *Theological Institutes* there are few references to Wesley's own statements, and hereby hangs an important point. It is fundamental that from the beginning, John Wesley was not considered a framer of doctrine whose interpretations were definitive. The crucial issue, rather, is that Wesley pointed to the gospel of God in Jesus Christ, insisted upon biblical foundations for doctrine, and affirmed the sovereignty of God and the graciously granted worth of human life.

One particular change occurred in the time between Wesley's theological enterprise and Watson's *Theological Institutes*; there was a movement from a confessional to an apologetic stance. Wesley preached the truth he had come to know by God's activity in human life; he was a witness to the redemptive work of God as that has been and was being experienced. His attention was constantly focused upon the work of God in human life. Watson began with at least one cautious eye on those who surrounded the Christian community and were encouraging doubt or drawing the attention of believers to tempting but false notions. Wesley's theology served preaching for conversion and growth. Watson presented a defensive theology, intended to preserve the faith and keep it pure. In this transition there was a subtle yet clear move from a more experiential mode to an orderly, thoroughly formulated theology.

Theological Institutes is a substantial work. It opens with a defense of revealed knowledge, as opposed to notions of natural religion. The knowledge of God, which has been imparted through Jesus Christ and the witness of Scripture, is central and necessary; and what is revealed cannot be deciphered by the native ingenuity of humans. At the same time, Watson's purpose was to keep the primacy of the witness of God in balance with the rational capacity of human beings.[15] Watson held that revelation is necessary in order to know God savingly, but he also contended that revelation complements and completes our natural intellectual competence. Inadequate human reason must be aided by divine revelation so that it may become adequate to receive and understand the truth of God.

The outline of Watson's constructive theology is significant. He began with the importance of revelation and located this witness in the Bible; then in part 2, he expounded the "Doctrines of the Holy Scriptures." He insisted that all his arguments were based on experience; the only saving knowledge we have of God, he claimed, comes from our own experience of God and of the world. But because Scripture is the primary witness to God as experienced in human life and conveys "infallible truth," he actually began with biblical references.[16] Thomas Jackson, in his *Memoirs*, commented, "As a theologian, the distinguishing peculiarity of his mind was an absolute submission to the authority of Holy Scripture."[17] Scriptural revelation fulfills our human rational searching; so Watson, with care and sensitivity, shifted back and forth from the scriptural base to human reflection.

In this spirit, he pursued the question of the existence of God. The fact that he moves immediately to this issue once again illustrates his apologetic concern; but Watson's method of defense was not so much to analyze opponents' arguments as to make as clear as possible the claims of scriptural Christianity which, among other things, stand over against the opposition's general claims. For Watson, Biblical teaching stated that God is unitary, spiritual, eternal, omnipotent, ubiquitous, omniscient, immutable, wise, good, and holy. From this point he moved to a discussion of human ability. Since the Fall, it has been impossible for persons to come to these understandings of God on their own; they can only know God savingly through the biblical record. But once these truths are perceived through revelation, people are able to support them through rational arguments, or at least show that they do not contradict reason. The necessity of revelation for fallen human beings is especially met by the revelation of God in Jesus Christ, who, through his vicarious sacrificial death, has opened the way from God to people and from people to God.[18]

The doctrine of the Trinity illustrates Watson's strategy against external opponents. That God is Triune is a revealed truth. This cannot be known with clarity or certainty by unaided human cogitation. We know that God is Triune because, Watson claimed, the Scriptures say so. But once we see that this is the case, it is possible to reunderstand our religious intimations and recognize God's Triunity to be the truth to which they pointed.

In volume 2, Watson expended great energy in arguing that faith is a gift and that justification is by faith alone. Here he opposed the Pelagians, especially those among the Anglicans. But he also denied that grace is irresistible; in this he stood against the Calvinists. He stated his mediating position clearly and consistently. In both sin and redemption, there is a prior reality; we are related either to Adam or to Christ, and this identification is decisive as persons concur with sin or with righteousness. There is grace, and consequently there is human responsibility; everything is dependent upon God, yet in God's sovereign order there is a gracious gift of ability which persons receive and must utilize.[19]

A central emphasis in the *Theological Institutes* is the contrast between the "Extent of the Atonement" and the "Theories Which Limit the Extent of the Death of Christ" (chs. 25–28, a statement of some 176 pages, more than 10 percent of the entire system). This is a long detailed discussion which Watson claimed to have compressed "into as narrow lines as possible."[20] He was attempting, with biblical and rational answers, to meet the best arguments of the much-discussed issue of limited atonement. The fact that this issue loomed so large is reflective of the time, with its prevalent search for God's ways of relating to humankind; especially was this an important topic among evangelical Christians as they attempted to interpret their mission.

Watson stated his aim and exhibited the spirit of his argument:

> This inquiry leads us into what is called the Calvinistic controversy; a controversy which has always been conducted with great ardour, and sometimes with intemperance. I shall endeavour to consider such parts of it as are comprehended in the question before us, with perfect calmness and fairness; recollecting, on the one hand, how many excellent and learned men have been arranged on each side; and, on the other, that while all honour is due to great names, the plain and unsophisticated sense of the word of inspired truth must alone decide on a subject with respect to which it is not silent.[21]

Watson's conclusion was that the sovereignty of God must be affirmed, but that God, as sovereign, works through justice and goodness; and that these qualities have been expressed, not through an irresistible grace, but through a grace that both creates and relies upon human responsibility. Absolute determination by God and absolute freedom of human beings are persistent alternatives, but the greater truth, as revealed in Scripture, is found in holding divine sovereignty and human ability in proper balance. With these and similar themes, Richard Watson passed the Wesleyan tradition to his contemporaries and successors.

Richard Watson succeeded Wesley, not only in the historical sense, but also in the theological sense of taking a step beyond. In his *Theological Institutes* he objectivized and systematized the beliefs that Wesley had proclaimed with more abandon. He brought consistent structure to Wesley's creative thrusts, and some important things changed in the process. The assertiveness of Wesley became a more cautious and careful exposition; and although Watson deeply believed the same truths, protective action tended to replace vital proclamation.

Though such change was due in part to different temperaments, it also reflected a second-generation response to received convictions; and it expressed a changing stance in regard to the way Christian truth should be presented. The theological work of Richard Watson must be understood in the context of its time and in regard to its historical place in the Wesleyan movements. Our purpose is not to identify faithfulness or disloyalty in the succession of Wesleyan theologians, even if we should acknowledge that some are more creative than others. Our purpose is rather to ask, What is God doing through these persons who desire to be faithful witnesses to Christian truth? And having come to some conviction on this point, we may and should then ask, How does this achievement relate to the specific tradition we call Wesleyan, in terms of correlation, correction, or affirmation?

Some interpreters have tended to view the movement of Wesleyan theology as a degeneration from a pristine source to less pure streams.[22] The evidence in nineteenth-century British Methodism hardly supports this thesis, for Pope, whom we shall look at next, and Watson and Clarke understood the essential parts of Wesley's theology and intended to maintain these themes. But they faced new circumstances and attempted to respond to those challenges. For this they are to be honored. But there is also, on their part, a preoccupation with finding rational evidence for faith, with demonstrating the credibility of Scripture, and these emphases tend to change the character of Wesley's original theological effort. The value of that move, their successors will judge.

William Burt Pope

We move now across half a century, to William Burt Pope (1822–1903). Much had transpired, especially in the effort of Methodism to establish its identity. Yet central theological themes—themes that characterize the tradition—were continued across the expanse of time.

Pope possessed a richly textured personality. He was intelligent, widely read, and imaginative. One contemporary described him as "small in stature, with a grave, tender face capable of a most genial smile."[23] Pope was the New World's first major contribution to British Methodism. He was born in Nova Scotia, where his father was a businessman and Methodist preacher, but Pope returned to England to attend school.

Pope was both a Methodist minister and a catholic Christian. Shy and retiring, he was expansive and warmly sensitive to a great range of Christian tradition. Pope's intelligence developed rapidly; he finished school at age fifteen, went back to Nova Scotia, and worked for an uncle while pursuing his study of language. Then he entered Hoxton Theological College in England to prepare for the ministry. His years of training were effective, and as one biographer wrote, "He left Hoxton a Methodist by conviction, widely read in several tongues, with habits such as make a scholar of first rank, with sympathies that went out almost equally towards evangelism and towards mysticism—a polished shaft in the quiver of the Lord."[24]

Pope was a thoroughly learned biblical scholar and systematic theologian whose biblical study underwrote his theological work. Illustrative of his interests, his daily schedule set two hours for Hebrew, Greek, and Latin, three hours for theological study, and one for mathematics, with German, history, and biography filling "the nondescript hours and seasons."[25] Conservative by nature, he understood his task to be the restatement of the basic positions of his tradition.

Pope's scholarship was aided by a clear, engaging literary style which expressed his thoughts succinctly. His essay on "Methodist Doctrine," for instance, is a precise and vibrant statement of the spirit and content of Methodism.[26] Convinced of the deep worth of tradition, Pope wrote, "It is our rejoicing that, as to the whole compass of the Christian faith, we are one with the general confession of evangelical Christendom."[27] And again, "The staple and substance of Methodist theology is essentially that of the entire Scripture as interpreted by the Catholic evangelical tradition of the Christian Church."[28] This evangelical-Catholic tradition he found especially in the early pre-Augustinian church and in John Wesley.

Few theological teachers have carried a greater sense of the weight of their responsibility. With a moving humility, Pope called upon his colleagues:

> Remember that we are pledged to the truth which Christ has given to us, with all its difficulties. We cannot receive him without the severities of his doctrine. He does not only impose on us an ethical cross that rests upon moral nature. For my part, that would be easy indeed to bear in comparison with that other cross of his most precious doctrine, the whole fulness and integrity of His truth which He lays upon my spirit and commands me to bear.[29]

Pope's effort, in essence, was to set Methodist theology within the living thought of the catholic world. He described it as being

> Catholic in the best sense, holding the Doctrinal Articles of the English Church, including the Three Creeds [Apostles',

Nicene, and Athanasian], and therefore maintaining the general doctrines of the Reformation. It is Arminian as opposed to Calvinism but in no other sense. Its peculiarities are many, touching chiefly the nature and extent of personal salvation; and with regard to these its standards are certain writings of John Wesley and other authoritative documents.[30]

The central idea in Pope's thought was that of divine grace as effected in human life by the Holy Spirit. This grace is expressed preveniently in justification and, finally, in sanctification. The explication of these themes is found in Pope's major work, *A Compendium of Christian Theology*. In orderly fashion, he arranged his discussion by stating each theme in a concise paragraph, then elaborating upon its meaning. He opened with this proposition: "Christian theology is the science of God and Divine things, based upon the revelation made to mankind in Jesus Christ, and variously systematized within the Christian church."[31] As with the Gospel of John, the meaning of this whole study is expressed in the introduction. If one understands the prologue, one understands the whole. But the introduction, for most people, requires elaboration.

Pope's opening paragraph contains five basic theses: (1) God is the source, subject, and end of theology. (2) God is known through revelation, hence God's activity comes first; nevertheless, (3) unless there is human capacity to receive divine truth no communication would be possible. (4) Again, revelation is central and the definitive revelation is Jesus Christ—therefore this is Christian theology. (5) All this is arranged through general rational induction and systematic ordering and, in this sense, theology is a scientific enterprise. Theology may be expressed as biblical or historical interpretation, as doctrinal development, or as systematic arrangement. This last form was Pope's method, and in this he exhibited a confessional stance that takes doctrine as its framework, is illustrated from history and verified by Scripture.

Scripture is the "Divine Rule of Faith," the medium of revelation. There is a general revelation, which includes every manifestation of God and is the ground of natural religion and natural theology. There is also, and more important, special revelation: the "unfolding of the eternal counsel" of God in Christ. Scripture and Christian truth, Pope maintained, coincide exactly. Pope, like Watson and Clarke, was precritical in his understanding of the Bible. The impact of higher criticism had simply not been felt. Pope was direct: "Biblical criticism does not extend its range beyond the judgment exercised upon the verity of the text."[32] And he used fewer then four pages in discussing the critical effort to establish the best text as the basis for theological interpretation. The Bible itself is the primary compendium, but since it is historical, it is not structured as a systematic theology— hence the need for an organized approach. All systematic theological constructions are arrangements of the original and sufficient biblical source.

There is little in the *Compendium* that differs from Wesley, Clarke, or Watson. The same issues are discussed and similar conclusions are reached. The distinctive quality of Pope's writing lay in his style of expression, his lucidity, and his completeness. He carried out the Wesleyan emphases and his chief contribution was perhaps his continuation of the doctrine of the universal range of God's gracious redemptive activity, which is free in all, to all, and for all.

Yet Pope, with all his brilliance and disciplined study, was isolated from the newer currents in British intellectual life—Darwinianism and idealistic philosophy. This separation was caused in part by Methodism's place in British society and its disassociation from the established church and other dissenting groups; in part it was because of Pope's own conservative disposition and his tight focus on biblical truth. Whatever the cause, Pope was not engaged in the swirl of Victorian struggles with religious doubt, the new dynamic of biblical criticism, the changing philosophical scene with the rise of idealism, or the transforming power of evolutionary ideas. His position was formed prior to the 1860s, the critical period for many of the issues, and although the *Compendium* was published in 1875–1876, he was not responsive to these new currents. Catholic in his range of sensitivity to traditional Christian positions, Pope was uncongenial toward contemporary developments, although a slight familiarity with Friedrich Schleiermacher's theology is evident. He also mentioned F. D. Maurice and Samuel Taylor Coleridge, but these he rejected because of their moderating positions on biblical critical studies. At no point did he engage other dimensions of new themes in British theological discussion. He did speak once of Darwin in the *Compendium*, but only to show a logical gap in Darwin's theory. Consistently, Pope presented a confessional theology and in so doing, attempted to reinvigorate original Wesleyan witness.

Pope both represented and perpetuated the conservative stance of British Methodist theology. The tensions between inheritance and anticipation, between retention and exploration were relaxed, and he sacrificed the latter possibilities for the sake of the former values. In this, Pope preserved, with strength and increased clarity, the essential thrust of the Wesleyan position; but he also encouraged lack of attention to the imposing intellectual issues of the day. There are times when conservation is meritorious, and Pope, through his caution, kept sharp focus on the redemptive grace of God in Jesus Christ. That, in a fluid age, was no small contribution.

Hugh Price Hughes

A new spirit was evident among Methodist theologians at the close of the century, and a changing set of sensitivities was projected through one man, Hugh Price Hughes

(1847–1902), who cut different paths for some Methodists to follow. Grandson of a prominent Welsh Methodist preacher and a remarkable evangelist himself, Hughes' influence was effected through his editorial work as well as by his gift of oratory. In 1884 he established the *Methodist Times*, and of his work, another editor of the era observed, "Mr. Price Hughes has been a constant force upon which you could always depend whenever a wrong had to be routed."[33] In Hughes Wesleyan theology was married to a fierce social conscience.

Through his periodical, Hughes took up such issues as education, temperance, peace, labor, and economic life. The application of the gospel message to the social context became a burning passion, a singular obsession. He seemed to be controlled by the words written to Charles Kingsley by an Oxford friend: "Get hold of some one truth. Let it blaze in your sky like a Greenland sun, never setting day or night." These concerns, carried under the banner The Forward Movement, were a challenge to Methodism from within. Hughes charged that the church had dealt too exclusively with individual piety and that it must now attend to "business, pleasure and politics."[34] In 1887, in evidence of this social concern, he helped to establish the West London Mission. Typical of his stance was his warning that Christians should never "think of ourselves apart from Christ [or] think of ourselves apart from mankind."[35]

Christianity of the Methodist variety was now involved in the political life of the nation. Hughes' theme was the phrase "non-conformist conscience"—the moral stance of nonestablished Christians—and with vigor he entered the political realm, endorsing, opposing, organizing, and speaking. One writer commented that "Hugh Price Hughes is always to me the embodiment of *force*."[36] His theology was practical; it involved proclaiming the Kingdom and serving its causes. Hughes regarded theology as the constant handmaiden of social concern; thought must evoke action.

71

To complement Hughes' work, his wife, Mary Katherine Howard Hughes, organized a "sisterhood," modeled on the ancient order of deaconnesses and called Sisters of the People. This group was given special responsibilities and served through the West London Mission. Mrs. Hughes emphasized that the women were to develop all their talents, devote themselves to work for which they had special aptitude or preparation, and be accessible to people in need.

Hughes' interests also included ecumenicity, and in 1890 he, along with many prominent Free Church (non-Church of England) leaders, originated The National Council of Evangelical Free Churches. The inaugural congress of this organization was held in Manchester in 1892. Arguing that the new council should be theologically defined, Hughes became permanent chairman of the committee to draw up a doctrinal statement.

Hughes was aware of the importance of theology, but he was even more interested in progressing to the consequences of theology. He was not a scholar in the sense of Clarke, Watson, or Pope. He possessed neither their intellectual discipline nor their technical knowledge. He was a practical theologian—all of life, he insisted, was to be transformed. "Christianity does not say to us, 'Sit and be convinced,' but 'Arise and walk.' "[37] He never forgot or failed to advise that the beginning of faith is personal trust in a personal savior; Christianity, he often remarked, is Christ. But more and more he pushed beyond the initial evangelical experience to stress the gracious working of love.

Hughes related that Andrew Fairbairn, the leading Congregational theologian of the era, had commented that ministers' libraries had been completely revolutionized in the last half of the nineteenth century. Books on abstract theology were being replaced by commentaries on the New Testament and biographies of Jesus; higher critical study was gaining strength and was now influencing theology. Hughes rejoiced in this transition. This biblical study, he said, emphasized two themes: "The Fatherhood of God and the kingdom of God."[38] These were also the ascendent themes of Protestant liberalism. British Methodist theology was moving toward closer identification with that general liberal stream.

Hughes always spoke in the present tense. He preached on the present sovereignty of God; he reminded his hearers of their daily prayer, "Thy kingdom come"; he spoke of religious life not in terms of monastic orders or the next world, but in the immediate context. He encouraged his contemporaries to seize the day for the work of love. The social issues upon which Hughes concentrated were of long standing, but now were newly intruding upon the Christian conscience: racism, militarism, the subjection of women, irresponsible wealth, the ranking of classes, the opium trade, torture of animals, and the sale of spirits and gunpowder to "uncivilized" peoples.

Yet he attempted to keep these present social interests in balance with more traditional themes. In *Essential Christianity*, he argued that Christianity basically stresses "spiritual blessings," that it keeps an eye on eternity, and that essentially, it is union with Jesus Christ. These realities lie at its heart, and from this center radiate the propulsions of Christian service. So he concluded "Let us submit to Christ, let us yield ourselves to Him in all simplicity and heartiness; let us permit Him to do what He will in us, and with us, and through us."[39]

Hugh Price Hughes represented a change of time and a new awareness. British Methodism was being drawn from its isolation; it was becoming sensitive to different responsibilities; and it was finding enlarged theological interests. Hughes was a spokesman for the linking of evangelism with mission tasks directed toward the social order. He invigorated the interaction of preaching and service.

Conclusion

The five men we have looked at in this chapter were remarkable. They represented enormous energy and dedication, disciplined living, and faithful scholarship; they combined evangelical zeal with a great range of service.

John Fletcher was the prototype of a saintly theologian. Following Wesley's lead, he centered his life and thought on grace. The merciful sovereignty of God, he argued, makes possible the response of faith. Grace creates, continues, and consummates Christian life; so Fletcher stressed the sanctification that crowns faithful existence. In all this he represented the development of a distinctive theological perspective. Wesley published Fletcher's biography in serial form in *The Arminian Magazine* in 1790:

> Within fourscore years, I have known many excellent men, holy in heart and life. But one equal to him I have not known; one so uniformly and deeply devoted to God, so unblameable a man in every respect, I have not found either in *Europe* or *America*. Nor do I expect fo find another such on this side eternity.[40]

Adam Clarke also was remarkable. After twenty-five years of labor on his biblical commentary, he walked into his parlor and,

> without speaking to anyone, but beckoning to his youngest son, took him into the hall and said, "Come with me, Joseph, I wish to take you into my study." His son had no suspicion of anything unusually extraordinary to be seen, and followed mechanically; but his astonishment was indeed great, when Dr. Clarke opened the door, and pointed to his large study table, and the stand at his right hand, cleared of all their folios, etc., and nothing remaining on either but his study Bible:—"This Joseph is the happiest period I have enjoyed in years: I have put the last hand to my Commentary: I have written the last word of the work: I have put away the chains

that would remind me of my bondage; and there (pointing to the steps of his library ladder) I have returned the deep thanks of a grateful soul to the God who has shown me so great and continued kindness; I shall now go into the parlour, tell my good news to the rest, and enjoy myself for the day."[41]

To see this work through the completion of its printing would require another fifteen years, but a milestone had been passed; he had accomplished a strenuous task, working, as he said, until he was half dead and praying until he was wholly alive—and all this amidst an unusually active life as preacher, scholar, family man, pastor, educator, and conference leader.

Richard Watson, in the last three years of his life, was continually ill, but he was an active superintendent of a circuit, delivered a series of lectures on Romans, visited the sick, gave one afternoon each week to missionary work, arranged his *Theological and Biblical Dictionary* and composed many of its articles, wrote his commentary on Matthew, and "meditated" on an exposition of the Old Testament when he had completed the New; he also began a biography of Charles Wesley, "which he intended to pursue as a sort of relaxation from severer studies."[42]

William B. Pope was of the same character. His long days were filled with devoted study and sensitive service. His care for the Christian inheritance drew him into colloquy with his predecessors, extending his sensibilities while deepening his understanding of the faith. The strain eventually proved too much; his health broke. But he had produced his major work, and he bequeathed a spirit as well as a system to his successors.

All these men exemplified the union of vital piety and sound learning for which John Wesley had so much hoped. They were good men who honed their talent to love God and serve their neighbor. They remained perpetuators of their tradition.

Dominated by a biblical orientation, all were committed to the Scriptures as the sure and complete guide to Christian thought. The authority of the Bible, as they understood it, was consistently expressed through every passage unaffected by internal or subsequent historical changes. Their basic thesis was the grace of God expressed in Jesus Christ—all Scripture witnesses to him. This approach produced great clarity in central gospel emphases; and with this foundation, the Methodist movement was well served and served well its time. However, insofar as the changing times were not directly engaged—Watson made tentative moves outward, but Pope drew back—there was limitation of theological leadership. Although the contribution of early and mid-nineteenth-century Methodist theology preserved the power of its past, it was less vigorous in directing that power toward its present or into the future.[43]

It was at this juncture that Hugh Price Hughes came on the scene, representing a redirection of theological interest for some in the Wesleyan movement. Hughes came from the tradition of Wesleyan evangelism and never forgot his foundation in the biblical message of personal salvation. Reclaiming his inheritance, Hughes attempted to build ethical strategies that would speak directly and challengingly to his social setting.

John Wesley had attempted to explicate faith as working through love; he had held together the dual thrusts of saving faith and redemptive service. His followers also attempted to hold these dimensions together through the integrating motif of grace. In Clarke and Watson there was a principal emphasis upon the dimensions of personal faith, but also upon moral responsibility—a moral responsibility expressed primarily within the life of the Christian community and secondarily through benevolent service beyond the bounds of that community. In Pope, there was some loosening of the ethical imperatives and a reassertion of qualities of the interior life; in response to the challenge of his time, as he understood it, he attempted to conserve the central emphases of evangelical revivalism. The bequeathed theological base was accepted, acknowledged, and utilized by Hugh Price Hughes, but his stress was placed upon the implications of the theological tradition for Christian life in the world of social interaction. Benevolence and the ethical mores of Christian life were recognized but also superseded, in an effort to attack corporate and organized systems of evil. Personal ethics with social implications became transmuted into social ethics derived from a personal base. The context and the internal life of the Wesleyan movement were undergoing change.

CHAPTER 4

THE AMERICANIZATION OF
WESLEYAN THEOLOGY

NORTH AMERICAN Methodism, separated from
England by geographic distance, existed in a
different cultural setting. Professor Perry Miller
argues that a chief characteristic of American culture was the
religious revivalism that dominated the first six decades of
the nineteenth century. The passionate extension of Christian faith through the preaching and hearing of the gospel of
personal salvation was a shaping force. From the beginning,
it was clear to Francis Asbury and the Methodists that their
special mission to the New World was, following their
founder's example, to spread the gospel message across the
land. It is not surprising, therefore, to hear Nathan Bangs say
that the Methodist movement was "begotten, fostered, and
grew up under the influence of the spirit of the revival."[1]

Methodism was introduced into the colonies by lay people.
Robert Strawbridge established the first Methodist society in
Maryland in the mid 1760s, and Barbara Heck was
instrumental in establishing a society in New York City.
Richard Boardman and Joseph Pilmore, the first missionaries

sent by John Wesley, arrived in 1769. The coming of Francis Asbury (1745–1816) in 1771 was crucial. Asbury's contribution to Methodism was enormous; he was the director and example, the overseer and chief advocate of the movement. But he did not make a theological contribution beyond preserving, by reiteration, the chief themes of Wesley.

Several other people also made contributions that would become significant in later Methodism: Philip William Otterbein (1726–1813), Martin Boehm (1725–1812), and Jacob Albright (1759–1808), all of whom carried young, evangelical movements into the nineteenth century and built them into denominations. Otterbein and Boehm were instrumental in founding the United Brethren (1815), and Albright's legacy was brought to fulfillment in the Evangelical Association (1816).

These revivalists preached their theology, they were evangelistic in effort and committed to the active transformation of human life. In basic beliefs they identified with the Wesleyan tradition. The course of study established by the United Brethren in 1815, for instance, included Wesley's sermons, Fletcher's *Appeal* and *Checks*, and Adam Clarke's theological writings. But the deposit of written theology left by early United Brethren and Evangelicals is meager. General revival convictions were enough: Jesus Christ as Savior, the authority of Scripture for theological interpretation, and sanctification. Evolving independently of the Wesleyans, and developing a polity of their own, these groups recognized themselves as sharing a common cause with the Methodists. They maintained a friendship founded upon spiritual and missional affinity.

Asbury and the other leaders knew that their roots, like Wesley's, were in classical Christianity as carried through the Reformation. The dominant theme was the salvation of people through Jesus Christ. This emphasis is clear in Otterbein's sermons and those we have of Asbury and the

United Brethren and Evangelical preachers. The revivalistic plan of salvation, with special interest in Christian holiness, constituted the common core of their witness. Originally related, these traditions, a century and a half later, would realize organic unity.[2]

American Methodist theology was aware of its changed context. But notwithstanding the distinctive emphases that were to develop in North America, this tradition utilized and intended to be a continuation of John Wesley's interpretation of Christian faith. In a succinct paragraph, Sydney Ahlstrom has described the general condition.

> There is no justification for the conclusion of many historians (including the most fervent Methodists) that the Methodist message was a "democratic theology" or a "frontier faith." In the earliest part of the nineteenth century, at least, its theology was derived not from American democracy or the frontier but from John Wesley. . . . And the starting point of this theology (as of all Reformed theology whether "Arminian" or not) was the sovereignty of God and the depravity of man. No one spoke more forcefully of man's abject need for divine grace than Wesley, and the true Methodist demand for repentance . . . stems from the heart of the Puritan movement. Arminianism in this context meant not an optimistic view of human nature . . . but a reinterpretation of the strict Calvinistic understanding of atonement, grace, and the sanctifying work of the Holy Spirit. Had this not been the case, Methodism would never have been the moral force that it was on the frontier. Decades of vulgar, simplistic theological polemic between Wesleyans and Calvinists ultimately forced both sides to exaggerate their distinctive tenets and banish subtlety from theological discussion. . . . One must insist that the force of primitive Wesleyan theology constituted a major factor in Methodist explosion on the frontier.[3]

This comment is perceptive and accurate, and its implications need to be explored. For North American Methodist theology, John Wesley constituted the background; the sovereignty of God and human sinfulness, the content; and personal salvation finally realized in sanctification, the goal.

Theological Beginnings

One of the earliest Methodist theologians, Asa Shinn (1781–1865), later to become a Methodist Protestant, in 1813 published *An Essay on the Plan of Salvation: in Which the Several Sources of Evidence are Examined, and Applied to the Interesting Doctrine of Redemption, in its Relation to the Government and Moral Attributes of Deity*. The emphases in the title are important—salvation was central in theology as in experience. For the next half century, the issues of God's providential ordering and moral attributes were of special concern in developing pivotal aspects of the divine/human relationship.y Asa Shinn is symbolically important because he represents the tension between inherited Wesleyan thought and responsiveness to a specific culture. Self-educated, Shinn was especially open to his immediate context, but as with his predecessors, the foundation of his position was scriptural. He wrote,

> Each one is bound under a sacred obligation, to go to the Bible for his system of divinity, and so far as any man is governed by a regard to any human creed, in the formation of his religious opinions, so far he is deficient in the very principle of Christian faith; and pays that homage to human authority that is due only to the Divine.[4]

Shinn further commented, "An appeal to *experience*, in support of any doctrine, is not to be received unless in accord with the oracles of God."[5] The order of priority was set: Scripture is the primary and commanding source for theology. For Shinn, human depravity, redeeming grace, and sanctification were keynotes; and with specific emphasis

81

he stressed that grace is freely offered to all people because of the moral character of God.

Asa Shinn foreshadowed distinctive North American modes of theological work. In *An Essay on the Plan of Salvation,* his initial discussion was concerned with the basis of religious knowledge. He built his position upon the Scottish common-sense philosophy that was pervasive at the time. This philosophy presented a theory of knowledge that affirmed the epistemic continuity between the mind and the real world, the unity of truth, a rational soul, an orderly world, and the reality of God providing this order. It is not the use that Shinn made of this philosophy that is significant, but the fact that he entered into the current American discussion as a part of his responsibility. The sign was small but clear; American Methodist theology would respond to, be shaped by, and contribute to the presiding issues in the intellectual and moral sensibility of its culture. The Wesleyan tradition in the United States was developing an indigenous character.[6]

Wesleyan and Calvinistic Theology

Differences among revival groups soon became prominent and Methodism found its chief contention with Calvinism. The relation of Methodism to Calvinism in North America is often referred to as "controversy." In part, this notion comes from the earlier Wesleyan-Calvinistic polemics of the 1770s and 1780s in England. But in North America there were not two solid lines which confronted each other. Rather, Methodism took a position that cut through the spectrum of positions in nineteenth-century Calvinistic theology.

To understand the situation it is necessary to glance backward. In the seventeenth century, a federal, or covenent, theology had dominated New England Congregationalism—the belief that God has initiated a covenant relationship that carries moral obligations. This school of Reformed thought deflected and softened the harsh determinism of strict Calvinism by introducing the idea of a "conditional" covenant. Predestination, they claimed, is not absolute; God obligates human beings to play a role in the process of salvation. Hence one must prepare one's heart, use the means of grace, and practice morality. While none of these activities guarantees redeeming grace, they do fulfill the prerequisites for salvation and, in this sense, a person participates in the process of regeneration.[7]

Jonathan Edwards (1703–1758) had led the attack on this position earlier, attempting to reclaim the sovereignty of God; and Samuel Hopkins (1721–1803), his most able student, continued the battle. Hopkins produced the first American systematic theology, developing a position called consistent Calvinism. He emphasized total human depravity and absolute divine sovereignty, insisting that one must accept the decree of God concerning election and be willing to be damned for the glory of God. Hopkins allowed this volitional element by including human freedom within the divine decrees, since the efficacious exercise of decreed freedom brings redemption. Even so, in this life one may only hope for salvation, since the final decision always remains with the sovereignty of God.[8]

Hopkins' position was not accepted by many of his fellow Calvinists. In 1818 Nathaniel William Taylor (1786–1858) of Yale published *Man, A Free Agent Without the Aide of Divine Grace.* Taylor agreed with Hopkins that human consent is fundamental in relationship with God. Free agency, inherent in humans, is evident in understanding, conscience, and will. Hence he emphasized the volitional character of sin: For an act to be sinful, it must be willfully done. But Taylor argued that the freedom to sin is an ability that lies outside grace. Redemption is found as the sinful will, by the gracious permission of God and aided by the Holy Spirit, chooses to accept the redeeming work of Christ. On this basis, one may experience not just hope of salvation, but personal certainty of it. The Holy Spirit necessarily operates in conversion and sanctification, but this "never violated the great laws of moral action or contravened the freedom of the subject."[9]

The Wesleyans looked at the divergencies among the Calvinists as representing vastly different approaches; yet all Calvinists, they claimed, continued to hold that only elected people will utilize divine grace. When one surveys these positions and then reads the Methodist theologians, it is clear that the Methodists were seeking to establish their position in relation to these differing ways of relating grace to human freedom. Nathan Bangs (1778–1862), who deserves the title of the first significant Wesleyan theologian in the United States, represents this effort.

Originally editor of *The Methodist Magazine*, Bangs was instrumental in establishing the *Christian Advocate* (1826) and then served as editor of the *Methodist Magazine and Quarterly Review* (1832–36).[10] In *The Errors of Hopkinsianism* (1815), Bangs argued that Hopkins and his followers had unsuccessfully attempted to combine the primary efficient causality of God and human free agency. Seth Williston, a colleague of Hopkins, rejoined that Bangs failed to recognize total depravity, and therefore the impotence of people in their sinful condition. Bangs replied, accepting the fact of human depravity but emphasizing prevenient grace and, on this ground, defended human ability for moral conduct. "Those gentlemen who urge the doctrine of total depravity against this truth seem to forget one very important trait in the Gospel system, viz., the atonement of Christ, and the benefits which universally flow from it to mankind, by which they are graciously restored to the power of action." In providing his answer, Bangs claimed that human beings have moral obligations and the means of fulfilling these obligations through God's grace. Grace is present because

"Christ the true light, has come, the Spirit of truth is sent into the world."[11] Through Jesus Christ there is renewal of human ability to respond to God.

The issue, for both Bangs and the Calvinists, hinged on the relation between God's sovereignty and human capacity; each wished to stress both, but the ability of human beings was differently understood.[12] Wilbur Fisk (1792–1839), in *Calvinist Controversy* (1835), a sermon followed by explanations, continued this debate. He identified four different branches of Calvinism and disagreed with all of them, but his chief target was Hopkins. Predestination is wrong, he argued, for it requires that God be the author of sin, destroys the accountability of persons, arrays God's secret decrees against his revealed Word, destroys God's moral attributes, and leads to Universalism and infidelity. Against this, Fisk maintained, election to eternal life is conditional upon human response. The Calvinists also spoke of human motive, but in their interpretation, there is no power of choice, only a passive susceptibility to being drawn to God. This they called volition. In contrast, Fisk said, the answer is prevenient grace that empowers the mind for spontaneous free response.[13]

In order to counter the Calvinists, Fisk moved to philosophical positions which affirm human freedom. Since both sides of the controversy were referring to grace, Fisk sought to differentiate his position by using analogies of human independence and freedom.[14] Both Fisk and Bangs were seeking distinctively human models for descriptions of human action as had Wesley. In an age of scientific advance, predicated upon scientific models of tight cause-and-effect relationships, the effort to find an alternative model was exceedingly difficult; but it was this issue that Methodist theologians pursued throughout the better part of the century. In this endeavor the doctrine of prevenient grace assumed basic significance.

In their emphasis upon prevenient grace which restores human ability, Methodist theologians touched a critical issue in the analysis of human nature.[15] Fisk presented the argument sharply:

> Arminians do not mean that man's ability to use grace is independent of and separate from the grace itself. They say that man's powers are directly assisted by grace, so that through this assistance they have ability of strength *in those powers* which before they had not, to make a right choice. To talk of ability to use gracious ability, in any other sense, would be absurd.[16]

Bangs and Fisk established a position for American Methodism within revival theology. Calvinism was viewed as offering quite different internal alternatives and as precipitating extreme reactions. The Methodists intended to combine prevenient grace and human freedom in such a way as to insure both the primacy of God's sovereign rule and the integrity of human life as rooted in God's grace.[17] Each side saw causes for disagreement; nevertheless it is difficult to distinguish the Methodist position from that of Nathaniel Taylor. The New Haven theologians and the Methodists each claimed to give clearer emphasis to divine grace, but functionally, they were closely aligned. The polemical posture in which the discussions were cast tended to magnify their small differences and made agreement difficult to acknowledge.

Growth and Division

The struggle with Calvinism controlled the first efforts of North American Methodist theology, but the growth of the Methodist movement and its inner diversities soon became prominent and problematic. Ecclesiastical issues—growth, racism, and the splintering of the body—influenced theological activity.

AMERICANIZATION

The growth of Methodism was phenomenal. In the 1760s there were some 600 Methodists in America. By 1805, there were 120,000, and by 1865, more than 1,380,000. Characteristically Methodist expression so penetrated American religious life that some interpreters have designated most of the nineteenth century as The Methodist Age in America. Winthrop S. Hudson dates this period from 1825 until the eve of World War I, and he finds, in contrast to the Puritan evangelicalism of the eighteenth century, a romantic-perfectionism that stressed the ability of persons to respond to God, a simple gospel stripped of subtle theological distinctions, warm-hearted interdenominational fellowship, increased lay leadership, more informality in worship, and the widening pursuit of Christian holiness.[18] Some of these features were rather clearly attached to Methodist style and practice, but they tend to be generalizations, playing down the theological interests of Methodism. Nevertheless, these characteristics were present, and the fact that Methodism was the most representative religion in America during that period is important. Methodism was affecting American life.

But separatist tendencies were also present, and splintering of the church was to be a major problem as differences over polity and theological emphasis developed. In 1792, the first Conference after Wesley's death, Virginian James O'Kelly challenged Asbury by objecting to the authority and life tenure of bishops. A temporary compromise proved unsuccessful and O'Kelly withdrew and formed the Republican Methodist Church. Thereafter, other movements continued to arise, usually stressing some of O'Kelly's themes, and by 1820 a reform group was organized. Three issues were paramount: election of presiding elders, representation of lay people in decision-making bodies of the church, and the role of local preachers in General Conference. Democratic sensitivities were being expressed, but the General Conference of 1828 denied all reform petitions. On

November 2, 1828, a convention composed of eighty-three ministerial and lay delegates (including Asa Shinn) was called in Baltimore, and the Methodist Protestant Church was formed. A major division had occurred.

The chief social, political, economic, and religious issue in nineteenth-century American life was slavery. No other issue so tore the life of the nation. In the initial stages of Methodism in North America the position of the leadership was clear: They were stridently antislavery. In 1780 the Conference required all itinerant preachers to free any slaves they held, and they were to advise all other Methodists to do the same. The Christmas Conference in 1784 voted to exclude from the Lord's Supper and expel from membership all Methodists who sold slaves or bought them for nonhumanitarian purposes; but this rule was suspended in 1785 due to great pressure. By 1799 Bishop Asbury was wondering whether amelioration might not be wiser than emancipation.[19] As cotton became the base of agricultural life in the South during the first decades of the nineteenth century, the value and importance of slaves increased rapidly. In 1817 the Methodist Episcopal Church had a black membership of 43,000, and by 1826, blacks constituted 40 percent of Methodists in the Carolinas and Georgia.

Racial separation had come early in the life of Methodism. In 1796 the African Methodist Episcopal Church received its original impetus in Philadelphia and struggled to find its own appropriate life and expression. Richard Allen (1760–1831), a man of remarkable gifts and strength, and Daniel Coker, a schoolteacher and persuasive spokesman, were leaders in that movement. Allen, a successful businessman as well as a friend of many political leaders in Philadelphia, was, in 1799, the first black to be ordained by Francis Asbury. After two decades of exploration and tentative moves, the group consolidated, and in 1816 the African Methodist Episcopal Church was officially formed. This is the oldest organization of any type established by blacks in North America.[20] In addition, blacks in New York City sought to form a separate conference in the Methodist Episcopal Church, but the effort failed, and in 1820 the African Methodist Episcopal Zion church was organized.

Racial tension and church separation continued. In 1835 a major controversy over abolition within the Methodist Episcopal Church was initiated when LaRoy Sunderland and four other antislavery proponents published an "Appeal" to members of the New England and New Hampshire conferences.[21] Pronouncing liberty "the inalienable gift of the infinite God to every human being," the declaration provoked a vigorous "Counter Appeal," drafted by Daniel D. Whedon of Wesleyan University and signed by eight prominent chairmen, including Wilbur Fisk and Abel Stevens, a Methodist historian. The response denied that slaveholding was necessarily sinful, basing the argument on the general spirit of the gospel and the specific directions of the New Testament.

The debate escalated, with the active bishops taking the conservative side—that slavery was a civil institution exclusively in the custody of the civil power. The Wesleyan movement, which for so long had been only loosely related to political affairs, was now, along with the nation, drawn ineluctably and thoroughly into the controversy over slavery. The issue was sharp: Is the owning and selling of slaves compatible with Methodist Episcopal principles?

Through the decade of the 1830s, small numbers of abolitionists left the church, and in November 1842, a large contingency led by Sunderland and Orange Scott, a fellow minister, formally withdrew. The dissidents' objection was twofold: the failure of Methodism to disentangle itself from slavery, and the episcopal form of church government. In May of 1843, the Wesleyan Methodist Connection of America was formed with an initial membership of 6,000, which increased within nine months to 15,000. The Wesleyan Methodists rejected episcopacy, required the participation of lay people in both annual and general conferences and that conference officials be elected, prohibited fellowship with slaveholders, and adopted a rule forbidding abridgment of the rights and privileges of any member or preacher on account of race.[22]

The life of the Methodist Episcopal Church had suffered serious disruption. But the case that brought the racial issue to a fundamental crisis was that of Bishop James O. Andrew of Georgia. Andrew was not a slaveholder when elected to the episcopacy in 1832, but by inheritance and marriage had acquired slaves. Andrew acknowledged that he was a slaveowner, but he claimed that this was involuntary and consequently he had not violated the *Discipline;* further, that the laws of Georgia made emancipation impractical. The General Conference of 1844 took up the matter and engaged in the crucial debate. No resolution was reached, and the Methodist Episcopal Church, South, thereupon came into being.

In spite of this split, Methodism continued to grow. There was, some critics claimed, an unhealthy accommodation to the presiding cultural mores and a loss of the sense of scriptural holiness. Modes of dress, types of recreation, and attitudes toward money represented a changing sense of values. Some members of the Genesee Conference in western New York state became concerned about the acceptance of popular social standards by members of the church. They spoke about decline in class attendance, family prayer, quarterly fasts, and congregational singing. Their concerns included the church's tentativeness toward abolition, temperance, membership in secret fraternal organizations, and, most central, its failure to stress instantaneous sanctification. As a consequence, another separation occurred as the Free Methodist Church came into existence in

1860 "to testify that the new church was delivered from secret societies, slavery, rented pews, outward ornaments of pride, and was at liberty to have 'the freedom of the Spirit' in its worship."[23]

When the Confederate states declared their independence and war ensued, Methodism, as the church of the common people, was the most heavily involved of all the religious bodies. President Lincoln commended the Methodist Episcopal Church for contributing more soldiers and nurses and offering more prayers for the Union than any other church. Similar representation of southern Methodists was found in the Confederacy. The war brought devastation to the South, and embittered relations prevailed across the Mason-Dixon line. After the war, the branches of Methodism fought for possession of church property and competed with one another in mission activity in the southern states.

During the war the Methodist Episcopal Church, South, experienced a reduction in its black membership from more than 200,000 to less than 20,000. The African Methodist Episcopal Church and the African Methodist Episcopal Zion Church absorbed most of these members. Neither church had a southern constituency prior to hostilities, but both evangelized in the Confederacy, and by the end of the war their membership had more than quadrupled. The Methodist Episcopal Church also worked assiduously to gain black members in the South and to serve the free black populace.[24]

In 1866, the General Conference of the Methodist Episcopal Church, South, took action in regard to those blacks who, although restive, remained within its membership. Legislation was passed to provide for the organization of a separate black church, and in 1870 the Colored Methodist Episcopal Church was formed in Jackson, Tennessee. The establishment of this church was a definitive sign of the continuing segregation. White Methodists were unwilling to accept blacks on an equal basis, and blacks were unwilling to accept second-class status in the church. The newly formed church was a symbol of frustrated possibility, even as it offered a new structure for black Methodists.

Holiness Controversy: An Internal Debate

We have diverted our discussion to historical matters because they directly affected the theological life of the church. The struggle centered on Methodism's relation to its culture, expressed principally in two issues: race, and the doctrine of sanctification. Both issues caused division in the Methodist Episcopal churches.

There is considerable evidence that the message of early Methodist preachers in America—in spite of Asbury's efforts—gave primary attention to conversion, and much less to sanctification.[25] Holiness teaching never entirely died out, but fresh interest in the experience of entire sanctification was created among Methodists when in 1835, Sarah A. Lankford, and later her sister Mrs. Phoebe Palmer (1807–1874), held Tuesday meetings for the Promotion of Holiness in New York City. Phoebe Palmer was determined to make the reality of holiness available to Christian believers, and she insistently raised the question, "Is there not a shorter way" to the holy life. Her answer was Yes.[26]

The "long way" to sanctification required one to wait, often with uncertainty, upon direct witness of the Holy Spirit. More explicit means of assurance would, Palmer believed, be of great practical help to seekers. The answer she found was that one should simply trust the promises of God given in Scripture. Complete sanctification could be acquired by being *fully conformed to the will of God, as recorded in his written word.*" God has promised sanctification, therefore the work will be accomplished. It is then up to believers to accept this truth. There are two actions: God's gracious and sure promises, and the believers' responsive commitment of their lives to God. In her autobiography Phoebe Palmer wrote, "Instead of perceiving any thing meritorious in what she had been enabled, through grace, to do, i.e., in laying all upon the altar, she saw that she had but rendered back to God that which was already his own." And again, *Faith is taking God at His word,* relying unwaveringly upon his truth."[27]

Palmer proposed that the uncertainties of personal relationship with the Holy Spirit be replaced by a more objective and specific base. If a person accepts the scriptural promises, surrendering entirely, then God will fulfill the scriptural promises. Primary emphasis was placed upon human action. She stated her thesis:

> It was thus, that by "laying all upon this altar," she, by the most unequivocal Scripture testimony, as she deemed, laid herself under the most sacred obligation to *believe* that the sacrifice became "holy and acceptable," and virtually the *Lord's property,* even by virtue of the sanctity of the altar upon which it was laid, and continued "holy and acceptable," so long as kept inviolably upon this hallowed altar.[28]

The success of Palmer's movement was quick and extensive. Many, principally Methodists, responded to the attraction of a short and sure way. Nathan Bangs, who welcomed the renewed vitality and professed sanctification himself, was nevertheless appalled at the dismissal of direct witness of the Holy Spirit and at the limitation this approach placed upon the Spirit's initiative and confirmation. First it will be helpful to hear Bangs' positive statement about sanctification.

> By Methodist I understood those peculiarities of the system by which it is distinguished from all other *isms;* hence it not only includes the doctrines [characteristic of general Protestant theology] enumerated above, by which it proves its orthodoxy, but it brings out more prominently than is done in other denominations . . . that of Christian perfection, or the

entire sanctification of the whole man to God, or holiness of heart and life.[29]

Bangs argued also from a negative perspective—that in Palmer's method, the sanctification process becomes mechanical, predictable, and too simple. The chief contention concerned the mode of the Spirit's operation. Was it to be understood as working through the word of Scripture, already given, and requiring only acknowledgment? Or was it to be understood as a present, immediate encounter, in which assurance is found through dynamic relationship? Bangs maintained that the second alternative was truer to traditional Wesleyanism.

Attending a meeting at Phoebe Palmer's home, Bangs felt it necessary to speak against her position. His chief points were that although Scripture describes sanctification in a general and objective manner, the experience of being sanctified must be personally appropriated, and this occurs only by the gracious presence of the Holy Spirit. This is the believer's only confidence—and it is possible that a person may be deceived. One can investigate one's life, however, to see whether the fruit of the Spirit is present. Without this evidence, there is no sanctification, in spite of the scriptural Word. Bangs reiterated his support of the teaching of Holiness and also stated that he believed Phoebe Palmer and her followers might have experienced more than they were stating theologically. But he expressed concern that the experience be properly interpreted.[30]

The renewed Holiness teaching penetrated rapidly through the branches of the Wesleyan tradition and found strong endorsement among Free and Wesleyan Methodists. We shall follow this development more fully in chapter 6, "Holiness Theology." Within episcopal Methodism, one of the more representative statements on Holiness was Randolph S. Foster's *Christian Purity* (1869). A minister, a professor of theology at Boston University, a special friend of Borden Parker Bowne, and later a bishop, Foster was an eloquent spokesman for sanctification. In his book he set his course by naming his predecessors: Wesley, Fletcher, Watson, Methodist preachers Timothy Merritt and George Peck, and Bangs. "Holiness," he wrote, "is the greatest good, the highest destiny of the militant Church, and the most precious interest of the race. A holy Church would soon make a holy world." In his discussion, he discriminated four understandings of the doctrine. According to the first understanding, regeneration does not imply entire sanctification; regeneration is all that can be hoped for in this life; entire sanctification comes after death. The second view of the doctrine holds that regeneration is the beginning of sanctification; sanctification will be completed just before death. The third view maintains that regeneration and sanctification are not identical—that sanctification is only a point in the process of regeneration, not a separate and additional work. Nevertheless, on this theory, sanctification may be reached and enjoyed in this life. The fourth understanding of the doctrine holds that regeneration and sanctification almost always represent markedly distinct dimensions of experience. Sanctification, in this case, may be experienced either instantaneously or gradually, and it may not be known at the moment it transpires; but when sanctification is reached, a line is passed, and new life, different in kind and degree, fulfills the regenerate life.[31]

The major objective of Foster's book was the explication of this last, or "ultimate," theory, for one must be holy in this sense or life cannot be lived at its highest level. The sanctified life is the goal of Christian experience and is a promise to all Christians. Quoting extensively from Wesley and the Scriptures, Foster opposed Palmer's interpretation. He mentioned her thesis, then argued:

We must believe that such instructions tend to delusion, and have been the fruitful source of many spurious though sincere professions. It is well, nay, it is indispensable, to make an entire surrender of all to God; and when this is done, God will acknowledge it by sending the witness of his acceptance; but let no one, at his peril, conclude that he has made this surrender, and is consequently sanctified, without the requisite witnss; he will only deceive himself, and receive no benefit. His faith, however strong, being false, will do him no good. It is the Spirit which sanctifies, and he sanctifies through faith—faith not in any act of ours, but faith in God; and when by faith he sanctifies, he will impart the witness.[32]

With Foster, there was a return to the free action of the Holy Spirit and the assurance that comes from direct personal relationship. But there was another emphasis that must be noted, for when the author was pressed to state how this experience is authenticated, he responded with a twofold test: There must be a witness of the Holy Spirit with our spirits, and there must be an outward manifestation of the fruits of the sanctified life. It is important to note that the Wesleyan tradition, in which free moral agency became so central a theme, found in Foster an affirmation that it is not human action, but God's grace that brings sanctification and that this grace is decisive in the fulfillment of human life. The stress upon the fruits of the Spirit represented a concern for empirical evidence as witness to the reality of holiness. In some cases this interest led to a subtle shift of emphasis to moralistic descriptions of authentic Christian living; but at its base this theme represented the connection of sanctification and morality. Perfect love of God was indissolubly joined with love of the neighbor.

Foster brought free will and free grace together in the doctrine of complete sanctification, with each achieving its ultimate goal through interaction with the other. Both themes had their foundation in the idea of prevenient grace—that the atonement of Christ has given every person the power to respond affirmatively to God's call. Further, this grace is sufficient to enable people to carry out the implications of that response in their lives. Divine grace is available to hallow human life.

Conclusion

A number of changes were notable as Wesleyan theology moved to the new continent. Remarkable growth gave Methodists a distinctive place in American society. The Methodist Age was characterized by an interaction of the Wesleyan tradition with United States' culture, each helping to shape the other. Consequently, Methodism in North America possessed a different social status than it had in Great Britain, and as a result, its place in society influenced its theological construction.

Fraternal controversies among revival theologies represented varied efforts to be faithful to inherited Christian understandings while also engaging current intellectual and social values. The nature of God and the nature of human beings were matters of fundamental importance, and differences in theological position—on the issues of divine election and human freedom, for instance—revealed divergent assessments of both the divine and the human moral character. Bangs and Fisk, especially in their emphasis on prevenient grace, reflected the dominant Methodist response to these issues.

Theology never exists in isolation from its context, and the tumult of American life—from new nationhood to slavery, to questions about accommodation to culture, to church separation, to civil war—affected the theological development of the Methodist movement. Hence discussions of abolition and the full realization of human character became fundamental theological and ethical confrontations within the church and between the church and society. The Holiness movement was in part a rejection of accommodation to the imposing culture and a call for the demonstration of peculiarly Christian characteristics. In a basic sense, the desire for abolition and the desire for sanctification represented searches for full realization of human life as created and renewed by the grace of God.

Perhaps a personal illustration can help depict the era. In an interesting way, the life of Nathan Bangs not only spanned this time, but characterized the Methodism of the period.[33] Abel Stevens, the nineteenth-century Methodist historian, ranked Bangs second only to Asbury among builders of his church and commented that he did more than anyone else to stimulate its intellectual life. A brief biographical sketch makes the important points. Born in 1778 in Connecticut, Bangs moved to the "wilderness" of central New York state while a child. Migrating to Canada at age twenty-one, he was soon converted and shortly called to preach. In 1801 he was licensed, sold his "earthly belongings," purchased a horse and saddle bags, and went into service as a frontier itinerant. After serving as a missionary in Ontario and Quebec, Canada, he returned to pastorates in New York state and became a presiding elder in the rapidly expanding church. In 1820 he was named book agent of the Methodist Book Concern, a position he filled for twenty years.

Bangs had begun to write in 1809, although his lack of formal education left him with a rough and colloquial literary style. In spite of the labor required, he produced *Errors of Hopkinsianism* (1815), *Predestination Examined* (1817), books on Methodist polity and history, a biography of Freeborn Garrison (1829), and a treatise on sanctification (1851), among other works. He was also the editor of Methodist journals (1820–1836).

In addition to his regular preaching duties, he was possessed by an intense interest in missions. He was instrumental in establishing the missionary society of his church, and from 1820 until 1836 (coterminous with his time as book agent) he served as corresponding secretary and treasurer of the society. Mission activity seemed to bracket his active ministerial life. At age seventy-five, while the Civil War raged, he died.

A number of aspects of Bangs life present suggestive analogies for interpreting American Methodism during its first three-quarters of a century. The movement moved quickly to the frontiers; it was missionary and evangelistic in intention and action. Though roughhewn edges showed at times, there was continual involvement in theological discussion and controversy. With the rapid growth of Methodism, an adequate sense of history, polity, and doctrine was fundamental to ecclesiastical self-identity. Theology was understood to be important, and Methodists, although it is often overlooked, significantly participated in the development of North American theology, especially in their attempt to provide full-orbed interpretation of human freedom and divine grace, as experienced in conversion and sanctification and in their interaction with changing social conditions. But intellectual activity always lived within a more inclusive frame of interest, as simultaneously and ultimately there was commitment to continuing missionary responsibility at home and abroad. In less than a century, Methodism had become well established, even as it sought its distinctive place and role.

CHAPTER 5

DIMENSIONS OF BEING HUMAN:
The Late Nineteenth Century
in North America

T HE UNITED STATES has been, throughout its existence, a heterogenous collection of people and cultural traditions, and this diversity has had a direct effect upon theology. There were fresh winds from other than British sources: German immigration, the increasing black presence, Scotch-Irish immigrants—people from predominantly Lutheran, Calvinistic, and Roman Catholic backgrounds—all came together in the new nation. As a consequence, North American Wesleyan theology was immediately thrown into contact with other religious traditions, intruded upon by the social and intellectual impulses of its surroundings, and affected by the openness of geographical expansion.

Perhaps most important of all, Methodism was, along with the American spirit, pragmatic. Reasons for the success of the Methodist revival in North America were multiple, but among them was the fact that this movement not only adjusted to the New World but also accommodated itself to the growing edges of the new land. In these moves,

Methodism separated itself from the earlier religious establishments in America.

The struggle of the Wesleyan movement in the United States centered in the dual effort to maintain the identity of its own tradition while at the same time remaining responsive to new developments. This was no small task, for the revivalism of the early nineteenth century was not clearly marked by denominational affiliation; there were a number of positions which—to the outside observer—appeared to be relatively close to one another; and there was a continual flow of social change that often challenged inherited assumptions.

Nathan Bangs and Wilbur Fisk had led the Methodists in the early confrontation with Calvinism. In attempting to establish a mediating position for Wesleyan theology among the various alternatives of divine sovereignty and human freedom, they staked out territory that would need to be continually defended. After Bangs' time, Wesleyan theology tended to become more deeply affected by the currents of new ideas: the increasing references to New England transcendentalism, the romantic movement as mediated through Samuel Taylor Coleridge and Friedrich Schleiermacher, the recent German biblical criticism, the writing of Frederick Denison Maurice of England, and the new theological emphases of Horace Bushnell. These influences appeared, first as brief ripples, then as more persistent waves. Methodist theological categories began to undergo revisions that would, by the end of the century, produce a differently sculptured character.

A Change of Emphasis

Two men represent the increased focus on the issue of free will: Albert Turner Bledsoe and Daniel D. Whedon. Both understood Jonathan Edwards to be their chief opponent, and both attempted to counter his arguments in the interest of vindicating the operations of God and the integrity of human beings. Both had studied law and both had come into Methodism from other denominations. The arguments of neither were original, but the vigor with which they prosecuted their case revealed the earnestness of their efforts.

Albert T. Bledsoe (1809–1877) was educated at West Point and was a friend of Robert E. Lee and Jefferson Davis. He taught at the University of Virginia (twice) and at the University of Mississippi and served in the Confederate army. Strong-minded and confident, he insisted upon the absence of irresistible external compulsion upon the human will and in 1845 his *Examination of President Edwards' Inquiry into the Freedom of the Will* was published. Its major thesis was that morality cannot be compelled and that God's sovereignty is not exercised so as to necessitate human response. Bledsoe's primary objection to Edwards was similar to that of Fisk—that he confused human desire, affection, and feeling with the act of willing. Affective experience, Bledsoe claimed, is distinct from volition, and no clear causation links one to the other. Further, he made a distinction between originative, "self-active" causes and necessitated moral experiences. The human will, he contended, is a self-active cause and is, therefore, free. This freedom was the pivotal issue in his theology.[1]

Of special importance was Bledsoe's *Theodicy: Or Vindication of the Divine Glory, as Manifested in the Constitution and Government of the Moral World.* The issue of evil was important as American theology dealt with the moral nature of God and the free agency of human beings. Bledsoe explored the problem of evil in his own way, asserting that the solution must be found in the interaction of human freedom and divine government, which stresses the goodness and holiness of God. The goal of creation is the realization of the greatest amount of moral good. Such good can be realized only as actual conditions allow the possibility of sin and evil. In regard to human beings, moral character—the ultimate end of human existence—requires both human freedom and God's moral sovereignty. Once again, voluntaristic categories were foundational; and in Bledsoe's insistence upon this theme, Methodist theology was expressing its distinctiveness.

Daniel D. Whedon (1808–1885) served as editor of the *Methodist Quarterly Review* from 1856 until 1884, and from this position he provided theological leadership for a generation of Methodists. A man of fine quality, Whedon possessed quiet strength. He followed his conscience, even though his opposition to the extension of slavery cost him his position at the University of Michigan. Intellectually exceptional, he was able to build upon a good education and an early teaching career. As an opponent, he was both fair and forceful; as a theologian, he was more a servant of the truth than eager to score debating points.

In reading Whedon's writings, one immediately recognizes his Wesleyan convictions. The major outlines of his theological structure covered all the traditional themes, but the weighting of the themes was shifted: Interpretation of human nature moved to a central position and other doctrines became variations upon this theme. This new emphasis reflected both the impact of the Enlightenment with its insistence upon human autonomy, and the new nation's interest in democracy and in the inherent capacity of persons for making a different life. Also important were the need for moral responsibility in a society of reduced external constraints and the dignity of the person, which required reaffirmation amid the clamor of increasing industrialization. People under God were Whedon's concern; and both terms—*people* and *God*—are always present. In this context, he believed, the ability and responsibility of the person must be secured.

To make good his position in theological terms, Whedon found it necessary to answer Jonathan Edwards. The fundamental issue was the radically God-centered theology of Edwards, and Whedon engaged the debate on the ground of human experience. He recognized the quality of his opponent: "In acuteness the intellect of Edwards has scarcely been surpassed. No cause, perhaps, ever had a keener advocate . . . and if his philosophy and theology are not triumphant, it is not, we repeat, for the want of about the acutest advocate that ever framed a special plea."[2] Yet Whedon fundamentally disagreed with Edwards and sets his course in the opposite direction.

Whedon stated succinctly the Edwardian Maxim—"God judges us as he finds us to be, good or evil, and holds us responsible without regard to the means by which we come to be so."[3] Whedon did his best to refute this maxim, and in so doing much follows:

> From our rejection of this maxim . . . we differ from some or all classes of Calvinists on the subject of *freewill, divine sovereignty, predestination, election, primary responsibility for inborn depravity, partial atonement, and final perserverance.* To this maxim . . . we oppose the counter maxim that *in order for responsibility for a given act or state, power in the agent for contrary act or state is requisite.* In other words: *"No man is to blame for what he cannot help. Power underlies responsibility."*[4]

The way human freedom became the center of Whedon's theology may be seen in his article "Doctrines of Methodism."[5] He began with the fact of free will in human experience; then he indicated the way this theme is related to such issues as divine sovereignty, foreknowledge, sin, redemption, justification by faith, regeneration, the witness of the Spirit, and entire sanctification. He concluded with a statement on the "Perpetuity of Man's Free Agency."

The emphasis on the power of contrary choice was not

uniquely Wesleyan, for Nathaniel Taylor, among many others, had asserted this principle. The crucial aspect for Whedon, as for his Methodist predecessors, was that this power is itself a gift of grace, the result of the atonement. Without the reality of prevenient grace, people would be incapacitated in their wills because of original sin.

The consideration of human ability, even though graciously given, as the cornerstone of a theological system entailed basic implications. An initial interest in human character and ability began to suggest the ways in which God may be perceived. There was also a shift from a scriptural base to a philosophically derived interpretation of human experience, and grace was given a more restricted function, in that once gracious ability was set, attention shifted to human activity, and this then became the dominant concern. A basic alteration occurred in Whedon's theology, but it must be fairly described, for Whedon did not intend for the interaction between God and humanity to become broken or one-sided. Nevertheless, the difference in choice of primary perspective did shift emphases and pointed to a new direction for some Methodist theologians.

Whedon was pivotal, even though his work and that of Bledsoe reflected a general consensus among many of their contemporary Wesleyan theologians. Whedon's work was a culmination of past tendencies and a point of derivation for the future. The earlier interest of Shinn, and Bangs, and Fisk now issued in Whedon, in a thoroughly articulated philosophic interpretation of human nature as the beginning point of theological construction. Building upon this base, Whedon set frames of reference which stimulated many succeeding Wesleyan theologians to respond to prevailing intellectual currents.

There were some who felt compelled to refuse these new tendencies. Daniel Curry (1809–1887), successor to Whedon as editor of the *Methodist Quarterly Review* (1881–1887), in the article "A New Orthodoxy" (the title is indicative of the common conviction among Methodist theologians in regard to the primacy of free will), objected to the shift of theological premises.[6] Curry, throughout his career, had supported more traditional Wesleyan doctrines, and he now resisted the implications of Whedon's position. He saw in the adoption of Whedon's philosophical base a compromise of the uniqueness and larger inclusiveness of Christian revelation. Against this, he restated the essentials of Richard Watson's position.

Systematic Theologians

The struggle over the interpretation of human freedom was, to a large extent, a debate among Christians. It had to do with the nature of God, who was assumed to exist, and the character of human life, which was assumed to have meaning in relationship with God. In this sense, the contention between Methodists and Calvinists was an effort to clarify and interpret these common assumptions.

There was also, within Methodism, another theological effort. This was the development of more fully orbed statements of Christian faith, more broadly based defenses of Christian truth, and more thoroughly organized systematic implications. This undertaking was the work of systematic theologians.

Among Methodist theologians, several southern thinkers represented this endeavor. The three most prominent were Henry Bidleman Bascom, Thomas Ralston, and Thomas O. Summers. Bascom (1796–1850) itinerated in Tennessee, became editor of the southern Methodist *Quarterly Review* in 1860, served as chaplain in the United States Congress, and eventually became a bishop of the church. Ralston (1806–1891) was a native of Kentucky. He was principal of a Methodist school for women in Louisville and wrote the influential *Elements of Divinity* (1847), the first Wesleyan

American systematic theology. Summers (1812–1882) was an English immigrant who became the editor of the Methodist publishing concern in the southern church. He was a prolific writer and the first professor of theology at Vanderbilt University. The chief effort of these three men was to present a coherent interpretation of Christian faith, its bases, and its doctrinal content. Systematic theology, they believed, was a way to convince cultured despisers of the faith that Christian affirmation was valid and to reinforce that faith for believers by demonstrating that its foundations were strong and its vision clear.

Ralston and Bascom were representative of "rational orthodoxy," which was built upon the belief that Scottish common-sense philosophy provided a theory of knowledge capable of presenting a persuasive case for the existence of God and for exploring natural, rational intimations of God's nature. Further, there was the conviction that biblical revelation gives account of and completes that which natural reason dimly recognizes: Natural reason and revelation provide a unity of knowledge. Finally, there was confidence that upon these foundations could be built a comprehensive interpretation of God, the world, and human beings.[7] Ralston and Bascom stressed these themes, and consequently they opened with arguments to prove the existence of God and the moral sense of human beings. To this they related the revelation of God in Jesus Christ, which conveys saving knowledge of relationship with God and an understanding of the character of God. In developing their systematic statements, they were confident that they had presented a defensible and convincing case for the central claims of Christian faith. There was little that was unique in their presentations of the content of doctrine, but their reach to be inclusive and to keep the different aspects of Christian teaching in complementary relationship gave substantial structure to their enterprise.

Thomas O. Summers shared their assumptions, but he found his principal source in Richard Watson's *Theological Institutes*. Summers' two-volume *Systematic Theology* is an extended utilization of Watson's position, and at each critical point he basically represented Watson's arguments and conclusions.[8] Some of the issues were closely related to the concerns of Ralston and Bascom, as Watson also countered the Deists and attempted to present persuasive arguments for Christian interpretation of God's nature. But Summers did not spend as much effort in establishing the existence of God, although he expounded particular doctrines more completely than had Ralston and Bascom. Abrupt, conservative, at times overbearing and abrasive, Summers was fearful of heresy and sought to prevent it in his own thought by carefully following trustworthy Wesleyan predecessors. He generated no new ideas, but with systematic patience, restated major themes.

The interest of these theologians was not centered upon human nature as the fulcrum of theological interpretation; rather, they were attentive to a more inclusive interpretation of God's activity, with human freedom a subordinate part of larger considerations. Interpreters of nineteenth-century Methodist theology usually follow the development of the struggle to establish human freedom and responsibility, and this was a major stream. It is necessary also to recognize that there was an alternative development, which undertook a somewhat different task and which, in its own way, achieved a more complete range of Wesleyan theology.

Two other contributors should be mentioned in connection with systematic theological effort: Miner Raymond and William F. Warren. Miner Raymond (1811–1897) was a self-educated man who pursued his studies while he taught rhetoric and mathematics, served as an intinerant minister, and finally became a professor of theology at Garrett Bible Institute. His *Systematic Theology* (1877-79) contains three volumes. Raymond accepted the general tenets of rational orthodoxy with trust in the coherence of reason and revelation. In tentative fashion he explored current advancements in psychology and the study of moral conscience for describing divine presence and human ability. But the biblical record remained his final court of appeal. Raymond was more suggestive than rigorous in his presentation. In explicating the content of Christian doctrine, he emphasized the "synergistic" interaction of God and persons and continued the interest in the governmental theory of atonement—that God has created a world structured on moral order and that it is this order that must be satisfied. This understanding of the atonement was affirmed by many theologians of his era. Among Methodists it already had been upheld by Ralston and Bledsoe, and later it would be expanded by John Miley. Raymond was aware of the diversity of themes passing through Methodist thought of his day and drew these issues together in his three volumes, but his attempt lacks structural coherence.

William F. Warren (1833–1929) was an American who studied and taught in Germany until 1866, when he returned to the United States to become a professor and later the first president of Boston University. His intellectual sensitivity was instrumental as he envisioned a move from a mechanistic to a more dynamic interpretation of human life and religious experience. Influenced by Schleiermacher, Warren completed an *Introduction (Einleitung)* to a projected systematic theology. This introduction presented a theory of knowledge denominated Christian realism, which ascribed fundamental reality to both thinking subjects (subjects with independent free will) and the external world. Warren was sympathetic to German historical-critical study of the Bible, and with his Methodist contemporaries, he sought an epistemology that would express theology in a manner congenial to reigning scientific convictions. But Warren did not complete his systematic theology. He became a university administrator and a leader of his church. As an educational statesman, he shaped the character of Boston University, and the general spirit of his thought helped prepare the way for acceptance of the work of Borden Parker Bowne and personalistic philosophy.

The Final Quarter

Through three-quarters of the nineteenth century, North American Wesleyan theology had been nurtured by its own past and by a sensitivity to its cultural context. The pace had been swift, but there was continuity of assumptions about the Bible and a sense that the Christian faith was compatible with the altering intellectual and social surroundings. There was also change, represented by Bledsoe and Whedon, and toward the end of the century this change was accelerated. New intellectual challenges demanded response. Chief among these were the impact of higher criticism of the Scriptures, the dominance of a naturalistic materialism in philosophic interpretation, the unsolved problems of racism, and a waning of revivalistic evangelism. All these issues made inroads into Methodism, and the final years of the 1800s were characterized by reaction to these challenges.

By the last quarter of the century, at least three major streams of development were evident in American episcopal Methodism. The stream which continued the inherited theological themes was exemplified chiefly by John Miley; it was reflected also in two black theologians, Daniel A. Payne and Henry McNeal Turner. Another development was the exploration of more adequate philosophical bases for theology, a venture led by Borden Parker Bowne. A third stream moved into biblical research that acknowledged the influence of higher criticism and adopted its implications. Hinckley G. Mitchell, of Boston University, and Milton S.

Terry, of Garrett Biblical Institute, were early representatives of this endeavor.

Divergent streams were present, but they were not completely isolated from one another. Miley shared interest in the bases of theism with Bowne, Bowne shared interest in biblical criticism with Mitchell, and Terry shared theological interests with all the rest. There was interaction and a knowledge of others' work, but each of these developments was distinctive and each requires attention.

John Miley

John Miley (1813–1895) was a significant force in the stream of continuity. Scientific awareness combined with biblical literalism, responsible human rationalism combined with supernaturally revealed truth, and human worth combined with divine sovereignty were dominant issues in his thought. In these instances Miley attempted to set regnant cultural themes and Christian distinctiveness into complementary relationship.

Miley constantly fought on two fronts: in favor of science and the Bible, and against the narrow limitation of either. He maintained that theology is a science in that it explores empirical experience, but he argued against science that excludes religious experience as significant data. And he defended biblical revelation, while also contending for extra-biblical modes of God's revelation. This concern to relate theology and science, or revelation and reason, was typical of the time, but the need to oppose popular positivistic views of science was a growing concern. Affirmation of biblical truth was also typical, even though Miley moved beyond biblical exclusiveness to understand the relation of God to human beings. Negotiating his way through this complex of issues, Miley became an apologist or, as he would have said, a natural as well as a dogmatic

111

theologian. These two enterprises—defending and clearly stating Christian truth—constituted his understanding of the task of systematic theology.[9]

Wesleyan by thoroughgoing commitment, Miley nevertheless believed he served the tradition by directing it in new ways. Like many of his predecessors, he assumed that Scripture is central, but he refused to allow it to be the exclusive medium of God's relation to people (a position he wrongly assumed that Richard Watson had held). Here there was a decisive move, for to Miley, the Scriptures were a theological sourcebook, but the Bible's purpose was only secondarily the evocation of direct experience of salvation. Religious experience moves center stage; affectional and willing relation to God become primary. For Miley, the Bible did not evoke religious experience, but spoke to that experience and shaped it. It is in this sense that he claimed infallibility for Scripture: In interpreting religious experience, it does not err. Miley heightened the biblical truth but limited the arena of its impact. Theology is a second-order task. Hence the Bible is important as a resource for intellectual interpretation of Christian faith. Direct experience of God is the basic and crucial issue, and this experience may not be con...ined within biblical mediation. The experience of God is immediate; the Scriptures clarify and give normative expression to the source meaning of that experience.

Miley's views on the authority of the Bible clearly reveal the general persuasion of his time. He was opposed to notions of inspiration that come simply from human genius or from mechanical dictation. In distinction, he held to "the dynamical theory," which insists upon the initiative of God and the response of persons. Throughout, his emphasis was upon the agency of the Holy Spirit, which prepares the minds, communicates the truth, leads in written communication, and guides in relating these received truths to the truth found through other empirical and rational media.

There are several noteworthy characteristics of this approach to biblical inspiration. While it allows for a human element in the authorship of Scripture, it also grants the commanding role of the Holy Spirit, so that the basic truth of Scripture is not distorted by human reception. Miley narrowed his focus upon the "divine truth" that is communicated. Divine truth moves above, although it is not contradictory of experimental, historical, or scientific truth. The Bible conveys truth, but beyond its statements of truth lies relationship. Miley viewed the theological task seriously, but he did not view it as final or completely comprehensive of religious life. In principle, Miley's approach to Scripture was intellectual or doctrinal; the Bible communicates the "truth" of God and it is this truth that must be expounded. It is important to note that while Miley moved away from mechanical inspiration, he nevertheless held to the inerrancy of Scripture. In this he articulated the inherited Wesleyan view of scriptural authority in a new context and made tentative gestures in the direction of higher critical work.[10] It is typical and important to note that Wesleyan theologians placed the authority of Scripture before the question of inspiration; they assumed inspiration because of the Bible's authority. This ordering indicates the basic dependence upon the internal witness of the Holy Spirit. In this regard Miley continued the Wesleyan emphasis: Relation with God is through the work of Jesus Christ and the agency of the Holy Spirit, and the Bible is authoritative because the Spirit gives witness to it and enlivens it. This dynamic of relationship, as opposed to belief in the Bible as such, or allegiance to a confession, however biblical, is at the core of Christian faith. And this order of priority has given distinctive character to Wesleyan theology.

Miley called his position ethical Arminianism. From the time of Bangs, Fisk, and Whedon, the designation of Methodist theology as Arminian had been common on the

American scene. Moving from rather vague meaning, it came, especially in North America, to refer specifically to Wesleyan theology, with focus upon graciously given human free agency. Miley accepted this designation without question. The result of his identification may be seen in his *Systematic Theology*. Free personal agency is the critical and constructive principle of his work. Robert E. Chiles has summarized Miley's effort as an attempt "to eliminate all remnants of Augustinian realism by his critique of native guilt, his insistence on governmental justice as the key to the atonement, and his tendency to compromise the gracious ability of man's freedom in his philosophical doctrine of responsibility."[11] Chiles is correct in indicating these tendencies. Miley intended to preserve the theme of prevenient grace as the ground of choice, but he did compromise the immediate priority of grace by placing emphasis on human ability in decision-making.

A survey of Miley's *Systematic Theology* reveals his intention. After an initial statement on method, he dealt with the "ground truth" of Christianity, Theism. Then he developed the doctrine of God, concentrating on the Trinity. Anthropology was treated next, with extensive attention to human sin, and guilt as the result of personal decision. In the second volume, Miley took up Christology, giving central place to the atonement, and secondarily, speaking of human response to Christ's atoning work. The doctrines of justification, regeneration, assurance, sanctification, and the church were included in this section. A discussion of eschatology completed the work. In a systematic manner, Miley presented the order of salvation and provided a theological framework in which this order may be explicated.

Of special note is the fact that Miley, more thoroughly than his Methodist predecessors, developed a "governmental" or "rectoral" theory of the atonement (which he discusses also in *The Atonement in Christ* [1879]). That is, sin is a violation of

God's moral ordering of the universe. God, being moral, needs no propitiation, and justice is compatible with forgiveness. But as a ruler, God must honor the law; hence the need for the atonement. The redemption effected by Jesus Christ sets right the broken order. Both substitutionary and moral influence theories were denied as Miley emphasized the moral character of God's sovereign dealing with human beings.

Miley's *Systematic Theology* is a major work, in that he carefully developed the central doctrines of Christian faith. He presented his position with clarity and sought logical coherence; he was direct in his discussion of issues and attempted to give convincing reasons for his conclusions. In all these ways, his work is commendable. Miley stood at the collision point of the old and new in Methodist theological interpretation. He significantly represented the culmination of the preceding Methodist tradition as he turned the received positions into a logically coherent system. Yet most of the themes he discussed were, even in his time, being reappraised, and many of his most basic convictions were undergoing fresh scrutiny. The nature of biblical authority, the role of experience, the natural condition of persons, the nature of the atonement, and the adequacy of philosophical bases for theological construction—all were being reevaluated. Consequently, Miley's work was both a culmination and a point of departure. After him, many theologians in episcopal Methodism would move in new directions.

Black Methodist Theologians

Black Methodists were closely aligned theologically with episcopal Methodists, sharing a common sense of the central emphases of Christian faith as expressed in identical articles of religion. Bishop James W. Hood, of the African Methodist Episcopal Zion Church, stated that it was racism, the implacable separation of the races, that provoked the establishment of the black Methodist denominations. Differences in doctrine or church polity did not occasion the separation, "for in nearly every case they adhered to the same doctrine and form of government, as the church from which they separated."[12] The isolation of the races by denominational structure was tragic, but across the differences were stretched ligaments of common belief.[13]

Black theology in the nineteenth century was not a formally constructed or academically shaped expression—it was primarily preached and sung. The deepest thought and the richest sensibility were found in the poetic expression of sermon and spiritual. This was theology and it possessed authenticity. The sermons were not so individual as part of a tradition; they were "God's trombones." The spirituals were also powerful theological instruments, as interpreters from Miles Mark Fisher to James Weldon Johnson, John Lowell, and James H. Cone have shown.

But there were theologians who wrote. Daniel Alexander Payne (1811–1893) and Henry McNeal Turner (1834–1915) produced theology with special sensitivity to their particular situation. It was this sensitivity that made their theology a distinctive addition to the dominant interpretations.

Daniel Payne was born to free parents in Charleston, South Carolina, and was orphaned when very young. Working in a carpenter's shop, he learned to read and write, and upon his conversion at age eighteen he determined to become an educator for his people. He set about the task of learning on his own, he achieved his goal, and lived in an exemplary manner. Frederick Douglass said of Payne that his was "a life without flaw, and a name without a blemish."[14] Payne opened his first school in South Carolina in 1829, but in 1835 the state legislature passed a bill that forbade the teaching of slaves to read or write. This act convinced Payne of the gross injustice in human society and he began to ask serious questions about God's providence.

Raised in the Methodist Episcopal Church, he joined the Lutheran for a short time, then became a member of the African Methodist Episcopal Church in 1840 and was ordained an elder in 1843. Later, he was elected a bishop of his church and was also to become the first black president of a university in the United States (Wilberforce). In 1835, while still in Charleston, he wrote a poem, and its closing lines became his continuing prayer:

> A useful life by sacred wisdom crowned,
> Is all I ask, let weal or woe abound![15]

From its inception, the African Methodist Episcopal Church boasted that its roots were in historical Methodism, and Payne intended to keep the church in that tradition. He continued contact with other Methodist leaders and on his first trip to England visited the graves of Wesley, Adam Clarke, and Richard Watson.

Payne's theological work took the form of sermons and other occasional pieces.[16] These are written in a vital, engaging style, and it might be said, as Payne said of a Methodist sermon he heard in England, that they are "well digested, clear, systematic, beautiful, sublime, and deeply evangelical."[17] His own concerns were many faceted and largely of a piece with the evangelical preaching of his time, but he also possessed a deep interest in the problem of evil—as reflected in human relationships—and in the providence of God. Slavery was the issue, for it "brutalizes man—destroys his moral agency, and subverts the moral government of God."[18] Slaves and slave owners alike were denatured by this inhuman institution.

To counter the realities of the condition of slaves, Payne reasserted the sovereignty of God and, in spite of empirical contradictions, emphasized God's infinite wisdom and inexhaustible goodness.[19] God's sovereignty and human sin—these two realities remained for Payne. Neither could be denied, but they were not easily understood in relation to each other. With a strong sense of devoted commitment to God and with anguish over the condition of his people, Payne advised trust in God and a continuing effort to rectify the social situation. God, he believed, is active in history, and in the final analysis, that is the ground of hope. For himself and for his fellow blacks, he took a stand:

> I shall lift up my voice to plead his cause, against all the claims of his proud oppressor; and I shall do it not merely from the sympathy which man feels towards suffering man, but because God, the living God, whom I dare not disobey, has commanded me . . . to plead the cause of the oppressed.[20]

Henry McNeal Turner also was a South Carolinian and also was free born. He learned to read and write even though it was illegal to do so; by the age of fifteen he had read the Bible through five times, memorizing long passages. He was licensed to preach by the Methodist Episcopal Church, South, in 1853 and traveled for five years as a missionary through South Carolina, Georgia, Alabama, Louisiana, and Missouri. In 1858 he joined the African Methodist Episcopal Church and served as a minister for fifty-seven years until he was elected a bishop.

Turner's theological interpretation grew out of a sharp consciousness of the situation of black people. Since all persons are created in God's image, Turner believed it was not improper to think of God as black (in his term, a Negro): "Every race of people since time began who have attempted to describe their God . . . have conveyed the idea that the God who made them and shaped their destinies was symbolized in themselves."[21]

Turner believed, with Payne, that the sovereignty of God

was the foundation upon which theology and Christian hope must be built and that sovereign providence would bring judgment and freedom for all people now, and an ultimate expectation of redemption. Never doubting that blacks would eventually participate as equals in American society, he too placed his primary trust in God and in God's intentions for the entire human family.

Borden Parker Bowne

Methodist theology in the United States was heavily dependent upon its own tradition, successors responding to the influence of their predecessors. By the close of the century, however, a more extended awareness, especially an awareness of German thought, was becoming prominent. William F. Warren had studied and taught abroad, but most dominant in basing Methodist theology on German philosophy was Borden Parker Bowne.

Bowne (1847–1910) was born into a devout Methodist home. Although his family was poor, he showed early intellectual ability, and after a short period as a drayman in Brooklyn, he entered New York University. There he became an excellent scholar, graduating as valedictorian of his class. After earning a Master's degree, he entered parish work, but soon left for Europe, where he studied for two years in France and Germany. It was in Germany and through the work of Rudolf Hermann Lotze, who attempted to show that the demands of empirical fact, logical truth, and moral value can be interrelated, and that of Hermann Ulrici, a neo-Kantian philosopher, that Bowne's philosophy formed definite contours. Shortly after his return to the United States, Bowne joined the faculty at Boston University, where he was to spend his professional life, leaving a clear mark on that university's development.

A thinker of great strength and wide sensitivity, Bowne

attempted to mediate between his inherited Methodism and the current cultural context. Without intellectual peer in the American Methodism of his time, he brought fresh hope and concrete possibility to the reshaping of theology. Convinced that personal idealism, a position which stressed personality as the fundamental reality, is the most valid philosophical position, Bowne undertook the task of relating this philosophy to his religious heritage. This effort led to an appreciation of the positive value of biblical criticism, a more optimistic evaluation of human nature, and an intellectual interpretation that could contend with the significant intellectual issues of the time. It was Bowne's intention to combat—indeed, to refute—the materialism and naturalism of a scientific and secularistic environment. He believed that the modern mind had been seduced by philosophical assumptions which reduced reality to materiality, but which were invalid and could be shown to be deficient. The base for his response was a fresh exploration of the immanence of God.

Bowne's basic thesis was stated in his preface to *The Immanence of God:* "The undivineness of the natural and the unnaturalness of the divine is the great heresy of popular thought. . . . To assist in the banishment of this error by showing a more excellent way is the aim and purpose of this little book."[22] And this also was the purpose of his philosophic undertaking.

Bowne was optimistic and positive. Francis J. McConnell, in writing Bowne's intellectual biography, argued that the theme of Christian perfection is the backdrop for Bowne's moral ideal of human life; and that Bowne was convinced that the only existence in which human life can fully realize itself is a world of people, a divine/human society.[23] This conviction underwrote Bowne's lifelong effort to raise religion to a high ethical plane and to defend this faith through rational persuasiveness.

Bowne possessed fundamental confidence in the rationality of the world and the unity of truth. But unlike his predecessors, he was convinced that a new metaphysic, or interpretation of basic reality, was needed to describe the world most adequately. In this effort, he gave personality a central place. Bowne understood the self in inclusive fashion, balancing the emotive and volitional elements of human experience with rationality. Religious experience becomes an integral part of natural awareness and provides an additional foundation for natural theology. Rational argument can support the case for Theism, but the content of an understanding of God must come from a source other than general arguments derived from inherent human rationality. Here revelation—that is, the religion of Jesus Christ—plays a central role in the constructive task of Christian theology. The grace of God is revealed in Jesus Christ and acknowledgment of this graciousness leads to growth of character and a realization of God's kingdom. Through Jesus Christ, God is revealed as an infinite Person, whose will directs the purpose of the world and whose grace is expressed in creation, redemption, and ultimate hope.

Bowne was a child of the Wesleyan tradition. His emphases upon grace as the nature of God and the underpinning of human meaning, upon concrete experience, and upon the self-agency of persons, were themes continued from his Methodist forebears. But he was also indebted to other sources, so that his interpretation of experience had roots in Enlightenment rationalism; his stress upon the importance of persons, in romanticism; and his understanding of free agency, in antideterministic philosophies. Bowne stood at the confluence of many streams, and in his constructive philosophy he was a creative force in Methodism. The potency of his thought led Methodist theology to the possibility of a new and different path.

Personality as the key to reality became the central organizing principle of Bowne's entire philosophy. God exists and is personal. Upon this fulcrum Bowne placed his lever and turned his world. He was clear about this beginning point and thoroughly developed its implications. Ultimate Being alone possesses inner freedom and originality for free personal agency. Hence freedom is a necessary character of reality—without freedom there is no true reality and only by the exercise of freedom can truth be known. Both Bowne's theory of knowledge and his theory of the nature of reality were constructed on these assumptions, and the position was denominated personalism.[24] A succinct definition of personalism was given by Albert C. Knudson:

> That form of idealism which gives actual recognition to both the pluralistic and monistic aspects of experience and which finds in the conscious unity, identity, and free activity of personality the key to the nature of reality and the solution of the ultimate problems of philosophy.[25]

Bowne sharpened the themes of previous Methodists: emphasis upon personal salvation, the renewal of persons to true humanity, the centrality of human freedom. But he also represented a new moment in that tradition as he altered those emphases, forging them into a philosophical system. By basing his construction on the immanence of God, he placed stress upon moral and developmental aspects of human experience. Grace is the cornerstone, for grace characterizes God, the mode of creation, and relationship with human beings. Sharp distinctions between God and the world are removed when the moral character of God is understood as permeating all creation.

Many of Bowne's followers claimed that his philosophy was distinctively Christian. This contention is correct, since he began with principles derived from the Christian tradition and intended to expound those principles in ways that would support and enrich Christian thought and life. Of special significance for our study is the fact that once again, and now in a thorough way, we see a representative of Wesleyan theology relating resources from that tradition to new intellectual interests. In what was perhaps the most impressive Methodist effort of the century, Bowne set forth a clearly articulated foundation and framework for a special Methodist variety of theological activity.

Yet something more must be said, for while this was clearly Methodist "family" theology, it was also ecumenical; Bowne's influence was felt beyond the boundaries of Methodism. Others within North American Christianity found personalism an attractive and useful philosophical foundation for theology. Bowne opposed anti-intellectualism in his own tradition and what he took to be the false rationalism of contemporary materialism and naturalism. His special targets were Herbert Spencer's theory of evolution and those philosophers who moved toward impersonal notions of ultimate reality. In the course of Bowne's work, he also affirmed the value of higher criticism of the Bible and the freedom and right of Methodists to utilize this mode of biblical study.

Bowne was moving ahead too fast for his own denomination. In 1904 he was charged with heresy by George A. Cooke, a member of his annual conference. Cooke argued that Bowne denied the Trinity, miracles, and substitutionary atonement; in addition, he claimed that Bowne's teachings about divine government and the future of souls, sin and salvation, repentance, justification, regeneration, and assurance were at variance with Methodist doctrine. The resulting trial was important because, since Bowne was aquitted, it supported the openness of the Methodist Episcopal Church to theological exploration and construction.

Methodist theological self-understanding was changing. Such significant followers of Bowne as Albert C. Knudson, Edgar S. Brightman, Walter E. Muelder, L. Harold DeWolf, S. Paul Schilling, and Peter Bertocci were to carry on the personalistic tradition and carry out its contribution to Christian philosophy and theology. Boston University, during this period, was the major contributor to the growth of Methodist theology. With Borden Parker Bowne, it entered the mainstream of intellectual culture in the last decades of the nineteenth century.

Biblical Interpretation

Among the streams in this era there was an increasingly rapid torrent of critical interpretation of the Bible. Such waters had moved around the edges of Methodism for only a short time, for until the later 1800s, a higher critical approach to the Scriptures, when it was contemplated at all, was rejected out of hand. As the century drew to a close, however, this tide was beginning to make inroads.

Two men were of central importance in this move—Milton S. Terry (1846–1914), of Garrett Biblical Institute, and Hinckley G. Mitchell (1846–1920), of Boston University. Terry found the work of German biblical scholarship, which had been evolving for several decades, suggestive of new modes of biblical interpretation. In 1883 his *Biblical Hermeneutics: A Treatise on the Interpretation of the Old and New Testaments* was published. This volume was part of the same series in which Miley's *Systematic Theology* appeared. In *Biblical Hermeneutics*, Terry acknowledged the contributions of lower (textual) and higher (historical and literary) criticism, and, by means of a wide-ranging historical sketch, supported openness to the scientific study of the Bible, while he also stressed the continuous direction of the Holy Spirit in creating and conveying the meaning of the text to the Christian interpreter.[26] As a general principle, the Bible is to be interpreted by the same method as are other books, utilizing the perfected knowledge and skill (art) required in all authentic reading of texts. Yet there is a "special hermeneutics" of the Scripture—that is, a recognition of those peculiar characteristics of the Bible which aid the interpreter in discerning its essential message. Terry advised, "The Holy Scripture is no Delphic oracle, to bewilder the heart by utterances of double meaning. Taken as a whole, and allowed to speak for itself, the Bible will be found to be its own best interpreter."[27]

The door for biblical criticism was opening. Bradford P. Raymond, president of Wesleyan University in Connecticut; William North Rice, a professor at Wesleyan; C.J. Little, president of Garrett Biblical Institute; and especially Hinckley G. Mitchell, a professor at Boston University, led this advance. Mitchell was a man of honest, almost simple disposition, one who was responsive to the continental critical study of the Old Testament. For fifteen years he taught without undue opposition—until in 1895 he was charged by a group of students with denigrating the truth and authority of the Bible. The furor was renewed in 1900 (in this debate Bowne played a prominent role as a defender of Mitchell), and once more in 1905.

The controversy centered around Mitchell's view of the Pentateuch. He did not accept Mosaic authorship; rather, he followed the work of German scholars in discriminating among the various traditions and documents that had been brought together to constitute the first five books. In addition, he was presenting the findings of higher criticism in regard to the dating of other Old Testament books and was reconsidering their authorship. Mitchell clearly was breaking out of inherited positions on chronology, composition, and theological construction, and this move constituted not only a difference from, but a threat to established Methodist understanding.

The threat was felt deeply, and many of more conservative views quickly rose to oppose this new departure. Illustrative of the affirmative side of the controversy was a pamphlet written by Milton S. Terry shortly after the turn of the century, *Methodism and Biblical Criticism*. Terry argued that John Wesley's preface to his *Notes on the New Testament* indicate that Wesley had recognized his limitations in fully interpreting the meaning of the Scriptures, that his *Notes* were for common people and not for persons of learning, and that he had used the best scholarship of his day. Terry observed, "There is no prescriptive creed, confession, law, rule or standard of Methodism which defines or determines our liberty of thought and opinion on matters of biblical criticism and interpretation."[28] To further support his position, Terry pointed out a number of differences in textual use and interpretation among previous Methodist commentators, arguing that there was no dogma in regard to inspiration among Methodist doctrinal standards.

Such a contention did not go unanswered, and in 1905 L. W. Munhall undertook an extended attack on Terry's assumptions and conclusions. Munhall charged that the most dangerous people in Methodism were those who claimed to believe in

> Repentance, Faith, Justification, Sanctification and the Witness of the Spirit, and at the same time accept and teach the methods, principles and results of the modern Higher Criticism of the Bible, even to the extent of denying its supreme and infallible authority, not excepting the infallible authority of Jesus Christ and His Apostles.[29]

The issue was joined and the battle raged; and a singular victory for the conservatives was achieved in 1905 when Mitchell's appointment to the faculty at Boston was not renewed.

With inexorable force, however, the weight shifted during the first decades of the twentieth century, and episcopal Methodism, on the whole, accepted higher critical methods as being necessary to legitimate interpretation of the Bible.

The precritical approach of fundamentalism found little foothold in the Methodist Episcopal Church; biblical authority was set in more dynamic terms; general biblical teaching replaced proof texts. Henry C. Sheldon, also of Boston University, stated the dominant position: The Bible, he claimed, "is the most authentic record of the revelation leading up to and culminating in Jesus Christ. . . . It is enough to claim that the Bible in its trend and outcome affords to the candid and intelligent inquirer trustworthy means of ascertaining the essential content of the true religion."[30]

An Overview

The latter half of the nineteenth century was a time of basic change within North American Methodism.[31] The rapidity of church growth, new status and responsibility in society, and challenges to interpretation of faith and life—all were felt with unusual sharpness. Theologians in the tradition were sensitive to the need for explicating the meaning of grace in such a way as to represent the true nature of God and of human beings and to effect the transformation of life. In the process of reinterpretation, the meanings of inherited themes, especially the understanding of the relation of grace to faith, were altered. The concentration upon human freedom found in the work of Bledsoe and Whedon represented a philosophical effort to establish distinctive qualities of human life, to reinforce the integrity of personhood with responsibility for choice and action. Interpretation of God's sovereignty primarily as the exercise of power was replaced by emphasis upon God's moral character as expressed through the moral structure of the created order, serving the goal of divine and human holiness.

In contrast to earlier Wesleyan interpretation, grace lost its tight christological connection. Whereas grace previously was directly related to Jesus Christ and his saving activity, the prevenient graciousness of God became increasingly understood as a general endowment of humankind with ability for free agency. Grace remained the foundation, but the emphasis was shifted to human responsibility. Hence the action of grace in producing faith was transformed into an elaboration of the action of faith in appropriating grace. With Whedon and Bledsoe, this move to treat grace as a constitutive part of human life was evident; grace continued to be the presumed base of human free agency, but the focus was on that ability, and consequently the base receded as the focus sharpened. For Whedon and Bledsoe, self-agency was the point of the needle; all else followed. Some of the systematic theologians—Ralston, Bascom, Summers—continued to utilize broader foundations for the construction of doctrine and did not concentrate so singularly upon human free agency. So the tradition as a whole did not yield to this one dominant concern. But persistent voices stressed the theme and it became a cardinal issue for the Wesleyan tradition.

John Miley organized these changed understandings into a systematic statement. Meticulously, he drew the lines together and presented an interpretation of the integral relationship between natural theology and biblical revelation. Once again, grace was assumed, but again the stress was upon the use that human freedom makes of this ability. In Bowne, the change of emphasis was expanded as grace was moved back to the roots of reality and interpreted as constitutive of the immanental nature of God and the possibility for personal fulfilment. Clearly, a transition was taking place as an inherited theme underwent radical alteration.

An explanation of this change lay in the fact that all these thinkers were shifting to philosophical bases for interpreting human experience. Philosophical argument increasingly provided the groundwork upon which human free agency was constructed, and this was subsequently substantiated by scriptural and theological support. The search for convincing foundations for the distinctive quality of human life led interpreters to positions that were believed to carry general persuasiveness. Bowne shared these interests, and with him there appeared a new statement of philosophical foundations for Christian belief.

Changing attitudes toward the interpretation of Scripture also played an important role at the end of the century. Through the last two decades, especially with the work of Terry and Mitchell, new openness to historical-critical findings required a reconsideration of the nature of biblical authority and the utilization of Scripture for explicating the content of faith; and this was facilitated by the greater reliance upon philosophical foundations. The new assumption was that God's self-revelation is mediated through historical experience and development, while conservatives claimed that God's revelation is beyond historical limitations. The tradition had assumed that divine truth is not changed by the historical context in which it is received; that the biblical writers were not conditioned by history and that their message was clear, consistent, and eternal. Terry and Mitchell, on the other hand, argued that the biblical writers received God's presence and described it in their historical setting; that ultimate truth is expressed through changing historical conditions. This transition in biblical study began before 1900, but bore basic significance for the development of Methodist Episcopal theology in the twentieth century.[32]

The survey of Methodist theology in this era shatters one common stereotype—the presumption that Methodism did not espouse rational rigor. Often American Methodism is contrasted with American Calvinism: Methodism stresses emotional religion, Calvinism stresses rational theology. This stereotype carries weight because it captures some general features, but it is overdrawn. The real distinction is not intellectual seriousness or rigorous discipline as much as the understanding of the role of intellect in faith and the end that intellectual discipline serves. For a doctrinal tradition, rational assent to the formulation of faith is central, although dimensions of trust and obedience also are present. For Methodist theologians, there is a balancing of holistic human response in faith; there is careful weighing of affection, will, and obedience in relation to intellect. Consequently, the intellectual dimension is not given singular prominence. This does not mean that intellectual activity is less rigorously used, but that it is differently valued. In full-orbed faith commitment—which includes will, heart, strength, and mind—the scope of the intellect is more restricted, but its quality and disciplined use retain prime importance.

Like a stream, the Wesleyan tradition, moving from its fountainhead in John Wesley, was seeking new paths, coursing through different beds—sometimes diverging, sometimes merging with other waters—but continually finding new openings for movement.

CHAPTER 6

HOLINESS THEOLOGY

J OHN WESLEY taught that Christians should love God perfectly and, as his special task, he sought to spread this message. After Wesley's time, stress upon perfect love for God as the culminating expression of Christian life continued in Methodist preaching. But there was fluctuation of emphasis upon, and divergency of interpretation of Christian perfection. At times, preaching for conversion tended to eclipse the teaching of full Christian maturity. Theological interpretations of entire sanctification also varied. Nevertheless, even with its variety, typical nineteenth-century Methodist theology and preaching expressed strong interest in the doctrine of Christian perfection.

Through the middle decades, there were pulsations of intensity in concern for Christian holiness. In the 1830s a renewed effort to reinvigorate the search for holiness of heart and life won wide support. By the 1850s, increasing numbers of both lay and clergy in many denominations were captured by the search for personal holiness, and this movement took on special characteristics. Through the remainder of the nineteenth and into the twentieth century, this doctrinal emphasis provoked controversy even as growth of Holiness groups moved forward with impressive strides.

Although the holiness movement was interdenominational by profession, in its inception it was essentially Methodist and distinctively American.[1] (Later it moved across the Atlantic.) In 1867 the National Camp Meeting Association for the Promotion of Holiness was established, and while this association was intended to be transdenominational, its leadership continued to be Methodist. John S. Inskip and Phoebe Palmer were especially prominent. By the 1800s a group called the Come-outers began to call for separation from non-Holiness churches; and through the last decades of the 1800s a number of such groups established independent existence as denominations.[2]

Developments in the Methodist Episcopal Church and the Methodist Episcopal Church, South, also furthered the drawing of sharp lines encouraging the tendency toward separation. By the 1870s, there was heightened concern within these churches—where the vast majority of Holiness people held their membership—to reemphasize the place of sanctification in Methodist thought and practice. But tension remained. It is suggested by E. Dale Dunlap that the final issue between Methodists and Holiness separatists was not theology, but obedience to the discipline of Methodism.[3] But there were also basic theological differences, each side claiming that its position was more true to Wesley. The principal issues involved the means to the sanctification experience (illustrated by the Palmer controversy); the tension between growth and instantaneous sanctification (often set in terms of whether there was a continuum of Christian experience, or two distinct experiences—works of grace—in maturing Christian life); and the appropriation of Pentecostal language (emphasis upon baptism with the Holy

Spirit as the sign of entire sanctification). Disagreement about these issues was profound.

Methodist Episcopal interpreters, on the whole, stressed growth in grace and tended to doubt the validity of two distinct events in Christian experience. In addition, they retained an emphasis on the christological framework of Christian holiness and did not use Pentecostal language. Perhaps most critically, they challenged the idea of instantaneously experienced holiness. Atticus Haygood from Georgia, later a bishop, led the attack against instantaneous holiness and what he considered to be a move toward works righteousness; Wilbur F. Tillet and Daniel D. Whedon also challenged this teaching as semi-Palagian and an intrusion of novel doctrine. A statement adopted by the General Conference of the Methodist Episcopal Church, South, in 1894 affirmed the doctrine of sanctification, but deplored the idea of two distinct events in salvation experience, the tendency to distinguish classes of Christians, and separatism. In 1896 the Methodist Episcopal Church expressed a similar position.[4] Many holiness leaders felt they could not remain, and separation from both churches ensued.

The growth of the movement was impressive, and it has become a significant dimension of Protestant life in the United States. By 1971, more than one hundred fifty Holiness denominations and other groups were members of the Christian Holiness Association, successor to the National Camp Meeting Association. Today the largest of these groups are the Salvation Army, the Church of the Nazarene, The Wesleyan Church, and the Free Methodist Church.

People who played major roles in this development were Charles G. Finney, the American Congregational evangelist; William Arthur, a British Methodist whose *Tongue of Fire* generated eighteen editions within three years; and Asa Mahan, a popular American theologian.[5] Of the many factors that helped to produce Holiness, we shall concentrate on the

133

theological.[6] Donald W. Dayton of the Wesleyan Methodist Church stresses the change effected in the late 1850s when pentecostal language was introduced into the description of entire sanctification. Dayton sees several significant shifts from previous, more traditional Wesleyan interpretations: (1) There was a move from Christocentric (Christ centered) to Pneumatocentric (Holy Spirit centered) theological focus. (2) The interpretation of Jesus Christ as standing between the old and the new covenants yielded to a dispensational view developed along trinitarian lines, the present age being the age of the Holy Spirit. (3) The book of Acts gained acceptance as the pivotal New Testament text for understanding Christian holiness. (4) New attention was given to pneumatic (spiritual) themes of power, gifts of the Spirit, and prophecy. (5) The long-term goal of Christian perfection was played down as the immediately experienced event of a "second blessing" was lifted to prominence. And (6) increased emphasis was placed on assurance and evidence of having received the pentecostal baptism.[7]

Dayton holds that there was a clear difference between original Wesleyanism and these mid-nineteenth-century interpretations. Wesley, he claims, "was not only reticent about identifying sanctification with Pentecost, but specifically repudiated at least some of the common themes associated with that position." Further, Wesley associated the "baptism of the Holy Spirit" with conversion; but it was identified with entire sanctification only in early Methodism, especially in the thought of John Fletcher and Joseph Benson. These differences between Wesley and his immediate followers did not necessarily result in different understandings of the doctrine of sanctification. But after 1860 preference for one part of the tradition was shown. It is of interest that this change to Pentecostal language in Holiness theology was contemporary with the loosening of prevenient grace from an intrinsic relationship with Christology in episcopal

Methodism. Proponents of the new emphases were convinced of the importance of the change and affirmed, "Here finally is the great breakthrough for which the Wesleyan tradition had been straining for a century—and . . . the pentecostal vocabulary provides the most biblically appropriate way of explicating the doctrine of entire sanctification."[8] Significant change was underway; but some established interests continued.

The Holiness movement had traditionally viewed sanctification as a release from sin and an empowerment for service.[9] Christian perfection carried ethical responsibility, and many Holiness leaders related their theological position to benevolent ethical concern and action. For instance, Phoebe Palmer was actively engaged in social welfare projects: she founded the Five Points Mission in 1850 (initiating Protestant institutional work in slums) and joined a mission church in order to be more directly related to these efforts.[10] Such concern was characteristic. Timothy L. Smith, a prominent Nazarene historian, has documented the broad extent of social concern and action among nineteenth-century advocates of Christian holiness.[11]

The vitality of the Holiness movement was also expressed in theological writing. In 1908, E. P. Ellyson (1869–1954) wrote his *Theological Compend*, the first systematic theology produced among Holiness people.[12] Ellyson's theology (admittedly a very unassuming venture) was published to recognize the joining of the Holiness Churches of Christ with the Church of the Nazarene to form the present Church of the Nazarene into a national body. This book was an exposition of central Christian doctrines, holding together dominant revival themes such as sin, salvation, and final hope. As Paul M. Bassett, a Nazarene historical theologian has pointed out, there was, in the *Theological Compend*, no prior discussion of the nature of theology or theological method; and more remarkably, the doctrine of sanctification was given only "a

modest place within his discussion of the doctrine of man."[13]
The strength of Ellyson's presentation lay in his concentration on evangelical themes that constituted the underpinning for further development of specifically Holiness interpretations. The foundations of evangelical Christianity were clearly set. And the need for elucidation that remained was met before the middle of the twentieth century.

Systematic Theology

Two systematic theologies, both by Nazarene theologians, have become important foundational documents in the Holiness tradition: *Fundamental Christian Theology: A Systematic Theology* (1931) by A. M. Hills (1848–1935) and *Christian Theology* (1940) by H. Orton Wiley (1877–1962). Hills' theology, which was preceded by his widely circulated *Holiness and Power* (published while he was still a Congregational minister) had great influence upon ensuing Holiness thought. In many ways, Hills was indebted to Methodist predecessors, and his work evidences a close affinity to John Miley's, but its formative source is found in the writing of Charles G. Finney and Samuel Harris.[14] Both Finney and Harris were Reformed theologians, as were other of Hills' mentors at Oberlin and Yale. It was not until his first pastorate that Hills read Methodist theologians. The fusion of Calvinistic and Methodist theology, with Calvinism providing the primary foundation, provided his position with its distinctive character.

Theology, for Hills, was discourse about God, the moral creature, and the created universe. The pivot in this constructive effort was free agency of persons; and upon this Hills formed his systematic frame and constructed his other doctrines. Freedom is the linchpin, the basis of responsibility, and therefore persons are accountable for sin and capable of responding in faith. Freedom is a gift of creation; God has given every human being freedom enough to be able to profess faith. God also reveals saving truth and demands that people believe this truth on peril of damnation.[15] Also central is Hills' teaching of sanctification as the expected fulfillment of Christian existence. The importance Hills attached to these cardinal doctrines places him in close relation to nineteenth-century streams of Methodist theology that tended to root faith and sanctification in acts of the human will.[16]

Hills' systematic theology represented an amalgam of evangelical revivalistic and Holiness thought. He drew these strands together and utilized an understanding of human nature which emphasized the native free agency of persons; he set forth the dignity of persons in terms of Christian perfection.[17] Interestingly, Hills included no extended discussion of Christian ethics.

H. Orton Wiley

Orton Wiley used a range of theological literature to develop the most important theological statement of the Holiness tradition. Especially indebted to William Burt Pope, John Miley, and personalist philosophy, he made meager reference to Hills and little to Ellyson, as opposed to more than seventy references to Miley and one hundred fifty to Pope. These references indicated the direction of his thought.

Wiley's fundamental principle was his conviction that "truth in its ultimate nature is personal." The principal character of personal reality is the possibility of relationship: "The knowledge of God involves a filial relationship between the Incarnate Son and the souls of men, a relationship begotten and nourished by the Holy Spirit." The "synthetic," or coordinating, method by which he explicated this basic principle originates in the highest principle, the personal God, and proceeds to personal meaning in human life, in Jesus Christ, and in final consummation.[18]

The knowledge of God draws together a number of dynamics in Wiley's thought. Beginning with the assumption that truth is personal, he grounded his conviction in the personal nature of God and in God's personal relationship to human beings through the Holy Spirit. Christian experience is a source of theology. Immediate intuitive awareness of God is possible because of the affinity that exists between God and humans through creation. Theistic arguments support this general sense of God, but the arguments cannot reach a full and saving knowledge of God. The renewal of personal engagement through Jesus Christ is effected by the self-disclosure of God to humanity. Again, this objective historical overture, witnessed to by the Scriptures, requires response nurtured by the inner witness of the Holy Spirit.

> God alone can reveal Himself to man. This he has done in a primary revelation found in the nature and constitution of man, and secondarily, by the direct revelation of Himself through the Spirit to the consciousness of men. The first finds its culmination in the Incarnation, or the Word made flesh; while the second has its source in the Glorified Christ, as the foundation of the revelation of God through the Spirit.[19]

With the foundation laid, the attributes of the Triune nature of God were developed, using scriptural references to explicate the content of these doctrines.

Developing his understanding of human nature, Wiley stressed the original holiness of human beings, as expressed in Adam's moral rectitude and the presence and agency of the Holy Spirit. By their nature, humans are self-conscious, self-determining beings, but the original parents misused their freedom, and their descendants are born into the world as corrupt beings, without spiritual life. But people are not guilty of inbred sin; guilt ensues "only when having rejected the remedy provided by atoning blood, [one] ratifies it as his own." The same is said about free will: "All who will may turn from sin to righteousness, believe on Jesus Christ for pardon and cleansing from sin, and follow good works pleasing and acceptable in His sight. This free agency, however, is not mere natural ability, it is gracious ability."[20]

The fallen condition of humanity is met by God's new creative act in Jesus Christ. Stressing the reconciling and redemptive dimensions of Christ's atonement, Wiley gave central place to the universal inclusiveness of God's salvation. Again, the dynamic action of the Holy Spirit which draws persons to respond to the atoning work of Christ was a basic emphasis. "As the incarnate Son is the Redeemer of mankind by virtue of His atoning work, so the Holy Spirit is the Administrator of that redemption." The work of the Spirit initiates the impartation of new life; but there is a baptism with the Spirit into full privilege of the new covenant. This anointing with the Spirit confers authority and power; and there is a sealing with the Spirit which demonstrates God's ownership and approval.[21] Authority, power, and sealing are all parts of the second work of grace; and unlike Hills' theories, this emphasis upon the Holy Spirit played a large role in Wiley's discussion.

In his third volume, Wiley discussed Christian ethics as based upon the continuing presence of Jesus Christ, a presence expressed through holiness in personal and social life. Wiley held individual and corporate dimensions in relation to one another and understood the implications of ethical responsibility as moving in both directions: "Man not only has duties to God, to himself, and to other men, but he is a part of a social structure which demands certain organizations for the perpetuity of the race, for its conservation, and for its spiritual illumination and guidance. These are the Family, the State and the Church.[22]

The church is the "objective economy" of the Holy Spirit. In his discussion of the church. Wiley found its two principal tasks to be expressed in the ministry of evangelism and in worship.[23] His understanding of the church was close to the preceding Methodist tradition, as his discussion of the sacraments of baptism and the Lord's Supper indicated. The importance of the church lies in the fact that it is an intermediate community, looking forward to the coming of the full kingdom of God in the second advent, the resurrection, the judgment, and the final consummation. A paean of expectation anticipates the last events.

> The scriptures lead us to believe that God in time will set free these forces on earth which are now held in reserve, and use them to the purifying of that which has been defiled by sin. God destroys only that He may create something more beautiful, and upon the ruins of earth laboring under the curse, he will raise up another, which shall bloom in unfading splendor. This new heaven will be the consequence of dissolution and purifying—"the noblest gold, brought forth from the most terrible furnace heat."[24]

Both Wiley's relationship to received Methodist theology and the special emphases derived from his Holiness tradition are evident. His constructive statement is the most complete systematic theology the Holiness movement has produced, and it is an important marker of that movment's theological expression.

Connections and Differences

The discussion among Holiness theologians as to the origins of their distinctive teachings has concentrated attention upon their Wesleyan roots. An important part of this discussion has centered around the relationship of John Fletcher to John Wesley and an assessment of their theological agreements and differences. It is evident that Fletcher's use of Pentecostal language, his emphasis upon instantaneous experience of sanctification, and the shift to pneumatological themes in theology have been influential.

Timothy L. Smith, in exploring the relation of one man to the other, writes that in regard to "the power and availability by faith of the Holy Spirit's baptism. . . . Fletcher himself taught more clearly than Wesley ever did, the proper baptism of Jesus."[25] But the relationship between these two founding fathers is still under investigation, and their connection to nineteenth-century Holiness developments is fundamental to an interpretation of the Holiness tradition.

Rob L. Staples, a Nazarene theologian, has reviewed the historical discussion and clarified some issues of controversy. The debate was initiated by Herbert McGonigle, a British Nazarene, in a paper "Pneumatological Nomenclature in Early Methodism." McGonigle shows that Wesley and the first Methodist preachers say almost nothing about baptism with the Holy Spirit, this nomenclature having arisen in America. Even though Fletcher used Pentecostal language, especially in his last *Check,* the most important changes occurred through the influence of Charles G. Finney and Asa Mahan. Wesley's references to the Holy Spirit were related especially to the experience of conversion, whereas nineteenth-century interpreters related such references especially to sanctification. Several scholars have recently reviewed biblical materials and have reached various conclusions: Robert W. Lyon, of Asbury Theological Seminary, indicates that the phrase "baptism with the Holy Spirit" in Luke/Acts refers to conversion; Alex R. G. Deasley, of Nazarene Theological Seminary, argues that although the primary reference is to conversion, there is a possible enlargement of the phrase to cover the experience of sanctification; and George A. Turner, of Asbury, opposes both and supports the mid-nineteenth-century interpretation.[26]

Staples draws important conclusions from that survey. (1) John Wesley did not describe entire sanctification in precise Pentecostal language. (2) John Fletcher introduced that language, but since he spoke of many baptisms, he made no simple equation between sanctification and baptism with the Holy Spirit. (3) Wesley, in the 1770s, "*acquiesced* to Fletcher's use . . . but did not *approve* it." (4) Wesley did, on occasion, use pneumatological language in discussing entire sanctification; the issue is whether he "characteristically used a *very specialized type* of pneumatological language."[27] (5) After Fletcher's time, baptismal language was not used by Methodist theologians of the nineteenth century, even those who taught Christian perfection.[28] (6) When this language did become part of Holiness interpretation, according to Timothy L. Smith, it was introduced from an external tradition—from Charles G. Finney, a Congregationalist. (7) This acquired use is close to, but not identical with Fletcher's use. (8) Among those committed to the doctrine of sanctification, there are three major trends within Wesleyan theology:

> (a) that of Wesley and of such theologians as Adam Clarke, Richard Watson, William B. Pope, Miner Raymond, Olin A. Curtis, Thomas N. Ralston, and John Miley, (b) that of the American Holiness movement, under Finney's influence, and (c) that of John Fletcher, whose view is in many ways a mediating position between the other two.[29]

Staples indicates a further major issue—that the change in language may represent a shift in meaning. While Wesley described the holy life in christological terms, some nineteenth-century theologians described it in terms of the Holy Spirit. This raises a question of evidence to demonstrate whether a person has been sanctified. " 'Christlike' is its own evidence. 'Spirit-filled' requires evidence."[30] Further, Staples argues that Fletcher, while he differed from Wesley in use of language, also differed from many nineteenth-century theologians in that he stressed continuing outpourings of the Holy Spirit, since more than one baptism may be required to make persons perfect. (There is an exception in the "fire-baptized" tradition which distinguishes three blessings, found in the Pentecostal Holiness Church and in R. C. Horner in Canada.)

Holiness theologians are now assessing the roots of their doctrine of sanctification and are relating the implications of their positions to actual experience. Whatever the final conclusions, and whether or not consensus is achieved, the discussion has enriched the historical understanding of the teaching of Christian perfection.

Mildred Bangs Wynkoop

A major contemporary contributor to theological construction within the Holiness movement is Mildred Bangs Wynkoop (born 1908), a Nazarene theologian. Wynkoop is the author of two important books. The earlier, *Foundations of Wesleyan-Arminian Theology*, was an effort to clarify and consequently to emphasize the doctrine of Holiness by giving it its rightful place among other doctrines. This she did by studying its prenineteenth-century roots in John Wesley, where she found a balance that was lost in the nineteenth-century movement. The critical issue is not predestination itself, she claimed, but theories of predestination. She found Wesley's thought, as opposed to Calvinism, to be rooted in "personal predestination"—that is, the action of God in the lives of individuals. "Wesley's emphasis was not on free will, as is so often supposed. His emphasis was on free grace, on prevenient grace granted to any and all men and accounting for all the good found in the world. . . . Any good in any man is only by the free grace of God."[31] In the Arminian theme of personal predestination, Wesley primarily emphasized the presence and work of the Holy Spirit; and this emphasis, Wynkoop insisted, must become central in Holiness theology.

A Theology of Love, in which Wynkoop explores the founda-

143

tions and expression of the doctrine of Holiness, constitutes a contemporary systematic statement. She begins with a question: Can theology and human existence meet meaningfully? Love, properly interpreted, is the bridge that holds these two dimensions together. "Theology infused with a personal experience of God's grace—this is Wesleyanism." The relation of God to people and the relation of people to God and to one another are the themes around which all else centers. The whole person is engaged by God and is transformed by relationship with God. This engagement is processive and must be understood in terms of its dynamic characteristics. Static categories and an overly sharp delineation of "stages" of growth distort the dynamic of God's way of relating to people, of personal self-understanding, and of interpersonal relationships.[32]

> Entire sanctification draws together the two major cords into one strong twist of rope.
>   1) God requires man to love Him wholly. Sanctification is the moral atmosphere of that love. It has two movements, a total renunciation of the self-centered life and a total commitment to God. . . .
>   2) God accepts this living sacrifice and fills the "heart" with the Holy Spirit. As *religion,* this is loving God with the whole heart, soul, mind, and strength; in *psychology,* it is an integrated personality; in *theology,* it is cleansing.
>   Both crisis and process are recognized—crisis at crucial moments, process as a continuing life both before and after the more formative movements of decision.[33]

In keeping with Holiness thought, Wynkoop stresses two moments of special significance in Christian experience—conversion and sanctification—but these are set within the total development of Christian life. Even though the Holy Spirit plays an essential role, Wynkoop does not use Pentecostal language or refer to baptism with the Holy Spirit. The stress upon the two moments, she argues, points to the dual reality of the privilege (forgiving grace) and the responsibility (responsive self-giving) of Christian experience.[34] The thrust of Wynkoop's presentation is upon the primacy of relationship; categories to describe experience are useful only insofar as they elucidate relational reality.

In a prefatory thematic statement, Wynkoop draws her presentation into concise expression.

> LOVE takes the Harshness out of Holiness.
> LOVE takes the Incredibility out of Perfection.
> LOVE takes the Antinomianism out of faith.
> LOVE takes the Moralism out of Obedience.
> LOVE takes the Gnosticism out of Cleansing.
> LOVE takes the Abstraction out of Truth.
>
> LOVE puts the Personal into Truth.
> LOVE puts the Ethical into Holiness.
> LOVE puts Process into Life.
> LOVE puts Urgency into Crisis.
> LOVE puts Seriousness into Sin.
> LOVE puts Fellowship into Perfection.[35]

Concurring Voices

Howard Snyder, a member of the Free Methodist Church, has articulated the important current concerns of the Holiness movement. In *Problem of Wineskins* (1975) he calls for a recovery of ministry to the poor, a mission the Holiness movement traditionally has undertaken. And on theological issues, he calls for a return to John Wesley's position on sanctification, as opposed to the narrowing of that vision by nineteenth-century Holiness theology. "A careful reading of Wesley's sermons," he writes, "has convinced me that the fundamental strain in Wesley's doctrine of sanctification is that of process. . . . To this Wesley added . . . his doctrine of a second crisis experience in which the believer was entirely sanctified. . . . The fully Wesleyan understanding of

145

Christian perfection as combining both process and crisis must be recovered."[36]

Interest in social action and an attempt to reestablish its place in the Holiness movement has been generally affirmed. Timothy L. Smith, in his study of nineteenth-century Holiness social activity, set the background, and it was emphasized in Wynkoop and Snyder. In 1974 the annual convention of the Christian Holiness Association adopted the Chicago Declaration of Evangelical Social Concern. Currently, Ronald J. Sider, of the Brethern in Christ, is a significant leader in interpreting the implications of sanctification for the totality of life.[37]

Conclusion

Holiness theology is one of the streams of the Wesleyan tradition. Consciously aware of its foundation, it took on special character in the nineteenth century and recently has undertaken a serious investigation of its development and future. The relation of sanctification to Jesus Christ and the Holy Spirit, and the tension between continuing maturation and crisis as completion are issues of special significance. These matters are not settled, but they have been creatively assessed by theologians of this tradition. Whether these investigations will draw this movement into greater confluence with other streams of Wesleyan theology is not yet clear. But as a vital part of Wesleyan life, Holiness theology is alive, and it remains a partner with others who claim Wesleyan roots and who wish to continue in the Wesleyan spirit.

CHAPTER 7

TWENTIETH-CENTURY BRITISH METHODISM

A S THE NINETEENTH century yielded to the twentieth, the stream of Wesleyan theology that had moved through rather well-defined channels now picked up influx from numerous new sources and overspread its neat boundaries. With British society and other churches, Methodism experienced a pervasive sense of change; the altering British situation called for new self-understanding and new mission strategies.

It is too easy to describe these challenging influences as the "secularization" of society. But clearly, a change in value-commitment on a cultural level was taking place. The central importance of spiritual well-being, of ultimate hopes, and of divine/human relationship was no longer granted by the general populace. British culture was exploring new foundations, and religious thought was intensely involved in this search.[1]

John Scott Lidgett

A chief theological representative among the Methodists during that period was John Scott Lidgett (1854–1953). It is not easy to place Lidgett historically, for he lived half his life in each century. Molded by nineteenth-century developments, he continually moved to new frontiers and, with courageous imagination, reached toward new possibilities. More than other British theologians we have discussed, he was responsive to a wide contemporary intellectual context, including German theology. Open and independent, he cut his own path, breaking through narrow theological confinements. For Lidgett, theology was a practical science, and the transformation of society was the intended goal. To understand Lidgett theologically, therefore, one must be aware of his investment of decades of life and energy in settlement work in southeastern London. A man of enormous creativity, Lidgett identified with conditions of deep poverty and worked to alleviate them. Like Hugh Price Hughes, he was unable to separate his theology from practical activity; and the particular theological themes he emphasized expressed the relation of his faith to his ethical commitment.

Lidgett described some of the influences that had shaped his life:

> The Methodism of my grandparents and parents was in the true succession of John and Charles Wesley. They were Methodists but not Dissenters. Hence it has been both easy and congenial to me throughout my life to maintain and strengthen the tenets in which I was brought up. The doctrines in which we were instructed were the doctrines of the Catholic Reformed Church, with their Methodist emphasis, interpretation, and application. Strictness of doctrinal belief was combined with that generosity and geniality of temper which has from the beginning characterized Methodism at its best.[2]

Contributions that stimulated his interest were legion: the writings of John Henry Newman, the science of Charles Darwin, the philosophy of Herbert Spencer, the polemics of

George Tyrrell and Thomas Huxley, the new biblical criticism, and the prevailing interest in Kant and Hegel, along with the theological and practical activities of Charles Kingsley and Frederick Denison Maurice.[3] To mention these influences is to indicate Lidgett's awareness of a world radically different from that of his Methodist theological predecessors; it is as though everything that had been held back from those who had gone before was now rushing in torrents through Lidgett's experience. Lidgett presented the main thrust of the new sensitivity:

> The doctrine of Evolution in philosophy and science; accompanied by that of Divine Immanence in theology has raised a new problem that is alike religious, theological, and philosophic. . . . The grace that bestows, rather than the will that ordains, becomes determinative of religious thought, while the faith that aspires, rather than the will that submits, becomes the highest concern of religious life.[4]

"The grace that bestows "was a dominant thesis; and focus upon this theme, Lidgett claimed, sharply differentiated his time from the past. He found this difference expressed in several possible negative convictions: the impossibility of maintaining exaggerated notions of individualism or otherworldliness, a Calvinistic understanding of God's sovereignty, a biblical fundamentalism, a sharp distinction between spiritual and secular realms. Against these persuasions he sought to give fresh expression to the meaning of grace; hence he positively affirmed the Fatherhood of God (in contrast to a primary stress upon the omnipotent sovereignty of God), the immanence of God with its implications of divine kinship with the human spirit, radical self-giving as expressed in the character of Jesus Christ, and the conviction that reality is rationally consistent and coherent. He stated his thesis tersely: "Grace redeems and renews what creation has implanted from the first in potentiality and promise."[5]

149

Three underlying motifs in Lidgett's theology are of special importance. First, the ultimate character of the created order is spiritual, and the universe is, throughout, intimately related to God—it is sacramental. Consequently, Lidgett was concerned to see the world as a unity, to interpret the universe as a spiritual reality which comprehends and enhances the interrelation of all creation. Second, theology is rooted in personal religious experience. Hence in regard to his chief doctrine of the Fatherhood of God, Lidgett claimed that "the foundation of the doctrine is wholly experimental." Third, Lidgett's was an apologetic theology, intended to make Christian understanding of God intelligible to and significant for contemporary people.[6] All these motifs were consonant with the dominant idealism in philosophy and the increasing interest in religious experience. It is both a compliment and a recognition of limitation to say that Lidgett's theological contribution was a reflection of his time. He represented, with sensitivity and clarity, some of the prevailing theological concerns of his era; and he led Methodism into the mainstream of liberal Protestant theological development. So remarkable was his influence that W. F. Howard, a prominent British Methodist biblical scholar, has called his work, "the statesmanship of thought."[7]

To present his point of view, Lidgett wrote a number of books. The themes of *The Spiritual Principle of the Atonement* (1898) and *The Fatherhood of God in Christian Life and Thought* (1902) set the direction for his constructive theology. He emphasized that the Fatherhood of God expresses the meaning of divine sovereignty; that Jesus' life of filial obedience renders the satisfaction that brings God's atonement and restores the relation of persons to God; and that this view is consistent with the Old and New Testament understandings of sacrifice and atonement.[8]

To read Lidgett's theological work is to enter the arena of contemporary German theology, especially that of Albrecht

Ritschl and Adolf von Harnack. But Lidgett was fully conscious of his primary setting in England and read these German writers through his own lens. More than any previous English Methodist theologian, he espoused the essential positions of Protestant liberalism, and he constructed his interpretation to make these themes clear.

Lidgett's leadership represented and stimulated British Methodist theology as it entered the twentieth century. The most recent significant aspect of that Methodism has been a dialectical tension between traditional theological interests and new forms of social mission and ecclesiastical life. Traditional emphases had focused upon biblical studies and Reformation influences upon Wesley; new configurations have resulted from the changing social and religious character of British life and thought.

Through the present century, British Methodists have recognized common commitments, interests, and goals with other Christians; Lidgett announced that denominationalism was dead. Obviously it was not yet so, but the attitude Lidgett represented has become dominant in British Methodism as an increasing interest in the ecumenical movement and in ecumenical theology is now characteristic.

Biblical Theology

While Lidgett must be prominently mentioned in twentieth-century Methodist theology, the truth is that British Methodism expended its greater strength in scriptural study and biblical theology. Most prominent Methodist theologians were primarily biblical scholars: one must recall Arthur S. Peake, W. F. Moulton, James Hope Moulton, W. F. Howard, R. Newton Flew, Vincent Taylor, Norman H. Snaith, C. K. Barrett, I. Howard Marshall, and James D. G. Dunn, among others.

In studying Methodist theologians, a strong sense of their

personal quality is conveyed. Time and again one pauses as evidence of a fine sensitive character emerges. Arthur S. Peake (1865–1929) continued that tradition. Here was a thoroughly good man, simple and profound in his commitments. Born into a Primitive Methodist parsonage and raised in that branch of Methodism, he was notable for both his academic achievement and personal attributes. Having won a scholarship to Oxford, he continued his education in that university and on the Continent, and then accepted a lectureship at Mansfield College in Oxford.

In 1892 he received a call from the young Primitive Methodist theological institute Hartley College, in Manchester. After much inner debate he left the university out of loyalty to his own church. Principal A. M. Fairbairn, of Mansfield, spoke for many: "It seems to me as if you have been especially raised up and trained for the very work that is most in need of being done. . . . And in many ways you are the only person that can do the work."[9] Peake's "work" advanced quickly. In 1897 his *Guide to Biblical Study* was published, followed by commentaries on Hebrews and Colossians and *The Problem of Suffering in The Old Testament*. In 1904 he became professor of biblical criticism and exegesis at Manchester University, the first time a non-Anglican had been elected to a such a post in an English university.

Peake's primary arena was biblical study, and his ability to make critical scholarship acceptable to a suspicious constituency was one of his chief contributions. Indeed, he may have done more than any other scholar to introduce his nation to critical study of the Bible on a popular level. With typical clarity he described his position, a position he would express in a number of different settings and ways:

The Bible is the record of revelation. It is not the revelation itself. That was given through history and experience, in life and personality. But a record of it was needed that it might be preserved for posterity, and this we have in the Bible. . . . We have the double process of revelation and interpretation, and the record of this is contained in Scripture. It lies in the nature of the case that the supreme value and authority attaches to the final stage of the process . . . Fragmentary and incomplete, marred by imperfection and impoverished by the limitation of the medium, yet the process of revelation in Israel is organically one with the revelation of God's only begotten Son, and he who would understand the climax aright must retrace with patient care the long and steep ascent by which it was finally reached.[10]

The work of Peake has endured remarkably well amid the changes in biblical scholarship since his time.[11]

There were other notable students of Scripture among the British Methodists. One sequence, each teaching the next, consisted of W. F.Moulton (1835–1898), James Hope Moulton (1863–1917), and W. F. Howard (1880–1952).[12] These men possessed fine technical competence and were committed to exact knowledge of the biblical text. They all worked carefully with the Greek language, and J. H. Moulton, with Egyptian papyri. Howard was also an exceptionally able student of the Fourth Gospel, as his *Christianity According to St. John* (1943) exemplifies, and *The Fourth Gospel in Recent Criticism and Interpretation* (1955) reaffirms. Other biblical scholars also have made significant contributions. George Gillanders Findlay (1849–1919) taught at Headingly, Richmond, and was the father of James Alexander Findlay (1880–1961), New Testament tutor at Didsbury College and author of *Jesus and His Parables* (1950). Charles Ryder Smith (1873–1956), tutor and principal of Richmond College and later professor of theology at the University of London, wrote several books on biblical themes: *The Bible Doctrine of Salvation* (1941), *The Bible Doctrine of Sin* (1953), and *The Bible Doctrine of Grace* (1956). Among contemporary scholars, the careful work of

A. Raymond George (born 1912), *Communion with God in the New Testament* (1953), deserves special notice.

This distinguished company must also include R. Newton Flew (1886–1962), who was a brilliant student at Oxford and later the principal of Wesley House, Cambridge. His service to the church was expressed especially through his leadership in ministerial training, but he also was an evangelist and a statesman, serving the cause of Christian reconciliation. Among his major books are *The Idea of Perfection in Christian Thought* (1934) and *Jesus and His Church* (1938). The first was wide-ranging, thorough, and continued the interest of Methodist theology in Christian holiness. Flew's second volume helped set British Methodism's ecclesiastical self-understanding after the union of British Methodist churches in 1932 and prepared the denomination for ecumenical discussions; this was also true of *The Nature of the Christian Church*, which was produced by a study commission led by Flew and approved at the Methodist Conference meeting at Bradford in July 1937.[13]

Vincent Taylor (1887–1968) was a steady and productive writer on New Testament topics. He introduced form-critical studies of the Gospels (studies of literary types and their settings in the life of the early church) to many English-speaking peoples and added valuable commentaries on Mark (this is of exceptional quality) and Romans. In these commentaries he also employed redaction criticism—that is, he used the entire text as we presently have it in its final edited form—in making helpful interpretations. Desiring to move beyond self-contained biblical scholarship, he explored theological implications of his textual work, especially in his trilogy on the atonement: *Jesus and His Sacrifice* (1937), *The Atonement in New Testament Teaching* (1940), and *Forgiveness and Reconciliation* (1941). Taylor's work represented a cautious reconsideration of reigning liberal persuasions. Accepting the fact of sin, he concentrated upon the atonement as a central contemporary issue. There was continuity in Taylor's constructive discussions of the atoning work of Christ. On the basis of careful New Testament study, he sought a middle path between moral influence theories, which stress that God's love prompts our responsive love, and legal substitution, which stresses a change in God's relation to people. He found the resolution in an emphasis upon the reconciliation accomplished by Jesus Christ. In Jesus Christ there are definitive loving acts: obedience to God's will, submission to the judgment of God upon sin, and intercession through the voicing of inarticulate penitence. Believers find the reality of salvation as they identify with Jesus through faith and are made one with him in his self-giving to God, especially through worship and the Lord's Supper.[14] Taylor also produced a trilogy on Christology: *The Names of Jesus* (1953), *The Life and Ministry of Jesus* (1954), and *The Person of Christ in New Testament Teaching* (1958).

Norman Henry Snaith (born 1898) was an Old Testament scholar at Wesley College in Headingly, Leeds. He wrote prolifically on Old Testament textual matters and produced commentaries on a number of biblical books, including Leviticus and Numbers, Job, and Amos. He also wrote an introduction, *The Distinctive Ideas of the Old Testament* (1944), in addition to special thematic studies such as *Mercy and Sacrifice* (1953) and *Inspiration and Authority of the Bible* (1956). In two small books, Snaith, with a direct, sometimes blunt style, has evidenced a strongly orthodox position. In *I Believe In . . .* (1959) he plainly affirmed the elements of the Nicene Creed, and in *The God That Never Was* (1971), he argues that this is the message contemporary people need. Identifying modern with ancient misconceptions that God is exclusively transcendent or immanent, Snaith reiterates the same themes he emphasized in his credo as providing the answer to modern false belief. Snaith is idiosyncratic, but he does indicate the continuing diversity that has characterized British Methodism.

Transition in biblical understanding has been continuous, and the scholars we have mentioned led the church through threatening yet promising new territory. A prayer of W. F. Howard describes the reigning sensibility remarkably well:

We give Thee thanks, O God, all-wise and all-loving, for the knowledge of Thy truth as truth is in Jesus. Grant us, we beseech thee, grace, that in times of perplexity and misgiving, when we are perplexed by new learning, when faith is strained by doctrines and mysteries beyond our understanding, we may possess the humility of learners and the courage of believers in Thee; give us boldness to examine and faith to trust all truth; patience and insight to master difficulties; stability to hold fast our tradition with enlightened interpretations, to receive reverently all fresh truth made known to us, and in days of unrest to combine new knowledge with the old honesty and loyalty as in Thy sight, and graciously deliver us alike from stubborn rejection of new revelation of Thy Spirit and from hasty assurance that we are wiser than our fathers. Amen.[15]

Contemporary Methodists continue this tradition of excellence in biblical studies. Most distinguished is C. Kingsley Barrett (born 1917) of Durham University, who has made and continues to make significant contributions to New Testament studies, especially in his two editions of *The Gospel of St. John*. He has also written commentaries on Romans on First and Second Corinthians, and on the Pastoral Epistles, as well as a study of the Holy Spirit in the Gospels. Morna D. Hooker, the first woman to hold the position of Lady Margaret Professor at Cambridge, also is a leader in the discipline. She has written on Gospel themes in *Jesus and the Servant* (1959) the *Son of Man in Mark* (1969), as well as on St. Paul in *Pauline Pieces* (1970). Professor of New Testament exegesis at the University of Aberdeen, I. Howard Marshall, has had a number of books published including *The Origins of New Testament Christology* (1976) and *Last Supper and Lord's Supper* (1980) Brian Beck, Principal of Wesley House, Cambridge, has recently written *Reading the New Testment Today* (1978). And James D. G. Dunn, of Durham University, has provided significant studies in *Unity and Diversity in the New Testament* (1977) and *Christology in the Making: A New Testament Inquiry into the Origins of the Doctrine of the Incarnation* (1980). The list is imposing, and the quality, as well as the quantity, is impressive. The positions expressed in these studies present a wide range of theological interpretations and critical interests.

As is evident from this quick survey, British Methodism has made a major theological contribution through biblical study. This is significant, for it indicates and reinforces the rootage of this tradition in scriptural Christianity. There is, in much of this biblical scholarship, a very practical turn, for it serves preachers and preaching. The careful study of biblical texts typically moves to interpretation, which can inform and guide the church. Theological distinctiveness has been neither espoused nor nurtured, but there is a firm commitment to the Bible as the basic source of Christian faith. That this is so does not make the Wesleyan tradition unique, but it does typify its character.

But even in biblical interpretation there has been radical change. Commitment to the Bible as the primary source does not imply a static set of interpretations. Quite the contrary, for commitment to biblical study leads learners through the multiple changes in understanding of authority, in exegesis of particular passages, in perspective on the essential message of the Scriptures, and in Christian responsibility for proclamation and service. Each of the people mentioned represents an effort to be faithful to his or her origins and present ecclesiastical context.

Theological Interpreters

A major area of theological activity has centered around the study of the Reformation, and especially Martin Luther, by the Methodist historical theologians E. Gordon Rupp (born 1910) and Philip S. Watson (born 1909). Both have explored the Protestant Reformation for its own value and have related their work to the Methodist tradition. These two scholars represent British Wesleyanism's response to the neo-Reformation revival in the post-World War II period.

Watson taught in English theological schools and universities, completing his career at Garrett Theological Seminary. His major contribution, *Let God Be God* (1949), was a seminal study of the sovereignty of God in Martin Luther's thought. This motif, Watson demonstrated, underlay Luther's understanding of salvation and the church. Insisting upon Luther's "copernican revolution," from person-centered to God-centered thought, Watson explicated Luther's theology under the theme of God's glory. He reexplored this theme in *The Concept of Grace* (1959) and also retained his interest in the Wesleyan tradition, editing *The Message of the Wesleys* in 1964.

Gordon Rupp, who became the distinguished Dixie Professor of Ecclesiastical History at Cambridge University, is a consummate scholar with unusual ability to communicate clearly and effectively. He made basic contributions to Luther studies in *The Righteousness of God* (1953) and has done primary work on the Reformation traditions, on the Continent and in England, in *Principalities & Powers* (1952) and *Just Men* (1977). Rupp has written on *Methodism in Relation to the Protestant Tradition* (1954), on Thomas Jackson, a nineteenth-century Methodist leader, and on the current status of British and world Methodism. He has challenged his own tradition to remember Wesley's "optimism of grace" against the background of the "pessimism of nature [sin]" and to meet its future with theological depth and acuity.

Other scholars also have expressed interest in Wesleyan theological themes in both general and specific ways. Three, in particular, have attempted more general theological statements—H.Maldwyn Hughes (1875–1940), Eric W. Baker (1899–1973), and Rupert E. Davies (born 1909). Each has drawn together a composite statement of general Methodist beliefs. Hughes wrote as an active practicing minister when he explored *The Theology of Experience* (1915). He understood experience in its widest sense—as every enrichment of life and thought gained by experimental knowledge. Keenly aware of his intellectual context and the current discussions of biblical and theological themes, Hughes predicated his position upon the affinity between God and humanity. Hence it is the immanence of God that establishes the basis for all religious experience, including Christian experience. Probing the relation of inner experience to historical fact, and analyzing the emotional, intellectual, and volitional dimensions of Christian experience, he recognized both the legitimate variety of Christian experience of God and the formation of doctrine. Throughout this volume and in *The Kingdom of Heaven* (1922), Hughes stressed the interaction of God's presence in the external world and in the human spirit, indicating that in this interaction, truth is found.

In 1927, Hughes' *Christian Foundations: An Introduction to Christian Doctrine* was published. Written for candidates for the ministry and basically an outline, this book was quite popular and was reissued into the 1950s. In developing his systematic statement, Hughes employed the theme of experience as the ground of certainty in Christian life and as the source for theology. Again, he stressed the interrelation of God's inward and outward working in making divine truth known. In addition, he now emphasized personalistic aspects of God and human beings. Within the general knowledge of God, Christian faith places primary focus upon Jesus as a divine/human person, so Hughes began with

Christology, then discussed the doctrines of God and human beings in terms of individual and social personality. Discussion of other major doctrines followed, including Wesleyan themes of justification, regeneration, assurance, and sanctification.

Hughes, who became the first principal of Wesley House, Cambridge, reflects the theological emphases current in his era. The distinctive place given to experience, the recognition of varieties of authentic ways of encountering God, the use of personalistic categories, and the employment of developmental and progressive themes were all consonant with dominant sensibilities. He grafted traditional Methodist teaching into this root and gave Wesleyan teaching contemporary dress.

Eric W. Baker was secretary of the Methodist Conference in Great Britain from 1951 until 1970. As such, he was considered by many to be a spokesman for British Methodism during the mid-century, and in this capacity he wrote a small popular presentation, *The Faith of A Methodist*. [16] Taking the doctrine of Christian perfection as the distinctive theological emphasis and as the organizing center of his thought, Baker explored the meaning of such themes as God, humanity, forgiveness, immortality, the Holy Spirit, and the Church. Interestingly, even though there was pervasive reference to Jesus, there was no separate treatment of Christology or special focus on grace. Baker intended to stand in the broad catholic tradition and to express his faith as a Methodist in such a way as to find the widest possible compatibility with other Christian traditions.

Rupert E. Davies, a teacher, writer, and spokesman for Methodism, has specialized in study of John Wesley, and in *What Methodists Believe*, he sets Wesleyan doctrine on the broad ground of beliefs many Christians hold in common. Only in a concluding chapter does he find distinctive characteristics in Methodism's combination of spontaneous and ordered forms of worship, its social concerns, its universal understanding of the scope of the gospel, and its utilization of the laity.[17] In *Methodism*, Davies gives a quick and lively view of Wesley's theology as rooted in the theme of grace, but there is no account of the historical development of this theological tradition. Davies has made his own contributions to particular theological themes, such as the meaning of authority, but his basic work has been based on John Wesley's theology.[18]

In the writing of both Baker and Davies there is, once again, keen awareness of Methodism's participation in the wider Christian movement and a strong desire for theological, as well as institutional union with other Christian churches. Theologically, neither recognizes any need to continue along separate denominational lines. Both illustrate a desire for Methodism to move into the more general and common stream. Methodism, they believe, should now serve in the wholeness of ecumenical Christianity.

One additional theological expression should be mentioned. Wesleyanism has been continuously conveyed through preaching. In the mid-twentieth century, three of the most prominent preachers in London were Methodists: W. E. Sangster (1900-1960), Leslie D. Weatherhead (1893–1970), and Lord Donald Soper (born 1903). Each was distinguished in the pulpit; each presented popular interpretations of theological issues; and each sought to renew the Methodist Church even as he believed Methodism should actualize its ecumenical promise. Sangster was especially interested in evangelical preaching and presented the doctrine of sanctification with fresh force in *The Path to Perfection* (1943). Weatherhead focused on psychological interpretation of Christian experience and wrote a provocative pamphlet on *The Will of God* (1944), as well as many other books. Soper, with his dynamic qualities and forceful style, stimulated the social conscience of the nation. Constantly attacking ethical issues, his has been a strong voice of Christian challenge.

None of these three preachers was an academic theologian; yet all presented Methodist theology to a wide audience and vividly demonstrated the interactions of theory and practice in the Wesleyan tradition. *Pastoral theology*, with weight given to both words in this common phrase, was their aim. [19]

New Voices

To this point, we have depicted a constant attempt to move British Methodism into the ecumenical setting; a double vision has held together the received past and the present. Two new voices have recently been heard. One, that of John J. Vincent (born 1929) has challenged his contemporaries by arguing for a reformulation of basic emphases in the Christian message. The other, that of Geoffrey Wainwright (born 1939), has related the Wesleyan tradition to the widest ecumenical context since the time of Wesley.

Consciously different from his immediate predecessors, and proposing a differing theological base to serve social needs, is John J. Vincent. In *Christ and Methodism*, he attempted to bring "reality into modern Methodism."[20] Stridently judging the dominance of personal and individual emphases in Methodist theology, Vincent proposed an opposing direction. In his concern for revitalizing Methodism, he was not alone: He and eleven others, calling themselves The Renewal Group, banded together from the late 1950s until the late 1960s. With Vincent as their leader, this group proposed to reform Methodist thought and life.

Vincent's thinking was influenced by John A. T. Robinson's *Honest to God*. This declaration of the need for Christian thought to be relevant to contemporary scientific assumptions and secular experience created a seismic shock in British religious life, and Methodism was inevitably affected.

Robinson's statement made it clear to Vincent that the liberal evangelical development, which Methodism generally espoused, was now at an end. The way ahead, Vincent argued, is to develop a theology that conveys a better understanding of Jesus Christ and that will free Christian thought from the deadwood of institutional religion and outdated confessional formulations.

First, Vincent's criticism must be noted. John Wesley's thought was centered on God's action in the human soul; therefore, fundamental in Wesley's theology was the priestly work of Christ, Christ as Savior. Wesley emphasized justification, the immediate assurance of God's forgiveness, and the necessity of holiness in life. All this must now be set aside, Vincent said, for pietistic themes, centering primarily upon the relation of individuals to God, cannot be successfully restated. It will no longer do to continually recast old doctrines.

Discipleship must now come to the fore; active following of Jesus Christ and participation in his ministry are the cardinal themes. Personal experience may be retained, but the traditional doctrines must be replaced by emphasis upon responsible vocation, by the application of Christian morality in stewardship of resources, and by social witness as a Church. Obedience is the issue; to be a Christian is actively to express God's will in and as the Body of Christ. Vincent looked on this as the most valid presentation of the theme of grace, for "grace is present in the deed of discipleship." Again he wrote, "This is what Christianity is—the continuation on earth of the whole pattern of Jesus which God demands and accepts."[21] Vincent stressed that Christ's service is central and that conformity of Christian action to the pattern of Jesus is the truest expression of Christian discipleship.

The greatest opportunity for Methodist theology, Vincent claimed, lies in the future. The characteristic attitudes of

Methodism—empirical seriousness, and pragmatic and experimental openness—provide the grounds for this promise.[22] Methodism's hope for grasping a new future through obedient discipleship depends upon freedom from historical restrictiveness and confessional fixity.

Geoffrey Wainwright

Recently a major new figure, Geoffrey Wainwright, has come upon the scene. Wainwright, who previously taught in Yaounde, Cameroon, and at Queens College, Birmingham, is now professor of systematic theology at Union Theological Seminary in New York. His study titled *Eucharist and Eschatology*, a careful investigation of the meaning of the Lord's Supper in the categories of biblical eschatology, was published in 1971. Attempting to develop what he calls a pictorial method of presentation, he explored the Eucharist as a messianic feast (the dominant theme), as the advent of Christ, and as the first fruits of the Kingdom.[23] Building upon this approach, in 1980 he authored a systematic theology, *Doxology*. Wainwright is the most significant systematic theologian produced by British Methodism since William Burt Pope.

The framework of Wainwright's theological presentation is crucial; again he intends to create images, to provide a pictorial way of understanding. In *Doxology*, he states that he has "a sharper visual than auditory awareness" and that his vision of faith is "firmly shaped and strongly coloured by the Christian liturgy."[24] Hence Wainwright describes Christian faith from within the practice of faith; worship is the beginning point and final confirmation of the truth to which a Christian bears witness. Worship is the context within which Christian vision comes to clarity; only in a believing community does theology function adequately.

The structure of *Doxology* is clearly formed. Beginning with the substance of theology (God, Christ, Spirit, and Church), Wainwright moves to the means of theological transmission (Scripture, creeds, hymns, worship, and doctrine), and then to the context of both the church and the world (ecumenism, culture, and ethics). His development of these themes is unusually rich and suggestive. Wainwright ranges across Eastern Orthodox as well as Roman Catholic and Protestant terrain; he is well-versed in many languages and draws together a range of material with remarkable cohesiveness. Throughout, Jesus Christ is central. God's intimate involvement in the world is the underlying reality, as grace works to honor and succor human life. Three pictorial statements present the main theses of *Doxology*: first, an early medieval tomb sculpture in Salamanca Cathedral, depicting Christ on the cross with his outstretched hands holding the sun and the moon; second, God's great self-emptying (*kenosis*, Phil. 2:5*b*), as represented in Charles Wesley's hymn—

> He left his Father's throne above,
> So free, so infinite his grace!
> Emptied himself of all but love,
> And bled for Adam's helpless race;
> 'Til mercy all, immense and free,
> For, O my God, it found out me!

Third, God is presently experienced, but God's full truth and final consummation are still to come. The Kingdom is both present and still ahead. In this dialectic the Christian life is lived.[25]

Wainwright states his thesis tersely: "Questions of worship and sacraments bring into focus all the major themes of theology: God, humanity, Christ, Spirit, scripture, tradition, and the place of the Church in human history and in the wider world." His chief intention is to demonstrate the interrelation of worship, doctrine, and life.[26]

165

Personal relationship is a central theme. Positively, Wainwright understands worship to present and reinforce this personal reality; negatively, he argues against such persons as John Macquarrie (*Principles of Christian Theology*), whom he interprets as denying the personal-encounter model of theology and the appropriateness of personal language in liturgy.[27] The sacraments are interpersonal events and are the focus of theological interpretation as well as the vital source of Christian life.

The relation of worship to doctrine may be illustrated by the fact that, liturgically speaking, the object of worship is Christ; the gift of the Holy Spirit enables people to love and, hence, to worship;[28] and the Church is the embodiment of corporate life, living both with present actuality of worship and in anticipation of future fulfillment.

In the interaction between worship and doctrine, and the debate as to which has primacy, Wainwright resets the traditional Roman Catholic/Protestant argument. In so doing, he moves toward Roman Catholicism, affirming the priority of worship, but he struggles to maintain the tension for the purpose of correction.[29] His stress upon worship, however, provides an openness to new doctrinal development and more inclusive Christian affirmation.

The implications of worship for ecumenism, liturgical revision, and culture and ethics form a major section of *Doxology*. Once again, the Eucharist is of central importance, for in this event common life is realized, culture is engaged, and community witness and work may be undertaken. Throughout, the creative act and the enabling initiative of worship is God's; people are called, by God's grace, to communion with God. God expresses divine glory in worship; Jesus Christ includes, in his own worship of the Father, the worship of those who gather in his name. For the Christian, Jesus Christ is the absolute authority, but this authority cannot be captured by human beings, as Jesus

Christ remains sovereign Lord over the apostles, the Scriptures, the Church, and over its teaching ministry. A gap remains between God's self-giving and human response and interpretation. The Holy Spirit guides people into truth, even when sin and error remain. Because of God, worship and its theological interpretation are adequate at present, but theology is always open toward the future, always seeking more adequate statement. Jesus Christ remains the "criteriological" norm of worship and theology, but there continues an openness to God's revelation through other channels and an openness to a fuller understanding of God's glory in Christian communion with God.[30]

Its range of issues and the awareness of problems, as well as its prospects for Christian theology, give Wainwright's systematic theology unusual breadth and relevance. But there is a constant effort on his part to retain the riches of the Christian past as he participates in the doxological life of the Christian church. In his construction, the Scriptures, the traditions of the church, and the reality of prayer retain a foundational position. As a systematician, he finds in worship a creative context for exploring ethical responsibility, cross-cultural interactions, and enriched ecumenical theology.

Through Wainwright, British Methodism has been carried into the widest ecumenical relationships. Extending the sense of tradition to include the common heritage of all Christians, he has projected a vision of actualized unity, setting issues that demand further exploration and critical judgments.

Tradition

We have surveyed twentieth-century British Methodist theology with quick glances; and the question remains, Is there—in all this—an expression of a continuing tradition? We have drawn together an important group, but is there a coherent movement?

In a primary way, the theme of grace and the tension between theory and practice have been continued. The work of John Scott Lidgett was an exploration of God's gracious character and action, in terms provided by his context; and with stalwart tenacity he related his theology to concrete human claims. The theme of grace has continued to play a central and binding role in British Methodist theology. It has been given special attention by Philip Watson, Vincent Taylor, C. Ryder Smith, Gordon Rupp, Rupert Davies, and Geoffrey Wainwright; and it has been implicitly influential in the work of most of the other theologians. In one sense, British Methodist theology of the present century has been characterized by considerations of grace as the axis of theory and practice.

Biblical scholarship among British Methodists represents interweaving interests. Basically, there is no distinguishing perspective that these scholars have held in common or from which they have worked. Yet in another way, there have been some noticeable characteristics. For instance, throughout there has been a close identification with the life of the church and an effort to provide resources for leadership in responsible ecclesiastical life. The scholars usually have been trained and taught in Methodist theological colleges and have understood biblical study to be in the service of preaching. In addition, they have sought an exact understanding of the language of the biblical text, and here the work of the Moultons, of Howard, and of Snaith is representative. More, the themes chosen for elaboration—atonement (Taylor), church (Flew), salvation and grace (R. Smith), prayer (George), apostolicity (Barrett), and Christology (Marshall and Dunn)—all reveal a decidedly practical interest in the presentation of the gospel. On one hand, as the discipline has grown in specialization and sophistication, the biblical theologians have become identified more with their peers in the scholarly guild than with their denominational life; on the other hand, for many of these scholars, responsible biblical study has been permeated by Methodist attitudes and interests.

In the historical field there has been some interest in presenting and assessing both John Wesley and the Methodist Church. The work of Gordon Rupp, Philip Watson, and Rupert Davies has renewed and enriched our understanding of Wesley and his followers. These historians of theology have set Methodist interests within the larger context of the Christian tradition. There is no special pleading or driving self-interest. On occasion, particular concerns do arise—Flew's or Sangster's work on Christian perfection, Davies' references to liturgy, and thematic variations on social action or optimism of grace. But even when Methodist interests are present, there is an overarching commitment to ecumenical relationships. Geoffrey Wainwright is most illustrative of the merging of Wesleyan emphases into a general Christian vision. Both in background and in spirit, Wainwright is a product of Methodism. But his tradition, rather than restricting, has freed him to enter an inclusive arena of Christian worship and theology. Methodism has been his channel into catholic Christianity.

The time of separable Methodist thought may now be past in Great Britain. Biblical, historical, and systematic theology do not claim unique denominational character or status. Yet there is awareness of participation in a tradition which, derived from the larger Christian reality, has moved through particular historical channels and is now moving toward riverbeds being freshly cut by merging streams. Into this common current the Methodist contributors have potential for encouraging an evangelical vitality, a concern for social justice, a willingness to challenge established structures, a respect for the Scriptures and forms of worship, a desire to read history fully, a catholic spirit of appreciative reception, and a continuing optimism toward God's grace.

CHAPTER 8

THEOLOGY OF EXPERIENCE:
The Beginning of a New Century

T HE COURSING of Wesleyan theology, which found new routes in the nineteenth century, was to become more unrestrained in the twentieth. Channels structured along previous lines were not adequate to hold the volume or contain the fast current. Swiftly spilling its banks and seeking fresh landfalls, the Wesleyan tradition found new beds through the religious, cultural, and social life of the United States, taking from and contributing to the terrain.

American Methodist theology was, by the turn of the century, increasingly diverse, and this diversity has continued through the century. Tensions evident in the heresy trials in Boston were overtly broken, and no other such doctrinal challenges would occur. This relaxation of tension released Methodist theology for identification with general, less denominationally specific modes of theology.

Diversity has been abetted among American Methodists by the tradition's sensitivity to its cultural context. From its beginnings, North American Wesleyan theology has been responsive to its intellectual and social ambience. Open cultural sensitivity has continued to characterize theological activity, especially in its effort to keep theory closely related to practice. Changing historical contexts have continually required new explorations and fresh interpretations.

During the first half of the twentieth century, Methodist theologians were denominationally conscious, but they were not denominationally restricted.[1] To investigate the range of theological positions in North American Methodism is to move across the spectrum of American theology. There has been a continuation of and new development beyond established themes among personalists; there have been participants who reflected the construction of theology upon the base of religious experience; and there has been increased attention to the implications of theology for social ethics.

Sheldon and Curtis: The Transition Begins

The turn of the century did mark a time of transition. In an important article, Albert C. Knudson argued that Henry Clay Sheldon (1845–1928) was a major transitional figure who brought newly found sensibilities to the work of theology. Sheldon, he claimed, both captured the genuine essence of Wesleyan thought and gave the stamp of modernity to Methodist theology. The older theologians, Watson and Pope, Knudson believed, failed to express the genius of Methodism—namely, the centrality of Christian experience; rather, their systems were "exotic, transplanted from other spiritual climes [i.e., Great Britain]," and stressed dogmatic rationalism and external authority.[2]

According to Knudson, nineteenth-century American Methodist theologians had failed to adjust to science and biblical criticism. This was characteristic of Miner Raymond, John Miley, and Randolph S. Foster. Those men, Knudson said, represented no advance over Watson and Pope, and their writings were "obsolete before they came off the press."[3] Unfortunately, Knudson stated, by the end of the century all these systems were burdens to Christian faith.

Sheldon had taught at Boston University through the last two decades of the nineteenth century and had produced multivolume studies in church history and historical theology. At the turn of the century he became a systematic theologian and published a number of significant volumes, including *A History of Unbelief in the Nineteenth Century* (1907) and *The Essentials of Christianity* (1922). Knudson claimed that a number of facets are clearly evident in Sheldon's work.

First, Christian experience, or "internal evidences," became central. The earlier theologians had sought assurance in external authority, with Christianity becoming a body of doctrine and a scriptural catechism to be memorized. With Sheldon, on the contrary, biblical infallibility and authoritarian rationalism came to an end, with the Bible gaining new authority through the convincing and convicting power of the truth it mediates. To be more specific, Sheldon was both more empirical and more philosophical than his predecessors; both science and human experience were acknowledged as crucial for theology.[4]

Second, Knudson continued, in regard to the interpretation of Christology and the Trinity, there is a division between the previous theologians and Sheldon. The older theologians' uncritical use of the Bible placed christological emphasis upon the full personality of the preexistent Son, upon miracle, and upon Jesus' possession of absolute divine attributes. Sheldon, in contrast, was interested in Jesus' human nature and his consciousness of oneness with God, his fidelity to vocation, and his spiritual Lordship. Hence Sheldon was little concerned with metaphysical dimensions of Jesus' nature and spoke of the mystery of God and Christ.

Third, according to Knudson, interpretation of atonement was undergoing transition. Previous theologians had interpreted the atonement in terms of satisfaction and governmental theories, while Sheldon, with tentative steps, was moving toward a moral influence theory such as that espoused by Bowne.

Fourth, in philosophical terms, the older theologians, Knudson stated, were committed to a naturalistic realism, which made a sharp distinction between the supernatural and the natural; Sheldon, on the contrary, stressed divine immanence and personalistic idealism. This new position assumed an intrinsic relation between natural and supernatural dimensions of reality and carried fresh interpretations of miracle, revelation, and inspiration.

These contrasts revealed Knudson's own sense of the theological transition that was taking place. Each of his points was sharply drawn and there is truth in the contrast he presented. A word of caution, however, for the preceding Wesleyan theologians had not been as exclusively committed to "external authority" as he claimed, nor had Christian faith become merely a body of doctrine, nor was their Christology as clearly one-sided. Yet there were different emphases, culminating in a fundamentally different theological outcome. The chief point of division lay in the historical consciousness of the newer generation. Sheldon reflected a developing conviction that history is the arena of God's activity and that all truth is mediated by historical existence. The theological foundation for this understanding was the idea of the immanence of God. Taking this conviction about history as the primary beginning point resulted in a thoroughly different theological construction. Knudson's discussion of Sheldon was, as a matter of fact, a good introduction to his own theological effort. Sheldon represents a transition. But, as with all significant changes, the moves were not orderly or easily made.

Olin Alfred Curtis (1850–1918), a professor of systematic theology at Drew, was representative of a tentative, rather different step. Determined not to produce an apologetic theology that would compromise with the false and presumptive spirit of the time, he nevertheless utilized personalistic philosophy and current psychology to develop his position. In his major work, *The Christian Faith*, Curtis began from both ends—personal idealism and traditional biblical foundations—and had difficulty meeting with exactness in the middle; but his effort was significant. He initiated his study with a long discussion of anthropology, stressing personality, freedom, and religious experience. His presentation, he acknowledged, was derived from D. D. Whedon, Borden Parker Bowne, and Thomas Carlyle, from whom he learned to value human nature. When, however, he turned to the system of doctrine as a whole, he insisted that "the source of all the data is the Bible, and the Bible alone."[5] In the Bible, Curtis found the doctrine of human freedom, sin as a volitional act, redemption as response to prevenient grace, and the promise of Christian perfection. On these issues, biblical teaching and his philosophical persuasions converged. But his central interest in Christology did not comport easily with the philosophical tradition; and in situating Christology as central, he set the other doctrines upon a stronger base of grace.

At another point Curtis made a distinctive contribution— his conception of the "organic whole" of the church.[6] The church, he argued, is an organism, a living reality; and just as a theological system is greater than its parts because it moves to the interrelatedness of its parts, so the church as a living organism is greater than the sum of individual believers. Further, the church is the concrete expression of the kingdom of God. As the embodiment of actual fellowship with God and other Christians, the church maintains a tension between individual and societal dimensions of experience and responsibility.

The influence of Curtis was deeper than it was broad. It is possible to see a connection from Curtis to John A. Faulkner and Edwin Lewis. Through the first half of the twentieth century, several members on the faculty of Drew University represented a critical stance toward the regnant liberal theological ethos, which also was represented on the same faculty.

Edgar S. Brightman

Borden Parker Bowne was the seminal source of the most generally influential school of theology produced by American Methodism. The number of able persons who have supported this distinctive philosophical and theological position has been impressive and has given impetus to a sustained development. For the first half of the century, personalism was the most prominent stream in Methodist theology, and it also reached into other denominations. The work of Edgar S. Brightman and of Albert C. Knudson exemplifies this development.[7]

Personalism holds philosophy and theology in a tight relationship; the two form an ellipse. The philosophy of personalism directly implies theological conclusions, and personalistic theology is directly rooted in personal idealism. The two are, finally, not to be sundered. Yet central attention might be given to either focus, and Brightman was primarily a philosopher.

Brightman (1884–1953) established his philosophy upon the base of experience—that is, with "any and all consciousness—and in particular, with specific sense perceptions, or consciousnesses, as organized and interpreted by the categories of the human mind."[8] The word *consciousness* is critical, for it is the conscious subject who reflects, feels, decides, and acts, and only through the action of a conscious agent do rationality, affection, or willing have significant meaning. Experience, then, provided Brightman's point of beginning and the raw material for his thought. An analysis

175

of experience reveals, according to Brightman, that there is a variety of content and intensity in human consciousness; there is experience of the external world, of moral responsibility, and of religious meaning. Each conscious experience gives rise to appropriate responses for the interpretation of that experience. Such interpretation must possess internal coherence, and coherence also with the reasonable interpretation of other experiences.

The basic conviction that arises from an interpretation of experience, Brightman claimed, is that the whole universe is personal. It is made up of minds and their consciousnesses. These are the primary values of reality, and experience mediates these values. *Value* is "whatever is desired, or enjoyed, or prized, or approved, or preferred."[9] Further, values, while objective and supersensible, may be ascribed to persons, and indeed, supreme value is ascribed to the Supreme Person. Personalism in philosophy appeals to the coherence of truth and to a supreme Mind in the universe.

> It has been shown that a reasonable and critical organization of our sense-perceptions reveals to us a realm of ends, where values are objective and where the meaning of the universe resides. Both realms, the argument has shown, are thought in fragmentary and inconsistent manner until we view them as expressions of the purpose of the Supreme Person.[10]

Religious experience, in Brightman's schema, conveys the most important values and is the most inclusive category of conscious awareness. While there are separable spheres of consciousness which retain persisting integrity, such as experience of the natural world and moral experience, religious experience comprehends all experience, and every experience may be an experience of God. God is the source and object of religious experience; "God is . . . a Supreme Person who embodies the highest goodness; that is, he is the source both of existence and of value."[11]

Religious experience assumes that God is "findable." God's revelation is the functional interaction of the Supreme Person with human persons, through which humans discover their special meaning in life. To find God is to find one's own best self.[12] "Personalism," Brightman wrote, "interprets the universe as friendly. It justifies hope. It finds in the relation of human and divine wills an inexhaustible meaning and purpose to life."[13]

To this point, we have followed Brightman's explication of the general position of personal idealism, and his position is in keeping with that of a number of his contemporaries. But Brightman followed a more narrow track as he stressed the finiteness of God. Religious experience, he argued, leads to a finite God. God, as discovered in religious experience, is capable of leading the world to higher and higher levels; but there are obstacles and difficulties. Those obstacles, "the Given," Brightman saw as residing within the nature of God. That is, God's consciousness contains within itself both freely chosen activity and unchosen passivity. "The eternal nature of God contains a principle of delay and suffering within itself."[14] But God is on the side of growth in goodness, and God's power is sufficient to maintain eternally the process of realizing his growing purposes.

The philosophical base of personal idealism, forcefully articulated by Bowne and restated and extended by Brightman, constituted the foundation for the development of liberal theology within Methodism.

Albert C. Knudson

Albert C. Knudson (1873–1953) attended the University of Minnesota and Boston University. He was the chief theological successor to Bowne and represents the utilization of philosophical personalism for constructive theology. Deeply pious, Knudson's parsonage home had established the daily practice of religion, and he consistently exhibited spiritual sensitivity. His work had two major focuses: Old Testament and theology. From 1905, when he joined the faculty of Boston School of Theology in the Old Testament chair, until 1921, when he succeeded Sheldon as professor of systematic theology, his writing dealt with Old Testament topics. But after assuming his new responsibilities, he wrote extensively in the field of theology.

Religious experience provided the point of intersection for Knudson's interest in Methodist theology, modern scientific thought, and personalistic philosophy. Religious experience has a divine/human source: It is a combination of God's creative action and active human reception; Christian theology is constructed upon that foundation.

> The ultimate basis for belief in the validity of religious experience is to be found, not in its immediacy nor practical utility, but in the native religious endowment of the human spirit, an endowment that is as fundamental, independent, and trustworthy as is our native capacity for sense experience, moral experience, and aesthetic experience. Religion, we have argued, is structured in the human mind.[15]

It is important to note that several streams of influence affected Knudson's thought. He accepted the need for empirical study of the Scriptures and human experience; he was rigorous and open in the use of scientific methods for biblical interpretation; and he found psychology helpful in explicating human nature. From Bowne came his philosophical perspective, especially in regard to God's personalness and immanence; he also followed Bowne's evaluation of human capacity for scientific, moral, religious, and aesthetic experience. From the Methodist tradition, Knudson utilized the decisiveness of conscious Christian experience and the integrity of persons in relation to the grace of God. He found

178

the vitalizing center of Christian experience in "a direct personal relation to a living Christ."[16] Here he stated the heart of his understanding:

> All that Christian experience affirms is that God was in Christ and that he was in him for the purpose of reconciling the world unto himself. It says nothing about the mode of the divine immanence or the method of reconciliation. All that Christian experience is concerned with is the fact of Christ, the fact of his unique relation to God, the fact of his reconciling activity. If God was actually in him reconciling the world unto himself we need nothing more. That is sufficient ground for assigning to him the position of divine leadership which he has occupied in Christian experience from the beginning.[17]

With the focus of Christian experience resting upon Christ, Knudson was content. Particular interpretations, whether from the past or in the present, are not final. But some interpretations are better, more congenial, release more possibility for experience, than others; and it is in this spirit that Knudson found modern thought a helpful tool.

Knudson's systematic theology is found in two volumes, *The Doctrine of God* and *The Doctrine of Redemption*.[18] In the first, he set forth his understanding of the theological task and began the presentation of content; in the second volume, he dealt with the world, anthropology, and salvation through Christ.

The chief characteristic of Knudson's thought was its comprehensiveness; his purpose was to hold multiple dimensions of experience together. Consequently, he began with an investigation of religion and attempted an inclusive understanding: Religion is a personal attitude toward an objective realm of value, and as such it includes direct awareness and trust. There is also a rational content to religion, and theology focuses on this content; hence Knudson's definition: "Theology [is] the systematic exposition and rational justification of the intellectual content of religion."[19] Religion is richer than theology, but theology helps to indicate that richness.

One of the basic balances in Knudson's position was the correlation of object/subject facets of religious experience. Religion is a personal commitment to objective reality, and both these factors must be stressed. It is prophetic religion (rather than mysticism) that holds most promise for full theological development. Knudson insisted that the source and norm of theology (that is, the primary witness to normative experience of God) is the Bible, and subordinate sources are Christian tradition, reason, and religious experience. The first two subordinate sources have added content to Christian understanding, although religious experience, if understood as direct and unmediated—that is, as mysticism—has made only a "regulative," not a "creative" contribution. Theology gathers relevant data from all four sources and "erects" a norm, or standard, by which they may be evaluated. "The accepted norm of determining what is truly Christian and what is not will be found in Jesus Christ."[20] The stage for his theological work had been constructed. By beginning with religious experience, by exploring Christian faith and theology, and by pursuing his understanding of the object/subject character of knowledge, Knudson had determined that personal experience of God is the entrance to theology.

Knudson proceeded in a complex fashion. For instance, as he initiated his doctrine of God, he stated, "In the beginning, then, in our exposition of the Christian faith with its doctrine of God, we are adopting a method suggested not by the uniqueness of Christian teaching, but by the logical structure of religious belief in general." Yet the doctrine of God comes to its normative fulfillment in the central intention of the doctrine of the Trinity—the incarnate expression of sacrificial love. The Christlikeness of God and the Godlikeness of

Christ convince people that God must be ethically conceived and worshiped. "Christ was for them the 'express image' of the eternal. In this conception we have the basis of all that is distinctive in the teaching of the New Testament and the Church concerning the divine grace."[21]

In his second volume, *The Doctrine of Redemption*, Knudson drew out the implications of this commitment in terms of the salvation effected by Jesus Christ. His Christology was built upon personalistic foundations; it stressed Jesus' ego-identity and conscious relationship with God. Jesus Christ is a unique expression of God's character as revealed in creation. There is continuity from creation to redemption. In the life and death of Jesus, God-consciousness is brought to fulfillment.[22]

The positions of Knudson and Brightman, and of the personalists in general, clearly continued several themes from their Methodist past: integrity of personhood, freedom of will, cooperation of humans with God (though unequals), and cultivation of spiritual living. But there were also changing emphases, as personalism attempted to meet its contemporary culture on the culture's terms. So, for instance, experience became more primary, there was an increased use of philosophical rather than biblical foundations, human integrity was more closely identified with innate goodness, there was an increased utilization of the category of creation rather than re-creation, biblical criticism was assumed and used, and there was a greater desire to meet the intellectual challenge of a scientific world-view. Both continuity and change were important. Inheritors of the evangelistic vigor of their predecessors, the personalists recognized the received tradition as they also charted new directions that altered its emphases. [23]

Harris Franklin Rall

Harris Franklin Rall (1870–1964), a contemporary of Knudson, embodied many of the representative streams and attitudes of early twentieth-century Methodist Episcopal theology. The son of a German itinerant preacher in the Evangelical Association, he was raised on the plains of Iowa and Nebraska. He received his advanced education at the University of Iowa, at Yale University, and in Germany, and taught primarily at Garrett Biblical Institute. Rall possessed several dominant characteristics: Deeply religious by commitment, he was always ready for new frontiers, expansive in his vision, and open toward ecumenical Christianity; he was conscious of the changing patterns of social, economic, and political life and intended to serve the cause of justice; finally, he was optimistic about life, social change, and theological activity.

Rall stated that his interest in theology arose from the meaning religion had given to his personal life and to social expressions of Christian faith.[24] His study of Albrecht Ritschl, the German theologian, sanctioned his conviction that his general approach was correct: Experience is the source of religious knowledge. The knowledge of God is experimental, not theoretical or speculative. Christian theology is a reflection upon Christian experience—that is, experience as shaped by Jesus Christ as he is mediated by Scripture. A living relationship connects Jesus Christ with people and induces their personal and ethical maturation.[25]

Rall's theological effort was an apologetic defense of the value and meaningfulness of faith against the forces of challenge and indifference. Modernity's secularizing effect takes its toll from inherited, settled religious convictions. This, he claimed, is a pervasive fact. And since the fissures of modern life run through every individual and every group, one must also interpret faith for those who claim to be Christian. Theology is a defense of faith for those both inside and outside the circle of faith.

Rall's struggle for acceptable interpretation of experience was focused in his assessment of the role and authority of the

Bible. In terms of background and one's personal development, Scripture is central and creative; from the standpoint of
modern historical interpretation, Scripture must be interpreted through modes of higher criticism. Since tension
between personal formation and objective description tends
to mutual debilitation, Rall felt the two should be held
together; the inner spirit continues, even as higher criticism
cuts away unhistorical, dogmatic, limiting interpretation.
The Bible must be free to breathe life into human experience.
In a typical statement, Rall posed the interplay between the
Bible and faithful sensitivity.

> Not only is the Bible a book of life, a revealment of the living
> God in the life and faith of man; it is only through life that we
> can apprehend its truth. This great Word of Jesus is
> fundamental for the theologian, as it is for the seeking
> disciple. If the Bible were a mere textbook, then mere reason
> could understand it, and any skeptic could be an equally good
> theologian with the Christian. But Christianity is not a
> philosophy. It is an experience and a faith; its truth is truth for
> faith and experience and its theology must be experiential.[26]

Committed to the authority of Scripture as its message is
conveyed to the believer by the Holy Spirit, Rall was also
open and sensitive to the changing intellectual environment.
He was convinced that intellectual honesty and strong
commitment can exist together, and his ground for this
conviction was the belief that the truth of God is both
completely comprehensive and thoroughly consistent. God
and God's truth are communicated to individuals through
the natural world, through moral conscience, and through
human relationships and historical development. Supremely,
God is present in Jesus Christ.[27] At the same time, the claims
of Christian faith and the claims of science can stand together;
truth is one.

Rall's primary emphasis was upon religion as relationship

with God. Religions may come and go, but religion—primary relationship with God—persists. Religion begins with God, and human response follows God's initiative. Human beings are created for God. This relational purpose runs through all of creation, but it is focused in human life; people are made for God and find their highest meaning in "the deepest response of the self to the highest that we know."[28]

Religion, for the Christian believer, centers upon Jesus Christ. Relationship with Jesus Christ is the central meaning of life. But Jesus is not the ultimate, or final, reality. It is God who relates to persons through Jesus; Jesus is a medium through which God engages human experience. Through the power of the living presence of Jesus Christ, individuals are given "creative good will"—that is, the courage to believe that God is redemptive and that the spirit of Jesus Christ rules in their lives.[29]

> My general position can be briefly stated. It is evangelical; it sees as central in Christianity the gospel of a God of mercy and help, come to man in Jesus Christ. It is biblical, though not biblicistic or literalistic. It sees the Bible as the witness to God's saving work in Israel, in Christ, in the Church.[30]

Rall recognized the reality of sin and defined it in three ways: (a) refusal of good, (b) selfishness, and (c) wrong-doing in relation to God. The consequence of sin is the vitiation of personal and social life; it is the loss of right relationship with God. But in sin there is hope, for God does not leave people alone; grace seeks to bring new life. Relationships are reestablished; salvation is found; personal and social life are reconstituted by the renewal of relationship with God.[31]

Harris Franklin Rall combined a strong social activism with his theological interest. Concern for the social order began in his college days and grew over the years. He joined the Methodist Federation for Social Service in its first year (1908). Through all his succeeding service as pastor, seminary president (Iliff), and professor (Garrett), he continued his social involvement and attempted to give it a major place in his thought.

> Here is the test of Christian faith: to surrender our own life in unfaltering trust and obedience to the God of saving good will, and, then, with equal courage and confidence, renouncing force and selfishness and guile, to build the individual life and our social order upon this same principle.[32]

Several matters are clear in Rall's theology. The development of Wesleyan theology in twentieth-century America had retained some strong connections with its past, especially the emphases upon biblical centrality, personal experience, and social implications of Christian faith. There was, however, a resetting of these elements. Personal experience had become the hinge upon which the other themes swing. In this Rall kept close affinity with Knudson and Brightman. With others of his era, he utilized a German theological position to build his own interpretation. Traditional Wesleyan theology was brought into integral relation with a larger cultural setting; and it was in this period that ecumenical sensitivity became typical of American Methodist theology.

An Intruding Voice

John Alfred Faulkner (1851–1931) represented the voice opposed to the dominant liberal persuasion. A professor of church history at Drew University, he was extremely well-read and wrote on topics as widely diverse as the early church, Erasmus, and Methodist history. He was, as W. K. McCutcheon, a significant commentator on American Methodist theology, said, the one exception in his era among the major theologians of the Methodist Episcopal Church.[33] His most important book was *Modernism and the Christian Faith*.[34]

Faulkner's arguments were directed principally against several pervasive assumptions of his liberal peers: the nature of authority, inspiration, miracles, Christology, atonement, and the Trinity. In his discussion he did not advocate a rejection of his opponents' positions, but a larger, more inclusive understanding. The central point of his effort was an attempt to counterbalance what he felt was an over-weighting on the side of subjective experience. There is, he maintained, a true external authority, an independent work of God; so authority should not be limited to individual, internal, spiritual influence, but should hold, along with human receptivity, that which is objectively given.[35]

Objecting to the claims of many of his peers, Faulkner insisted upon the possibility of miracles—that is, "any deed in an order which is impossible to the forces ordinarily working in that order." His presentation attempted to prove that miracles are accepted, in various ways, even by the liberals who deny them. Agreeing with Augustine that miracles are not against nature but against nature as known, Faulkner maintained that all creation and all orders of creation express God's volitional sovereignty, which continues to be innovative even as it is faithful to itself.[36]

In three chapters on Jesus Christ, Faulkner reviewed recent discussions that had focused on the moral or practical Jesus, as distinct from the metaphysical Christ. Acknowledging the importance of the former emphasis, he reasserted, in addition, the necessity for relating the qualities of Jesus' life to his character as divine. Faulkner pleaded for no particular metaphysical position, but insisted that awareness of divinity in Jesus Christ is communicated by the perpetual experience of Christ as the originating giver of life.[37]

Recent discussions have brought out that we must have in mind ethical and spiritual considerations rather than legal, judicial, governmental or such like, in our thought of atonement. We all agree. But I think the true method is the catholic one of seeking the truth in the old theories by universalizing or spiritualizing the kernel of truth in them.[38]

In a central challenge to his Methodist colleagues, he raised the issue—"Ritschl or Wesley?" Faulkner had read Ritschl and his interpreters with care, but he had a sharp complaint: There is a fundamental gap between Wesley's plan of salvation and Ritschl's theology. The theology of Ritschl, he contended, is more subjective and leaves out too many themes that have been important to Christian tradition. After stating his appreciation of Ritschl's emphases and of his success in overcoming a cold and intolerant orthodoxy, Faulkner nevertheless complained that Ritschl is "too minimizing, too reserved and critical, too much afraid of his sources."[39] The chapter concluded with a challenge.

The sons of Wesley can also take whatever stimulus he offers toward the larger light. But . . . if in these central verities of our Christian religion which Wesley again made regnant among men we forsake him for Ritschl, it will indeed be the Great Surrender, sad and causeless, and so far a betrayal of the faith once delivered to the saints.[40]

Faulkner represents a dissident voice; he warned against a subjective view of Christian faith and argued for a renewed recognition of the truth as expressed in inherited doctrines. He did not clearly indicate the pattern of integration; but he was a judicious thinker who critically assessed some prevailing convictions and held to the wisdom of keeping a wide vision.

Wilbur Fisk Tillett and Gilbert T. Rowe

Theologians in the Methodist Episcopal Church, South, shared the dominant convictions and perspectives of their counterparts in the northern church. Two representative figures in the southern church—Wilbur Fisk Tillett (1854–1936) and Gilbert T. Rowe (1875–1960)—reflect the common themes.

Tillett was professor of systematic theology and dean of the theological faculty at Vanderbilt University. He considered himself "a modern-minded man, possessed of an open attitude towards the results of modern scholarship, bearing as it does the marks of an honest and sincere spirit of truth-seeking."[41] In his earliest book, *Personal Salvation,* he reflected this spirit as he explored doctrines that have practical bearing upon spiritual living.[42] The content of that initial volume reflected both an awareness of contemporary theological interest (the title of his first chapter and his dominant concern was "The Fatherhood of God") and a utilization, in his structural outline, of basic Wesleyan themes (gracious ability, justification, regeneration, sanctification, and the witness of the Spirit). The old and the new in theology were melded; but in this earliest book, inherited themes played the more basic role.

Tillett's purpose was to present the divine plan of salvation. He began by asserting that the chief characteristics of God are personality, spirituality, and unity: Christ has revealed God as a loving Father who makes himself accessible to all persons. The corollary of this doctrine of God is that of the dignity of human beings: "The Fatherhood of God . . . naturally carries along with it the sonship of man." Possessed of a spiritual nature, humans are rational, moral, free, immortal spirits. As such, they are in a probationary state—a temporal period of moral trial which will determine their eternal status.[43] There is, in actual human condition, a bias toward evil and a tendency to trespass the intention of God. Consequently, sin is the reality of probationary existence. Atonement is required.

Jesus Christ was central to Tillett's doctrine of atonement. The self-sacrifice of God in Christ is the wisest and best means of redeeming humankind; and it releases a power strong enough to satisfy the moral governmental necessities of created order. Further, it arrests persons in their fall and places them in a "saveable state" by endowing them with gracious ability. The interaction of God and humans is genuine: People are graciously enabled to offer repentance and faith, and God offers justification and regeneration.[44] Tillett maintained that God's grace is primary, for grace underlies, enables, and fulfills human possibility.

The new life given through the dynamic of God's grace and human response provides the basis for sanctification. Sanctification is consecration—"the cultivation of every virtue, both active and passive, and the performance of every Christian duty." Christian perfection—complete love of God and continuous service to the neighbor—is the goal. Through the work of the Holy Spirit, there is a conscious knowledge of forgiveness, resulting in an assurance of one's relation with God.[45] As is evident, Tillett's early work may be described as traditional Wesleyan theology, set within the context of changing sensibilities.

Tillet's open spirit was increasingly responsive to dominant religious concerns of his time; his theological convictions altered until there was thorough identification with the prevailing evangelical liberalism. John J. Tigert, Tillett's predecessor, had written *Theism: A Survey of the Paths That Lead to God*. Tillett, in 1924, took the subtitle as his title and developed his thought in ways that deviated from his earlier statement.

Paths That Lead to God was a defense of Christian faith in a scientifically minded culture. Doubt, Tillett acknowledged, is a dominant attitude toward religion. The sources of this doubt, he said, are clear: the atrocities of World War I, modern democratic ideals of government, scientific doctrines of evolution, biblical criticism, and increased knowledge of world religions. Only reinterpretation and rational restatement can draw doubters back to Christian belief. To present the faith, he explored a number of positive paths that will lead to God: the natural world and witness of science, human nature, the divine/human Christ, the divine/human Book, the church, other religions, suffering, and death.[46]

It is important to note that the Wesleyan skeleton of Tillett's earlier book had disappeared. No longer did he discuss traditional theological issues, and he made no effort to reinterpret themes such as the Fall, atonement, justification, regeneration, sanctification, or a probationary period. Rather, there was a general assumption that divine immanence is working through all things to bring the whole creation to its true end in God. The presence of God is ubiquitous and effective for the redemption of all. He now emphasized "Christ's Doctrine of God" as the foundation for his theological interpretation.[47]

Two years later, in 1926, he published *Providence, Prayer and Power* in which he reiterated his latest positions. It is the providence of God, he argued, that leads all things to their final end. "Those who place the emphasis upon the Divine immanence find it not only difficult but impossible to find any place where God is not."[48] Beginning with God's immanent presence and moving with a firm confidence in progressive realization of God's intention in history and eternity, Tillett closed his last two books with an affirmation that God's kingdom is coming.

> There is no doctrine of the Christian religion more certain and assuring than this—that they who in this life travel the paths that lead to God will find death a doorway into not another but a higher life, where they will, with the eyes of the spirit, see God "face to face" and be with him forever.[49]

The most direct application of God's providence, Tillett found, is God's intention to use the United States as the chief instrument for building the kingdom of God, a world of democratic institutions and social justice. In *The Hand of God in American History*, he stated this thesis clearly.[50]

Gilbert T. Rowe, at Duke University, expressed the same fundamental perspective. Rowe had served a long apprenticeship in local churches and as the general book editor of the southern church. Consequently, he did not arrive directly by an academic track; his thought and style exhibited idiosyncratic freedom. He was lively and engaging in his writing, progressive and undogmatic in his spirit. For Rowe, as for others of this period, religious experience was primary, and its most important characteristic was conformity to "the spirit of Jesus Christ." Spiritual community, or immediate relationship between Jesus and individuals, was the central theme of Rowe's thought, and from this perspective the entirety of Christian life—from initiation to fulfillment—was interpreted.[51]

Liberality, Rowe argued, is a birthright of Methodists. The restrictive rules governing the Articles of Religion were not intended to give final blessing to any one way of stating issues; rather they were intended to guard as much against more doctrine as against less doctrine and, consequently, against increase in the domination of dogmatic formulations. Wesley, Rowe claimed, had not considered his abridgment to be a systematic statement of Christian doctrine; he had not, for instance, included a statement of sanctification. The Articles had been a convenient way to indicate some essential aspects of Christian faith; and Wesley's freedom extends to his followers. "It is certain that Wesley did not intend to lay upon American Methodists a burden that he himself would not bear."[52]

Further, since the number and designation of the "standard" sermons varied, and since the *New Testament Notes* pointed to the biblical text and not to themselves, the cardinal intention of the articles, sermons, and notes had been to mediate a personal experience of fellowship with God.

191

To put it epigrammatically, the distinguishing doctrine of Methodism is that it had no distinguishing doctrine. It is enough for Methodists to think, feel, and live as Christians, without bearing a sectarian mark. Their joy is in their catholicity.[53]

Having used most of his discussion in securing the theological liberty of Methodists, Rowe turned to the primary theological affirmations of Methodists and found three emphases: universality of atonement, salvation by faith, and witness of the Spirit. Upon this foundation Methodist preaching and action are built, he claimed, and by these transforming experiences the Spirit of Jesus Christ is inculcated into human life.

In his first book, *Reality in Religion,* Rowe made his point of departure clear. He was committed to a scientific interpretation of religion: He accepted the immanence of God, the centrality of human experience, and the cardinal role of Jesus in explicating the meaning of life.

The time has come when Protestantism can no longer hesitate to place itself unreservedly and unequivocally upon the side of the scientist in so far as the method of ascertaining truth is concerned. Man's only teacher is experience, and the only method by which the facts of experience can be understood is by observation and experiment.[54]

"The facts in this field are open to observation," he stated. "They occur according to laws, and it ought to be as easy and as profitable to ascertain the laws that operate in the religious realm as it is to discover those that hold good in the material world." Rowe brought his argument to conclusion in his affirmation of the centrality of Jesus in the interpretation of human meaning: "The permanent element in Christianity is Jesus Christ, and the significance of Jesus comes through the capacity of the divine for the human and of the human for the divine."[55]

In all these persuasions, Rowe was in keeping with his Methodist theological peers, and he recognized that this was a liberal stance that differed from earlier Methodist orthodoxy. Such a change, he asserted, calls for vigorous and honest affirmation of belief and acknowledgment of a liberal spirit.

Transition

Wesleyan theology, as it entered the twentieth century, was undergoing basic change. Knudson stated the issues in his study of Sheldon: the centrality of Christian experience, the immanence of God, the true humanity of Jesus, critical study of the Bible, atonement as moral influence, and a positive sense that the kingdom of God is being realized in history. The contrast to nineteenth-century Wesleyan theology is sharp. The previous emphases were radically different: God's transcendence, the primacy of Jesus' divinity, acceptance of biblical teaching as direct doctrinal resource, satisfaction and governmental theories of atonement, and less exclusive emphasis on the Fatherhood of God or the historical realization of the kingdom of God. The basic point of divergence was God's relation to creation. For the new generation, the immanence of God was firmly established, and upon this foundation Christian interpretation was built.

A division separated the times. Leverage for change had come from many sources, but within Methodism, Borden Parker Bowne had been a potent influence. Followers of Bowne charted new paths for the Wesleyan tradition, yet they believed they were faithful to their heritage. The Boston personalists and evangelical liberals intended to honor the genius of John Wesley and to explicate the essential message for their own time. Two major Wesley studies—Francis J. McConnell's *John Wesley* and Umphrey Lee's *John Wesley and Modern Religion*—represent the intent to remain true to Wesleyan theology, even as that theology required new

193

interpretation. The emphasis on experience is an extension of the tradition's openness to the immediate working of the Holy Spirit. God's reality—as Creator, in Jesus Christ, and through the Bible—is made vitally alive to every succeeding generation by the witness of the Spirit. This fresh witness prepares the way for new discovery and growth. With confidence, the new generation of theologians welcomed the spirit of the age. Scientific advance, varied philosophical possibility, new understanding of human nature and religious experience, awareness of denaturing social conditions, and development of historical study—all converged to create new contexts to which theology could and must speak. People who lived in that radically altered setting wanted and needed a faith that was relevant, and a theology built upon the immanence of God was accepted as the most appropriate response. The times had changed, and Methodist Episcopal theology was set upon a different course.

The theological stance that ensued was life affirming. The innate quality of human life—in regard to self-consciousness, rational ability, free agency, and moral potential—was assumed. Developmental themes of personal self-fulfillment and social betterment were pervasive. God's self-expression was not manifested through sheer sovereign omnipotence, but nurtured human maturation through moral engagement. Human life and destiny were confidently viewed as realizing the goals of God's creative intention. There was, withal, an open, positive, generous spirit in the liberal theology of the period. It is remarkable that even the grim realities of World War I, which forced many theologians to reassess human nature, did not alter the convictions of these people. Viewed as an aberration in human history, the tragedies of war were set within the larger context of the coming kingdom of God. And, with confidence, this hope was served.

Of special importance is the change in the understanding of the role of Jesus Christ and the Holy Spirit that occurred during this period. The Wesleyan tradition had, from its beginning, stressed the central importance of the incarnate presence of God in Christ and the immediate personal witness of the Holy Spirit. Jesus Christ, in his life, death, and resurrection, reclaimed a fallen world, and God as Holy Spirit engaged lost and recalcitrant persons. With the change of emphasis to the immanence of God, and the ascendency of emphasis upon native human capacity for experiencing God, the roles of Christ and Holy Spirit were subordinated to the creativity of God in creation. Less attention was given to immediate, transformative engagement. As stress upon the ubiquitous presence of God increased, discussion of the re-creative incarnate presence and the person of the Holy Spirit decreased. Knudson made little of the Holy Spirit in his discussion of Christian experience, and Tillett shared that lack of interest. Rowe and Rall mentioned the Spirit more regularly, but even in their exposition, the presence was more confirming than re-creative. All kept an important role for Jesus Christ, but primarily as an example of God's gracious, all-pervasive presence, as One who awakens human beings to their created possibility and whose life informs and guides human spirits. Jesus Christ makes clear who God is, and the Holy Spirit is the ubiquitous Spirit of God intensely experienced.

The doctrine of the Trinity, in the eighteenth and nineteenth centuries, had been central to Wesleyan theological exposition, with emphasis upon the discrete person and the work of each member. With the move to emphasis upon God as Person and Creator, immanently present in all reality, a different weighting occurred in trinitarian discussion. The persons of Jesus Christ and Holy Spirit were subordinated to this more primary interest, as both became clarifications of a prior and known reality. The doctrine of creation was the dominant theological interest, and the understanding of Jesus Christ and Holy Spirit was noticeably changed.

Concentration upon their persons and functions was replaced by singular emphasis upon their functions as expressions of the immanent God.

An important personal characteristic of the people discussed in this chapter should be noted. They were, without exception, men of deep piety. Disciplined in their devotion, all these theologians wrote and lectured on spiritual growth; worship and prayer were essential parts of their lives. These qualities indicate a particular influence of the Wesleyan tradition.

One striking contrast between British Methodist and North American Methodist theologians is the role that biblical scholarship has played in the two Wesleyan streams. Twentieth-century British Methodism has been characterized by significant commitment to the biblical disciplines. In the United States, this has not been as true. There have been some excellent biblical scholars: W. F. Albright (1891–1971), B. Harvey Branscomb (born 1894), Clarence Tucker Craig (1895–1953), Ernest W. Saunders (born 1915), Bernhard W. Anderson (born 1916), D. Moody Smith (born 1931), and Victor Paul Furnish (born 1931). The work of these persons possesses unusual quality.[56] But biblical scholarship represents a smaller component of North American Methodist theological work than of British. This fact indicates the emphasis North Americans have placed upon philosophical foundations for constructive theological work, a characteristic that had been present since the beginning in Shinn and Bangs, was further emphasized by Whedon and Bledsoe, given new range and vitality by Bowne, and continued, as we have seen in this chapter, to form Methodist Episcopal theology in the twentieth century.

CHAPTER 9

CONTINUITY AND CHANGE IN NORTH AMERICAN METHODIST THEOLOGY

THE DEVELOPING tradition of Wesleyan theology in North America continued to undergo steady change during the middle decades of the twentieth century. The active movement of the tradition was projected by previous momentum, as well as by its own strength. In this chapter, we shall follow some paths of continuity and change within evangelical liberalism, through Georgia Harkness, L. Harold DeWolf, and Edward T. Ramsdell. We shall also hear the resounding challenge issued by Edwin Lewis from his altered perspective. And we shall review a renaissance of interest in John Wesley, as represented by Albert C. Outler and Robert E. Cushman, among others.

The theologians dealt with in this chapter have been and many still are persons of prominent influence in North American Methodism. They have taught in a number of theological schools, they have been systematic interpreters of Wesleyan theology, they have been leaders in councils seeking to unite Methodism, and they have been engaged in ecumenical activity. As teachers of ministerial students, as

interpreters of Methodist beliefs, and as practical contributors to the life of their church, these theologians have helped
to shape the belief-structure of contemporary Methodism in
the United States.

Georgia Harkness and L. Harold DeWolf

The characteristic commitments of the early twentieth
century were extended by many theologians. Two representative voices are those of Georgia Harkness (1891–1974) and
L. Harold DeWolf (born 1905), both of whom bore a sense of
the Methodist inheritance as transmitted through teachers of
the previous generation. Liberal assumptions were continued in their writings: the immanence of God, confidence in
reason, commitment to developmental modes of thought,
and ethical concern for social righteousness. Yet each
reworked these themes in distinctive ways. The style of their
thought was generous, tolerant, and wide-ranging. There
was a freedom in their presentations that tended to make
them less academic and more engaging for the general
reader. Both writers have been able to communicate to a wide
audience with a gentle, intellectual apologetic.

Georgia Harkness played an important historical role. Not
only was she the first woman to hold a major chair in
theology in the United States, but her thought represented a
wide range of Methodist faith and doctrine. She was what
many Methodists would like to be: creative, poetic, devout,
thoughtful, and able to express these qualities to others
through her life and her writing.

A native of upper New York state, Harkness graduated
from Cornell University, taught school for six years, then did
graduate work at Boston University. Philosophy of religion
was her field, and when her study was completed, she taught
at Elmira and Mount Holyoke colleges. In 1939 she went to
Garrett Biblical Institute and later to the Pacific School of

Religion. She held chairs in theology in these two institutions for some twenty-two years. Extraordinarily productive, she wrote thirty-six books and numerous articles.

Harkness' theology worked out themes derived from Boston personalism. Her use of personalistic philosophy provided the foundation for explication of the Fatherhood of God, Jesus as Lord and example of Christian living, and service to the kingom of God. Warm, confident, and irenic, Harkness believed there is a unity to knowledge found in faith, reason, and the Bible. Theology, which may begin at any of these points, moves toward the same center—that God is personal and gracious, that Jesus Christ renews human life for its highest achievement, and that the Holy Spirit is the continuing and sustaining expression of God's relation to humankind. There was also a consistent concern for the coming kingdom of God and for Christian responsibility to enable justice and love to prevail. Her style was clear and engaging and her mode of thought general. She understood herself to be an interpreter for the general reader and this responsibility she fulfilled with vigor and felicity.

Harkness consistently expressed a confidence in the possibility of achieving God's will in human society, but she was also sensitive to the development of personal virtue—since fulfillment of personhood tends to replace interest in sanctification—and she contributed to spiritual formation through her exploration of mysticism and her devotional books, poetry, and hymns.

The most impressive characteristics of Harkness' theology were inclusiveness and balance. Never sharp or intentionally provocative, she constantly attempted to draw themes together, to keep many dimensions in relationship to one another, to make a full-orbed presentation of what she called "redemptive evangelical doctrine."[1] She was unusually successful in her effort to make the living vitality of God both understandable and meaningful to her contemporaries.

199

Also representatively Methodist and influential was L. Harold DeWolf. A man of deep religious commitment and wide social sensitivity, he lived in close contact with the thought and life of both church and society. It is typical that he was the mentor of Martin Luther King, Jr. DeWolf was a graduate of Boston University, studied under Knudson, became a professor of theology in that institution and, after 1960, dean of the faculty and professor of systematic theology at Wesley Theological Seminary in Washington, D.C.

DeWolf's theology is intentionally liberal and evangelical and has continued to develop. In the preface to the revised edition of *A Theology of The Living Church* (1960), he commented that his stance had changed from evangelical liberal to liberal evangelical. By this he meant that "the redemptive power of the Christian gospel, always of great importance to me, has become central."[2]

The structure of DeWolf's systematic theology (although he argues that there is no necessary order) indicates the emphases in his position. He began with natural theology, assessing the nature of human reason and its relation to revelation. Christian faith assumes the existence of God and God's concern for creation. Native human ability carries the possibility of knowing God and of establishing a strong, coherent sense of God's reality. Although a general sense of God is possible, for Christians this awareness is principally mediated by the biblical record. Hence there is interaction between God's more general and God's quite specific modes of revelation. DeWolf attempted to establish the superior reasonableness of Theism. Although objective knowledge cannot be established, probability can. Faith, in this context, is commitment of the will to that which it is reasonable to believe is worthy of that commitment; and the value of faith is found in the courage and vigor with which believers act. On the bases of general and special revelation, DeWolf developed his doctrine of God and his interpretation of the nature of persons. The importance of the reciprocal relation between gracious gift and human capacity is evident, since this discussion consumes about 60 percent of DeWolf's entire systematic statement in *A Theology of the Living Church.*

Once the framework was set, particular aspects were logically put into place. Jesus was a man in a full, unqualified sense; his uniqueness is found in his mission, which is spiritually decisive for all time. Jesus' utter loyalty to God's will sets him distinctively apart. In keeping with DeWolf's more sharply defined focus in the revised edition "The New Birth" became the pivotal chapter. From the base of the reality of God's redemptive grace in personal life, this systematic statement reached toward the reality of the kingdom of God. "Ye must be born again," DeWolf affirmed, and in so doing stressed the reality of actual change in human life. No stereotyped mode of transformation is assumed, but the reality of new life carries psychological, ethical, and theological implications. In the new life, there will be release from guilt, concern for others, centeredness upon God, clarification of ideals, and more inclusive loyalties. There is also a compulsion of grace to do God's will.

From his earlier *Religious Revolt Against Reason* (1949), through his *Case for Theology in Liberal Perspective* (1959), to the revised edition of his systematic theology, *A Theology of the Living Church* (1960), there has persisted a strong sense of the rationality of faith and the promise of human fulfillment in the kingdom of God. With the clarification that the center of his position is the power of God's redemptive grace, DeWolf moved beyond the earlier liberalism and emphasized a stronger dialectical tension between God and humans.

The systematic statement drew to a close with a section on "The Kingdom and The Church," in which DeWolf sharpened the focus of his development by emphasis upon God's immanental working, both in this world and for the ultimate realization of God's rule. It is important to stress the intrinsic relation DeWolf found between theology and ethics. His *Responsible Freedom* (1971) developed the inner connections between theory and practice. Upon this theological foundation he built social and ethical analyses, with suggestions for constructive activity in such areas as the natural environment, the economic order, technology, and world peace. Having set high goals, he concluded:

> To fail in such world-embracing goals for life is better than to succeed in the usual petty and provincial purposes for self and one's own ethnic group. God and current events alike call us to the large vision and the daring effort.
> This call to responsible freedom is a summons to faith.[3]

In DeWolf's thought the liberal impulse continues, but a sobering awareness of human capacity for sin and the systemic forces of evil make it clear that life needs to be reordered. Inherited immanental themes of personalism continue as a dominant assumption, but the re-creative incursion of grace in human life is given increased importance. The continuity of liberal themes will be evident in ensuing Methodist theology; but they will not proceed without challenge or alteration. DeWolf significantly represents deep rootage in and change of that received tradition.

A Manifesto

The continuity represented by Harkness and DeWolf was only one stream in a rapidly widening flow of Methodist theological interests. Through the mid-century decades, new currents were running and new emphases were gaining currency. For a moment we must step back in order to move forward, for the roots of these changes began in the 1930s. It was during that period that the sinfulness of human nature was being forcefully asserted by Reinhold Niebuhr and others. Chief among Methodists who reacted early and positively to these emphases was Edwin Lewis (1881–1959).

Lewis was an English Methodist who came to Canada as a missionary, migrated to the United States to continue his education, and eventually became a teacher of theology at Drew. He was, Carl Michalson said, the "rarest spirit most of us will ever know."[4] His career spanned the period of transition from an optimistic estimate of human nature to a somber sense of the pervasive power of personal and corporate evil. Influenced by British idealism in his earliest work, Lewis first assumed that Christianity has its foundation in the nature of persons; this was especially clear in the title and content of *Jesus Christ and the Human Quest*. Lucid and engaging in its literary style, Lewis' early theology attracted general interest; but a series of events occurred that set him on another course. Primary among those experiences was his part of the editorship of the Abingdon Bible Commentary (1929) and his reaction to the *Laymen's Missionary Report* (1931). His changing mind was symbolized by response to this latter book. Originally, he wrote a positive review, but then altered his assessment in "The Re-thought Theology of the Re-thinking of Missions." In this second evaluation he challenged the assumptions of immanental theology; for the report, as it stood, he believed, undercut Christian missionary effort.

Lewis was beginning to walk a different path. Determined to reclaim the treasure of the gospel, he expressed suspicion of the pervasive emphasis upon "religious experience," with its tendency toward subjectivism; and in contrast, he sought a more objective foundation for Christian life in the self-revealing of God in Christ. As a result, he relinquished the idealistic monism (belief that reality coheres in one absolute system) that had provided his previous philosophical base. Reassessing the theological situation, in 1934 he voiced a loud challenge in *A Christian Manifesto*.

Sustaining his intensity for more than two hundred pages,

Lewis argued against his most immediate background which, with much pride, he formerly had designated "modern." Classical Christian themes must be reasserted, he said. He assailed immanentalism, a position he now had come to believe placed too high a value on human goodness; denatured Christ's divinity; and denied the sacrificial, objective work of atonement. In contrast, Lewis stated that the transcendent reality of God should be central to theological interpretation: "No statement of Christian belief which does not include a supernatural reference—I mean, a reference to God as a Living God and to Christ as his embodiment by a process which involves God himself in sacrifice—is a true statement."[5] In a closing paean Lewis set his position in liturgical form:

Let us affirm the reality of God. . . .
Let us affirm the authority of the Word of God. . . .
Let us affirm the fact of sin. . . .
Let us affirm the divine Christ. . . .
Let us affirm the cross as the supreme event in the divine-human story. . . .
Let us affirm the gospel of God's provision for the salvation of the whole world. . . .[6]

The process that had begun as a rejection of liberalism now passed into a reassertion of the power of evil and the centrality of divine grace. Two volumes, *A Philosophy of Christian Revelation* and *The Creator and The Adversary*, carried Lewis' thought to its climax. In the first, he demonstrated that biblical faith implies philosophical structure. Christianity, he argued, possesses a metaphysical import that corresponds to the structure of human existence, an existence in which the fact of evil in human life must be given critical importance. In the latter book, Lewis developed an interpretation of Christian faith in terms of conflict. Both good and evil are fundamental realities of existence; God is confronted by an adversary who attempts to thwart the Creator's purposes in human and cosmic history. Struggle ensues, a struggle of life and death. God's sovereignty is not absolute, but it is victorious. God the Creator, incarnate in Jesus Christ, is greater than his adversary. By outsuffering and outloving the adversary, God triumphs and life is redeemed. Lewis' own pilgrimage is interesting, but in the history of Methodist theology, he is important because he rethought the reality of evil and challenged the tradition to consider that reality with utmost seriousness.

Edward T. Ramsdell

A marked indication of the changing situation in Methodist theology is found in the work of Edward T. Ramsdell (1902–1957). The transition in liberal theology, adumbrated in Harkness' thought and accentuated in DeWolf's changed emphasis, became clearer and more determinative in Ramsdell's theology. Born into a Methodist ministerial family in Michigan, he attended the University of Michigan and Boston University. He was a professor of theology at the Divinity School of Vanderbilt University, and later at Garrett, where he served until his untimely death. *The Christian Perspective* was his major theological contribution.

Ramsdell came from the Boston personalist tradition and acknowledged a deep indebtedness to Brightman and Knudson, as well as to William E. Hocking; he also expressed gratitude to Emil Brunner, Reinhold Niebuhr, and Gustav Aulén.[7] In his footnotes there are references at crucial junctures to H. Richard Niebuhr and Søren Kierkegaard, and throughout, there is close attention to, and sensitive interpretation of the Scriptures. These primal influences demonstrate the various—even contending—theological worlds in which Ramsdell lived.

Ramsdell affirmed the sovereign grace of God, the

fundamental importance of the Bible as the vehicle of God's Word to people, and the decisive disclosure of divine love in Jesus Christ. From his personalistic tradition, he continued to express confidence in human rationality, as well as the primacy of the qualities of personalness and goodness in Theism. In a new reconstruction of that tradition, he stressed the vision of faith as establishing the perspective from which reason operates, the fallen and radically marred human condition, and the new creative act of God in Jesus Christ.

The essential question, according to Ramsdell, is: *What is significant?* And to this he responded, "Christian faith is an understanding of significance. As such it is a perspective of reason. It is a way of looking at life, as well as a way of life." Basic trust is not in reason but in what is taken to be significant for reason; this issue is inevitably personal and, in the last analysis, is determined by the object of a person's worship. The gaining of a perspective involves the whole self, and the dynamic of how a point of view is gained has to do with response to crisis, with a sense of the adequacy or inadequacy of one's way of construing the world, and, in Christian faith, with the preaching of the Word of God, which opens the possibility of a new vision.[8]

> The unifying insight, or intuition, which comes to the Christian in faith is that of the Truth revealed in the life, death, and resurrection of Jesus Christ. Christian faith is the faith that the Word of God Incarnate, climatically expressed on the Cross as the power of the divine *Agape,* is the most significant fact in our total experience.[9]

The content of the revealed word, said Ramsdell, is the dynamic goodness of God. This goodness is revealed in creation, but the central expression of God's revelation is Jesus Christ, who is the Word incarnate. "The most important thing about the humanity of our Lord was the *quality* of His earthly life."[10] Yet this goodness was evident only to the eyes of faith, only to those who had been drawn into response and thereby transformed.

Against this backdrop of God as sovereign, and the Incarnation as definitive revelation, Ramsdell developed his doctrine of persons. Human beings, he argued, are "telic creatures," human life is purposely organized. This means that human beings are worshiping creatures. Unity of life should be found in the object of worship; yet the tendency to self-exaltation diverts this worship to idols, especially to the self. The fall is radical because it sets a different understanding of significance; persons become their own ends. The misordering of human life is expressed in anger, envy, avarice, sensuality, lust, sloth, and dejection.[11] Self-love becomes demonic and self-destructive, and this destructiveness has social consequences.

The culmination of Ramsdell's vision was reconciliation through the cross. The cross becomes the means of our repentance and the way to a new sense of significance.

> Faith is the channel of God's love in the believer's life and the Cross is its symbol. The love of God not only leads to repentance and makes possible the renewal of fellowship with Him, but it also transforms the heart of the believer. It frees us both from the burden of sin and from its power. It is regenerative. It changes the inner core of one's being.[12]

Ramsdell is important as illustrative of changing theological emphases. In his work, a reordering of root and branches had taken place. He had moved to revelation as the key category, and upon this theme he developed variations on God as the gracious initiator and on Jesus Christ as the fulfillment of faith; and he stressed the fallen condition of persons and the fundamental transformation of human life by re-creative grace. This was a Word-of-God theology, onto which branches of personalistic theism had been grafted. A new perspective had been set.

Neo-Wesleyan Theology

Direct lines of influence within the Wesleyan tradition are difficult to trace, and the investigation is complicated by the number of outside sources that are significant for theologians within this tradition. For instance, it is difficult to mark a clear course for the influence of Edwin Lewis, in part because his newly affirmed views about human sinfulness and the resetting of a christological focus for theological construction were held in common with contemporaries from several traditions. It is also the case that Lewis' newfound positions were expressed at a time when liberal Protestantism was being carefully reassessed and the theology of John Wesley was undergoing thorough reevaluation.

The reassertion of traditional Protestant themes was most directly expressed in the development of the neo-Wesleyan movement. The point of common concern was human salvation, its source, and its implications. With resurgent force, a number of scholars have undertaken a series of studies intended to trace the developed theological streams back to their source. Important among these, and a teacher and inspirer of many others, is Albert C. Outler. But the range and intensity of this effort is noteworthy. George C. Cell, in the 1930s, and William R. Cannon, in the 1940s, issued clarion calls. Subsequently Franz Hildebrandt, John Deschner, and Colin Williams have directed their studies to John Wesley, and David C. Shipley, Robert E. Chiles, E. Dale Dunlop, and Leland H. Scott have focused their investigations upon the growing tradition.[13] So clear is the parallel that it may be claimed that neo-Wesleyanism has been to the Wesleyan tradition what neo-orthodoxy has been to the Reformed tradition.

An important milestone in this development has been the effort to produce a definitive text of Wesley's works. In January 1959 this idea was initiated by Merrimon Cuninggim,

208

dean of the Perkins School of Theology, and Bernhard W. Anderson, dean of the Theological School of Drew University; backing the project with encouragement were Albert C. Outler and Franz Hildebrandt. Robert Cushman, dean of the Divinity School of Duke University, was approached and asked to edit the works. He declined, but accepted general leadership, and in January 1960 convened four deans for the preliminary considerations with William R. Cannon, dean of Candler School of Theology of Emory University, joining the other three. At the General Conference in April 1960, concrete steps were taken, and Walter E. Muelder of the Boston School of Theology was added to the group. Cushman invited Frank Baker (born 1910), an English scholar, to the faculty of Duke in order to edit the project.[14] It was agreed that The Clarendon Press of Oxford would serve as publisher, and an editorial board and a board of directors were established. In 1963 Joseph Quillian, of the Perkins School of Theology, assumed the chairmanship of the board; James E. Kirby, formerly dean of Drew Theological Seminary and now dean of Perkins, succeeded him in 1980. Thirty-four volumes are projected; these will incorporate all Wesley's original, or mainly original prose works, together with one volume devoted to his hymn books and another to selected extracts from the writings of others. The entire enterprise, which will include all substantive variant readings, represents a major scholarly undertaking.

Albert C. Outler

Albert C. Outler (born 1908), through his editing and writing, has provided signal leadership and brought broad historical knowledge to bear upon the neo-Wesleyan movement. His introduction to *John Wesley* and his important studies in theology, evangelism, and preaching in the Wesleyan tradition have made a major contribution to the revival and enlargement of Wesleyan studies. But Outler is also a theologian in his own right.

A native of Georgia, educated at Wofford College and at Emory and Yale universities, Outler taught at Duke and Yale, and then at Perkins School of Theology until his retirement. A historian of doctrine, his interest in Alexandrian and Antiochene Christianity, Augustine, and the meaning of tradition has also been put to the service of ecumenism.[15]

In addition, Outler's early and continuing interest in pastoral counseling is evidenced in *Psychotherapy and the Christian Message,* in which he related his theological understanding to dominant modes of psychological interpretation. This book exemplifies a critical dialogue of Christian theology with contemporary culture. Outler's goal was to develop a view of individuals that is psychologically sound and theologically grounded. He lauded the practical wisdom of psychotherapy but rejected the humanistic and naturalistic assumptions of the then prevailing psychological theory. The result is an interpretation that affirms human freedom and the transcendent mystery of selfhood. Historical life, however, is characterized by brokenness, for human freedom inevitably expresses itself in sinful pride and consistently results in malady. Nonetheless, there is possibility of authentic existence as God graciously acts to bring human life to its originally intended meaning. Outler's intention and achievement were concretely presented. In contemporary language the classical order of salvation was restated:

> The Christian Gospel is a joyous word from God to man in the depths of his existence. It speaks of the origins and ends of human life, of God as ground and sustaining power of existence, of man under God's command and blessing, of man in quandary and sin, of God in Christ reconciling the world unto Himself, of the Holy Spirit making for community of truly matured and fulfilled persons.[16]

In *Theology in the Wesleyan Spirit,* Outler sets forth his theological approach. The opening chapter, "Plundering the Egyptians," expresses his interest in utilizing resources gained from Scripture and from contemporary culture.[17] With bifocal attention to the Christian heritage and the present challenge, he develops three themes as central: the human condition, justification by faith, and holy living.

Diagnosis of the human condition constitutes an investigation, with contemporary sensitivity, of the reality of sin. Here Outler's previous study of psychotherapy is significant, for in that study may be found an extended discussion of this issue in the spirit and terms he is now suggesting. His analysis of human sin in *Theology in the Wesleyan Spirit* follows previously charted paths (yet paths not so common in early twentieth-century Methodism): stress upon the inordinate pride and free decision that lead to human prodigality.

Human fallenness brings Outler to the foundational theme of the gospel: justification. After indicating that Wesley's interpretation of justification was forgiveness and that that doctrine was grounded in the Reformation, Outler moves beyond notions of a legal transaction between God and humans to explore relational and therapeutic possibilities. He emphasizes the loss of a sense of guilt in modern culture and the consequent irrelevance of traditional guilt-oriented theology and evangelism. As in *Psychotherapy and the Christian Message,* there continues a strong sense of the initiating grace of God in Jesus Christ and through the Holy Spirit. Grace evokes repentance and faith. As the agent of God's redemptive compassion more than an appeaser of wrath, Jesus Christ brings meaning and joy and hope to human life.

The final chapter on holiness contains clear Wesleyan tones, while it also breaks narrow inherited boundaries by reaffirming aspects of the larger Christian tradition. Asserting that sanctification continues to be significant for contemporary Christians, Outler summarizes the meaning of Christian holiness.

> It is . . . an awareness of our radical dependence upon God's grace and our gladness that this is the truth about our lives. It means a sense of Holy Presence and of security and warmth in that Presence. It means our recognition of God's upholding love and our gratitude for his love. It means serenity in the face of death because of our confidence that God's love cannot be conquered or canceled by death. And, most of all, it means having no other gods of our own, since the *First* Commandment is also the *last!*[18]

An ecumenical vision dominates Outler's work. Setting the discussion in terms of increasing the strength of Christian witness to the world—unity is not an end in itself—he believes that the task is to present the gospel so that the world may believe. Hope is predicated upon God's providence and God's intention for the church and the world. With acknowledgment of the fellowship already achieved, and with cautious expectation projecting the future, Outler commends working and waiting for the unity of Christians that is yet to come.[19]

It is important to stress the ecumenical sensitivity and participation of the Methodist theologians of this period. Clarence Tucker Craig and Robert E. Cushman were substantial contributors to ecumenical theological conversations; and Harold A. Bosley and Garrett Theological Seminary were primary hosts when the second meeting of the World Council of Churches was held in 1954 in Evanston, Illinois. Other leaders in the ecumenical movement have been J. Robert Nelson, of Boston University School of Theology, and John Deschner of Perkins School of Theology.[20] This interest and commitment represent the persistent vision of Christian unity that has been expressed by the Wesleyan tradition since its beginning.

CONTINUITY AND CHANGE

Robert E. Cushman

The revival of interest in the basic work of Wesley has not produced a distinctive posture among Methodist theologians, but it has contributed to a renewed sense of tradition, a fuller understanding of the origins of Methodism, and the establishment of criteria for judging some of the directions of development.[21] Several positive aspects of this renewal are represented in the systematic work of Robert E. Cushman (born 1913).

Cushman succeeded Rowe as a theologian at The Divinity School of Duke University, and more contrasting positions would be difficult to imagine. A native of New York state and raised in a Methodist parsonage, Cushman was educated at Wesleyan (Connecticut) and Yale universities and became professor of systematic theology at Duke in 1945. Directed by the conviction that human nature is sinfully malformed, he challenged dominant positions of liberal theology by a frontal attack upon its understandings of religious experience and prevailing philosophical presuppositions. Claiming that religious experience had been misconstrued by many of his predecessors, Cushman reinterpreted its content. He presented a different philosophical possibility; he understood theological activity as faith seeking understanding.

In "The Shape of Christian Faith—A Platform," he stated his theses in concise fashion. First, religion is the finding and confronting of humans by God, it is not the seeking for God by humans. Second, "Religion is life in crisis calling for solution through reconciliation."[22] All of life—its intellectual, affectional, and volitional dimensions—is caught up in this crisis. Third, the basic concern of individuals in the religious situation is the disrupted condition of their lives. The religious problem is primarily moral (axiological), not intellectual. Fourth, the truth of religion is known only to those who are genuinely involved in the experience of

213

alienation and reconciliation. Fifth, apologetic theology is not concerned with vindicating the truth of a theistic perspective, but with making human beings aware of their problematic situation. Finally, it is Jesus who overcomes our estrangement from God and from one another.

> To treat the reality of God as something to be proved is to approach Divine Reality as if it were of the same order as all other objects. This is to step completely outside the circle of the true religious situation; for when a man is in the circle, he discerns that his first business is not demonstration but obedience.[23]

Cushman reshapes several themes. Neither philosophy as a metaphysical base nor science as a methodology is given first place. Experience of God is an experience that results from God's initiative. To be in the presence of God is to be called into question; it is to recognize one's thorough unworthiness (Isaiah's temple experience is a chief paradigm). God is primarily made known through a dreadful consciousness of alienation. "Who says sin, says God. Who does not confess sin, cannot say God." At the same time, to be confronted by God is to be affirmed. "If God finds man, he does not find an equal of his sanctity, he finds a sinner whose invitation is to become a saint."[24] Persons discover that they already have been discovered by God, and they are given new life. Religious experience is not an extension of a given natural potential; it is the experience of being judged and re-created by God.[25]

Theology is the intellectual task of faith seeking understanding. The order is crucial: Faith (as the experience of reconciliation) is the beginning; understanding is the working out of the implications of faith in all dimensions of life. Theology is derived from faith and serves to induce faith. Never an end in itself, Christian doctrine always is drawn from and is a means of Christian life.

Christian proclamation presents a vigorous call to self-examination. It is at this juncture that Cushman's philosophical study takes on importance. In his significant contribution to Platonic study, *Therapeia,* he went beyond the idealistic interpretations of Plato.[26] And in reinvestigating the Socratic-Platonic explorations of human existence, he wrote: "Plato is prepared to regard 'man as the measure' in virtue of the *essential* human *kinship* with and *potential* human *conformity* to a transcendent, supra-human, divine Reality which is the ultimate Source and Norm of all truth and value."[27]

In spite of this essential relationship, most people live as though they were asleep to ultimate Reality and moral obligation; they invert reality and are content with living an unreal or alien life. The task of the philosopher-therapist is to induce an awareness of the actual situation and the possibility of a rightly ordered condition of life.[28]

The correct understanding of the human condition (one's own condition) is made extremely difficult by the "willful human concentration of vision in 'the service of evil.' At the same time, the *possibility* of therapy rests in the faith that the divine *Light* of the Good, even though repressed and perverted, is nevertheless *shining,* however dimly, in the life of every human being." And here, finally, is the weak point in Plato's program of therapy: The means of therapy (the dialectical method) both intends to induce, and also presupposes, a suitable condition of moral character. At this point the philosophy of Plato presents its greatest dilemma; and here it has prepared the way for "a Mediator of God's own healing therapy."[29]

In Cushman's schema, grace and nature were set in a new dialectic. From the beginning, he challenged the Kantian notion of autonomous freedom. He objected to basing goodness upon the exercise of independent human freedom, since goodness in human life is established by God:

"Goodness is derived from a new nature. It derives from blessedness in which man is released from bondage. . . . Goodness derives, therefore, from being. Not from man's original being, as alienated from God . . . but by man's acquired being."[30]

A principal emphasis is the priority of faith in the attainment of knowledge. This has been advanced in his study of Augustine, in *Therapeia*, and also in the chapter "Worship as Acknowledgment" in *Faith Seeking Understanding*.[31] His exploration of the problem of knowledge and his constructive development of faith and understanding are among his most important contributions.

The center of Cushman's theology is Christology, and he persistently pursues this theme. Negatively, he argues against the historical skepticism of Rudolf Bultmann, John Knox, and Paul Tillich, who, he contends, allow the dissolution of the "historical Jesus." Positively, Cushman affirms the earliest Christian confession, "Jesus is Lord." He finds the chief problem to be an inadequate doctrine of creation; a satisfactory doctrine of creation is needed to support a viable doctrine of the Incarnation.[32] He concludes "Worship as Acknowledgment" with this thesis:

> The true worshipper is first, Jesus Christ himself, and true worship is attained for those who, "crucified with Christ," walk in newness of life. This is life in which God's dominion is regnant. It is life in which autonomy is no longer reserved, and in which the stewardship of all of life is acknowledged.[33]

A Present Direction

The investigation of John Wesley's thought continues, and in the last few years it has taken another direction, which indicates the ongoing conversation of Wesleyan theology with changing cultural contexts. Theodore H. Runyon (born 1930), of the Candler School of Theology, has recently related

Wesley to liberation theology. In the introduction to *Sanctification and Liberation: Liberation Theologies in Light of the Wesleyan Tradition*, Runyon argues that there is an affinity between Wesley's theology and contemporary movements for social change.[34] Approached with an awareness of the Marxist critique, he contends, Wesley's theology can be freed from the limitations of pietistic individualism and offer resources for rethinking theology. Wesley's emphasis on the present reality of the kingdom of God carried concern about economic life and condemnation of slavery. Even though Wesley was a political conservative, he understood *work* in a way congenial to Marxist theory; both systems emphasize that human life is activity and that work is directed toward some goal. Wesley's unique binding of justification and sanctification draws divine work and human work into close conjunction, so that divine love is brought into human history to affect actual life situations. Wesley's theology intends transformation, and sanctification becomes a "revolutionizing practice" that works its good in the social world of contemporary living. With his study, Runyon has suggested a new evaluation of Wesley's theological and ethical intention.

An Overview

With quick strides, we have traversed the North American terrain since the Second World War. In this era we have seen evidence of continuity with the previous generation of theologians as expressly carried forward by Georgia Harkness and L. Harold DeWolf. But in the thought of both these people, especially DeWolf, there was a change of direction which emphasized the need for transformation of human life. We also have seen increasing diversity in Methodist theology. Edwin Lewis represented a new sensibility that arose in the 1930s, stressing the reality of sin, the centrality of

Jesus Christ as God and man, the transcendence of God, and the authority of the Scriptures. While not directly dependent upon Lewis, Edward T. Ramsdell's theology reflected the impact of these changes as evangelical liberalism was thoroughly reworked. In the decades of the 1930s and 1940s, new interest in the theology of John Wesley and its relation to the Reformation was aroused, with the work of George C. Cell and William R. Cannon being most important. Theological construction fashioned upon this foundation became significant as expressed in the writing of Albert C. Outler and Robert E. Cushman. Recapture of Wesleyan thought has been related to renewed biblical interest, and new streams have been cutting fresh routes, some of which may be found in the work of Theodore Runyon on Wesley and liberation theology.

Through this period, the theme of grace has been sustained, but with a variety of emphases. The personalists and evangelical liberals identified grace primarily with the immanence of God in all creation, especially in human life. For Harkness, grace was understood as God's universal presence, particularly expressed in the spirit of Jesus Christ and in immediate relation to all human beings. With Lewis, Ramsdell, Cushman, and Outler, this view is challenged by a sharper concentration on the transformative and normative presence of God in Jesus Christ; and DeWolf moves from the former position to one tempered by this more explicit focus. In all these later thinkers, transcendence is held in tighter tension with immanence as the doctrine of the Holy Spirit is freshly emphasized. For some, there has been continued interest in biblical bases for constructive theology, although this has not played as clear or direct a role in American as in British Methodism. Biblical authority has been given new impetus during this period through Lewis' work on *The Abingdon Bible Commentary* and through the more general use of biblical themes by Outler, Cushman, and Ramsdell. While these theologians represent diverse possibilities, there is a

218

continuation of interest in utilization of the biblical witness.

In regard to a continuing exploration of human nature, there is continuity, even as there are, once again, variations. This tradition's concern for an adequate theory of human nature is not unique, but the strength of this interest and the continuing exploration of its meaning, especially in relating human freedom to God's grace, has been a distinct feature. Consistently, there has been a serious effort to find acceptable models for describing human selfhood; and this in differentiation from models originally designed for understanding naturalistic or mechanistic causality. This has been true of Harkness, DeWolf, and Ramsdell in the personalist tradition, of Cushman in his analysis of religious experience, and of Outler in his explorations of psychotherapy.

For many of these thinkers there also has been continuing commitment to the moral implications of theology. Practical divinity has remained a basic family characteristic. Throughout the twentieth century, ethical concern has been directed more toward the social order than toward personal piety. From the concern for ethics of Harkness and DeWolf to that of Runyon, it is clear that there is a persistent effort to demonstrate the way theology serves ethical responsibility. For the Wesleyan tradition, ethics cannot be legitimately neglected or unrelated to theological interpretation.

Finally, twentieth-century North American Methodist theology has grown in ecumenical identification in spirit and in fact. Rediscovery of shared historical sources and of current collaboration with the wider Christian church has permeated and enriched the investigation of the origins of the Wesleyan tradition, and it has inspired the search for common self-understanding and mission with contemporary Christians. With openness toward its past and its future, Methodist theology has struggled to appropriate its rightful place in the larger Christian tradition and to contribute to the ongoing life and service of ecumenical Christianity.

CHAPTER 10

RECENT AND CONTEMPORARY DIRECTIONS IN NORTH AMERICAN METHODIST THEOLOGY

RECENT DEVELOPMENTS have been chiefly characterized by their diversity. No neat pattern can shape the variety of positions. Rather, there has been a conscious participation in the general nondenominational ambience of post-World War II Protestant theology and a utilization of prominent philosophical positions. To survey the range of positions, we shall look at the contributions of Carl Michalson, Thomas C. Oden, James H. Cone, Major J. Jones, John B. Cobb, Jr., and Schubert M. Ogden, each of whom represents a creative effort to meet contemporary challenges to Christian faith. But their analyses of those challenges and their methods of meeting them vary widely.

Carl Michalson

Carl Michalson (1915–1965) felt that, after mid-century, American theology was coming of age. There seemed to be a new independence from German theology; there were no longer frontiers to encourage evangelical extension rather than theological reflection; and there was a fresh appreciation of the larger Christian tradition.[1] The decade of the 1950s, Michalson said, was an era of ferment, and the most striking characteristic of the times was theology's modesty about its own claims and a recognition of the challenge of the dominant culture. Michalson, as a Christian existentialist, was responsive to this challenge in his own way—that is, he believed that actual historical existence has priority over the search for the essential nature of persons or of reality as such. But he also mentioned other options: process thought, hermeneutical theology, secular theology. His distinctive theological construction represented his own response to his era.

Carl Michalson was from Minnesota. He attended John Fletcher College and Drew and Yale universities, and in 1943 returned to Drew as a teacher of systematic theology. Intellectually and spiritually, Michalson's inheritance was far-ranging; but he was especially indebted to twentieth-century theology and philosophy, particularly to the existentialists and phenomenologists for philosophy and to Rudolf Bultmann and Friedrich Gogarten for theology. After a brief but brilliant career, Michalson died at the age of fifty in a plane crash.

In his mature period, he rethought theological doctrines in terms of "history," especially as related to personal meaning—the meaning individuals find in actual conditions of historical existence. Michalson made a sharp distinction between the world of natural science—the objective world of "brute things"; and the world of human meaning—the "interworld," in which objective facts are subordinated to the meaning of events for human life. In this move, from an analysis of the meaninglessness of life—as exposed by existentialism—to answers found in concrete human history, Michalson developed a position that John D. Godsey has called "a theology of correlation founded on historiography rather than ontology."[2] In short, the Bible and all theological doctrines must be read and interpreted from the standpoint of their meaning for human existence. The realistic analysis that Michalson utilized is, nevertheless, related to an optimism toward grace and a positive expectation of God's transforming power. In contemporary language, Michalson restated some inherited Wesleyan themes.

His approach may be made clear in his discussion of Jesus Christ. In his Christology, Michalson set aside primary interest in the person of Jesus and stressed the impact of Jesus—"the hinge of history"—upon present life. The meaning of Jesus is found in the salvation he brings and is expressed in his confronting people in "speech events," as one who addresses individuals and evokes a living faith. By *faith*, Michalson meant an actual formation of life by a power that can ultimately sustain our living-meaning. The salvation effected by faith in Jesus opens individuals to their future. They are related positively to an eschatological reality in which anxiety is overcome and true responsibility for the world may be expressed. In slightly different words, Jesus makes evident the coming kingdom of God, the reality of which gives a new world of meaning for living as faithful and responsible neighbors.

In a radical turn, Michalson argued that Christians are not bound to the old separate and falsely limiting "scientific" world; rather, they are released from this restrictive perspective and are free to carry on mature activity within the world of personal relationships. In all this, Michalson's emphasis was upon preaching, for it is through human speech that God's Word is reexpressed through the vitalization of the Holy Spirit. The human word presents the Word-event of Jesus Christ; and hearing this Word reconstitutes human life in its authenticity, in its freedom for God and for the world, and in the development of responsible selfhood.[3]

In the final stage of his exposition, which was nevertheless a stage along the way and unfortunately not completed, in

Worldly Theology, Michalson enlarged his vision beyond individual meaning toward horizons of the meaning of the world for God and of the Christian responsiblity to serve God in the world.[4] This extended awareness is a mark of maturity in Christian faith and sets arenas of responsibility for Christian life.

Theodore Runyon has argued that in basic, although largely unexplicated ways, Michalson's mind "is patterned by the presence of Wesley."[5] The most distinctive indications of Wesley's influence are found in Michalson's emphases upon Christian faith as the foundation of a freeing and existence-transforming experience, upon human concurrence with divine grace, upon a new human history directed to the goal of sanctification, and upon Michalson's structuring (in his last writing) of Christian responsibility for the world. Michalson's dependence upon Wesley was, however, latent. His indebtedness was primarily at the assumptional level and was not a fully rationalized base for his theological construction; in this regard, Michalson is typical of the other theologians we shall consider in this chapter.[6]

Thomas C. Oden

Many contemporary theologians understand themselves to be living in a postliberal or postmodern era. That is, western culture now holds a new set of assumptions: Modernity—the Enlightenment ethos—it is claimed, has come to an end. To meet this situation, a variety of different responses have been fashioned by Christian theologians. Thomas Oden (born 1931) acknowledges the new situation and has recently determined to react by returning to previous themes of Christian doctrine, which must now be given new exposition.

Oden, native of Oklahoma, was educated at the University of Oklahoma, Perkins School of Theology, and Yale

University. He has taught at Perkins and at Phillips and Drew universities. In his recent work *Agenda for Theology*, he has characterized his earlier efforts as those of a "movement" theologian and now asserts his commitment to Postmodern Orthodoxy. Initially he was politically active, supportive of international interests and religious ecumenism. Soon he became directly involved in civil rights, pacifist, Marxist, democratic socialist, and women's liberation movements. He followed this by adopting psychological interests as the context of his theology, and with quick steps, moved through Transactional Analysis, Gestalt theory, and Esalen. Such exposure was invigorating, but represented a search for basic foundations, and in the last few years Oden has rediscovered orthodox Christian theology to be relevant to the contemporary era.[7]

After exploring the development of orthodoxy and its struggle with heresy, Oden attempts to probe for the vital center that is present in orthodox continuity. He locates this center in "Life in Christ": "Christianity is distinctive as a religious faith in that it understands itself (both originally and in the present time) to be living as a continuing community through the living Christ."[8]

"The premise of [*Agenda for Theology*]," he writes, "is that it is possible for the core of classical Christian belief to stand in critical dialogue with modern personal and social hope." And the task Oden sets for himself and for contemporary theology is to go beyond the identification of Christian truth with reigning cultural interests "to discover and reveal the message underneath the garish modern overlay." In more detail, he argues that the Christian tradition is the historical record of people's interpersonal encounter with the living Christ. This engagement is focused in the crucifixion and the resurrection, upon which the divine/human relationship and all human relationships are built. The theological dynamics of this fundamental interaction move through forgiveness, toward the exercise of new freedom for finding genuine community with God and with people.[9] This book hoists a banner, a call to rally and march.[10] Oden's theology is not yet fully developed, but an alternative route is set as he explores new directions. Both Michalson and Oden have taught at Drew, both have sought adequate foundations for contemporary expression of Christian faith, and both have challenged their tradition to recognize its resources and responsibilities.

James H. Cone

Specialized history and distinctive perspective have become increasingly significant in contemporary theology, and on the North American scene James H. Cone (born 1938) has interpreted Christian motifs in terms of his own social setting. An African Methodist Episcopal minister from Arkansas, Cone now teaches at Union Theological Seminary in New York. He is the most prominent black North American theologian and has interpreted Christian theology from a clearly envisioned black perspective. Cone's first book, *Black Theology and Black Power,* is a study of "the concept of Black Power, placing primary emphasis on its relation to Christianity, the Church, and contemporary American theology."[11] The major problem in American society to which Christianity must address itself, Cone claims, is "the enslavement of black Americans, and in *A Black Theology of Liberation,* he systematizes the themes of his first book. He speaks more clearly of Christian foundations, presenting "a rational study of the being of God in the world in light of the existential situation of an oppressed community, relating the forces of liberation to the essence of the gospel, which is Jesus Christ."[12] As this statement and the title indicate, the center of Cone's theology has become the liberation of oppressed people, a liberation that is to be achieved by demonstrating that the gospel of Christianity speaks and offers hope to those on the margins of society. In this process, Christian theology becomes the exploration of God's liberating activity in the world. The Christian hope, Cone believes, is for the freedom of all people.

His God is a dynamic deity who is actively involved in contemporary affairs. Cone denies a solely transcendent God and emphasizes that God is working actively in history. His theology is focused upon Jesus Christ, who is God's manifestation in history.[13] Pursuing this theme, Cone confronts established consciousness by relating Christ to the black struggle for liberation. God in Christ has become incarnate once again in the condition of black people. Cone is not merely asserting demands for blacks, since "blackness" is a psychological trait and an ontological symbol of all oppressed people. The biblical revelation, Cone insists, presents a God who battles oppressors and actively seeks freedom for those in bondage. This understanding also stresses the reality of concrete communities that are so strong that it is only in and as a part of community that authentic theology may develop. The black church, he asserts, is the chief hope of oppressed blacks, for in that community people find individual worth and corporate meaning.

Cone's theology is avowedly ethical in its focus and calls for radical world action by Christians. Christians must take sides and become "prophetic, demanding a radical change in the interlocking structures of this society."[14] To serve this end, Christians should not speak only of love but learn to express justice and power. Escape to otherworldliness is prohibited; theology must give hope for this present life. Suffering humiliation is the actual condition of many, but this is not God's intention. Suffering can have meaning only as a part of the struggle for liberation, and indeed, "Jesus Christ . . . discloses that freedom is bound up with suffering."[15] God participates in the historical situation, taking on the sufferings of the oppressed, overthrowing the powers of oppression. With strength and hope, Christians must confront the tragedies of life and struggle against those who perpetuate evil.[16]

Major J. Jones

A United Methodist black theologian, Major J. Jones (born 1919) has continued the discussion of black theology in the North American setting. A native of Georgia and educated at Gammon Theological Seminary, at Oberlin, and at Boston University, Jones, who is now president-dean of Gammon, has written two books which explore salient theological issues. In the first, *Black Awareness: A Theology of Hope*, he draws together two approaches in order to interpret contemporary Christian meaning. He begins with human experience—specifically, the experience of black people— raising questions about the meaning of God and a viable way of life. On the other hand, he points to the future and speaks of the nature of hope that is projected by Christian faith. An examination of black experience emphasizes the dimensions of social rejection, political and economic repression, and engendered self-hate. Only a gospel that is concretely historical, that alleviates the existing conditions of life, and that promises a future of self-love, racial affirmation, and a new binding of the total human community will be adequate for black people.[17]

Jones opposes programs of black power and the endorsement of violent revolution. He seeks a "humane" principle of revolution, for humanity is "much deeper than color"; and, he says, "The ultimate manhood or personhood sought should be, under God, fully human." Jones places his confidence in the ability of liberated people to join together in a collective No! to social and personal exploitation.[18]

The concept of God, Jones contends, must be one that is adequate for all people. In opposition to Cone, whom Jones feels overidentifies God with blackness, he proposes an inclusive understanding.[19]

> The God whose wrath is provoked is also the God of even those who have, by their very acts of evil, invited God's disfavor. God then is the redeemer of the oppressed as well as of the oppressor; he joins the struggle on both sides, seeking to transform both the oppressed and the oppressor.[20]

This God, Jones asserts, must work in visible ways to change the conditions in which people now live and to transform relationships among people. Reaching toward a "Community Beyond Racism," he argues, "Now the time has come when changes have to be pushed through into reality whether all parties of the community are ready for them or not. Hope is seen in the fact that such a time has come, no matter what the opposition."[21]

This theological base has immediate implications for ethics; and Jones pursues these consequences in his second book, *Christian Ethics for Black Theology*, which suggests "ethical formulations necessary to build a totally new creative relationship that has never heretofore existed between black and white people in America." To achieve this goal, all people of every race must relinquish their pasts, whether they were the oppressed or the oppressors, the privileged or the degraded, possessed power or were powerless, enacted injustice or were its victims; and they must reach toward "humanity beyond human particulars."[22] Espousing an ethics of liberation and hope, Jones envisions a future that belongs to those who hope for and who work to achieve this new humanity.

Cone and Jones represent different responses to the same reality. Both begin with the black experience, and both are acutely aware of the discrimination, oppression, and degradation in that experience. The fact of this negative experience sets boundaries for Cone that cannot be passed until the realities of the situation are thoroughly recognized; black experience must be fully acknowledged before it can be related to a larger context. With sharp perception and interpretive power, Cone vigorously forces attention upon the actual condition of black people, and he develops his theological construction upon that foundation. Jones, too, begins with black experience, but he finds in the condition of black people a paradigm of judgment and hope for all people. Evil in every form must be confronted, but to recognize these negative realities is also to find a route, under God, to the affirmation of all humanity. Cone refuses to release the tension that oppression has brought and continues to bring; reconciliation is difficult and distant. Jones is more optimistic and finds hope—through judgment and forgiveness—for early reconciliation. Both men maintain the tension of theory and practice. Cone focuses on the broken present, while Jones anticipates a significant realization of the kingdom of God. These two theologians have exposed willingly forgotten dimensions of human experience, and they have suggested alternative ways to develop Christian theological response.

Process Theology

An important group of Methodist theologians is identified with "process thought." This mode of theology is heavily dependent upon the philosophical work of Alfred North Whitehead and Charles Hartshorne. Whitehead, an English scholar, made seminal contributions to both mathematics and philosophy. His philosophical interests led him through a consideration of nature and its fundamental interpretation to wide humanistic interests, and eventually to a philosophy of religion implicitly presented in *Process and Reality* (1929). Whitehead's influence was immediate and widespread, but it tended, over time, to be continued only by a small but extremely able and faithful group of followers. In North America, Whiteheadian thought found common cause with the philosophy of values and empirical theology long regnant at the University of Chicago.

One of the chief reasons for the influence of process thought at Chicago was the presence of Charles Hartshorne (born 1897), a remarkably strong and original thinker who developed themes suggested by Whitehead. Hartshorne's interest centered in the idea and knowledge of God, and he argued tenaciously for a view of God that combines relative and absolute dimensions. Principally a philosopher of religion, he explored those interests in his interpretation of God and the world. It is Hartshorne's conviction that such philosophy provides the most intelligible, self-consistent, and satisfying reconstruction of Christian belief.[23]

John B. Cobb, Jr.

John B. Cobb, Jr. (born 1925), a Methodist theologian at the School of Theology at Claremont, is a major representative of process thought as applied to theology. Son of a Methodist missionary family, Cobb has carried his heritage and his wide-ranging sensitivity to new configurations of natural, social, and religious contexts. His central concern has been the doctrine of God and the distinctive way of understanding God provided by Whitehead's view of reality. Upon this base Cobb has constructed a systematic statement. His position has been consistent, though many-faceted. His thematic declaration, "We must choose God *and* the world," indicates the intention of his enterprise.[24] God and the world are intrinsically related, the knowledge of either implies knowledge of the other, and response to either is response to the other.

Cobb has developed a position which, if diagrammed, would resemble an hourglass. Basing his effort upon natural

230

theology, he brings the general sense of God to focus through concrete religious traditions, and then moves back into a comprehensive consideration of the natural world and human experience.

Cobb understands himself to be an exponent of liberal Christianity; he accepts the task of stating the themes of liberal theology in affirmative, persuasive ways; he expresses a gospel of grace in categories of thought and experience that are cognate with the modern spirit.[25] After a decade of setting forth his basic position, in 1969 he became acutely aware of the injustices in global society and the involvement of the United States in many of the most negative factors. The question of human survival has become crucial, and hopeful images for the future seem an absolute requisite. This realization of responsibility carries with it a renewed theological endeavor, which attempts to be comprehensive of the natural world—especially in terms of ecology—and of human quality, in terms of economic, political, and social amelioration. He believes that in order to be just and fair, a society must be truly global.

In the decade of the 1970s, Cobb states, he moved from a position of choice between two different religious ways toward a wisdom which includes the truth that is expressed in each. Following study of Andre Malraux, who traces the gradual disappearance of the image of Christ from western art, Cobb found a parallel: The image of Christ has also disappeared from theology, suffused in a pluralism of sensibilities. The Logos (the Word of God, John 1:1) as transcendent is timeless and infinite, but in its incarnate manifestations it is a specific and transient force. Because the incarnate Logos is grounded in the more basic transcendent Logos, Jesus as the Christ is the way to God, which excludes no other ways. The creative transformation represented in Christ is an expression of the transformative power of the transcendent Logos. This striving for inclusiveness has continued as Cobb works on the relation of historical religions to the Logos reality (his special area of research is Mahayana Buddhism) and clarifies his vision of a healed and whole world. His present project, "The Liberation of Life: From Cell to Community," represents his pursuit of this vision.

Schubert M. Ogden

Another major Methodist process theologian is Schubert M. Ogden (born 1928) of the Perkins School of Theology at Southern Methodist Universty. A graduate of Ohio Wesleyan and Johns Hopkins, Ogden did his doctoral work at the University of Chicago and, more directly than Cobb, is dependent upon Charles Hartshorne. From the time of his first book, *Christ Without Myth*, 1961, through his *Reality of God* in 1966, to his most recent, *The Point of Christology* (1982), he has presented a consistent and logically coherent view of the task of theology and its essential issues. For Ogden, as for process thinkers in general, the central issue is the nature of God. From this perspective, he has developed arguments that extend the implications of process understanding from the primordial possibility for human life as rooted in God's love, to the existence of God as the ground of secularity, to the presence of God in contemporary human struggle and hope.

The issue of God must be understood in its current setting. The scientific world-view sets the unavoidable intellectual ambience. "So far as his knowledge of the world is concerned, modern man long ago opted for the method of science and therewith decided irrevocably for secularity." The assertions of a secularist understanding of knowledge (logical positivism) and of morality (which rejects all transcendent justifications of action) require that the reality of God be persuasively stated. Ogden stakes out his position:

"The only way any conception of God can be made more than a mere idea having nothing to do with reality is to exhibit it as the most adequate reflective account we can give of certain experience in which we all inescapably share."[26]

The theological task is to demonstrate that contemporary secular people do have faith in God, whether they are aware of it or not. The effort of theology is to aid these people to recover a conviction that has been unconsciously (prereflectively) held; then to seek the connection between confident faith in the value of life and what is properly meant by the idea of God. This may, by careful analysis and explication, lead to an understanding of God as "the objective ground in reality of our ineradicable confidence in the final worth of our existence."[27]

The concept of God that can speak to secular people possesses two essential characteristics: (1) God is a reality who is genuinely related to life in the world, and to whose actual being people and their actions make a difference; and (2) God is di-polar—that is, God is at once supremely relative and supremely absolute.[28]

The conceptual tools for this reconstruction of Theism, Ogden believes, are to be found in the work of Whitehead and Hartshorne. Following this lead, he interprets selfhood as social and relational; and the basic category of the self is not substance, but process, or creative becoming. God, too, must be conceived of as a genuinely temporal and social reality—that is, as creative becoming. On this base, all the traditional attributes of God must be reconceived and restated. Such a view, Ogden argues, is also adequate to Christology, at least to the essence of Christianity as a discrete religious tradition; for Christianity is the representation to individuals and to the world that they are ultimately significant within the encompassing mystery of God's love.[29]

In the book *Faith and Freedom*, Ogden turns from more theoretical questions of belief and truth to practical issues of action and justice. As a consequence, he engages current liberation theology and means to contribute a more adequate statement of its possibilities. His foundations are clear: Theology must satisfy the criteria of appropriateness and understandability; of truth-finding and justice-seeking; of faithfulness to the original witness to Jesus as the Christ, which underlies Scripture; and of appeal to common human experience and reason. Upon these footings he builds his theology of liberation. Faith as existence-*in*-freedom (liberated existence) and faith as existence-*for*-freedom (liberating existence) constitute the basic dimensions of Christian experience. Existence-in-freedom is an expression of life as lived *in* God, who preveniently sets people free from all bondage and therefore redeems life; existence-for-freedom is life lived *with* God, serving the freedom of others through emancipating activity.

Ogden bases the gift of freedom in God's own nature. He argues for an understanding of God as both Redeemer and Emancipator. The implications of this position are spelled out in a series of tight definitions: *Redemption* is "the unique process of God's self actualization, whereby he creatively synthesizes all other things into his own actual being as God." *Sin* is "the rejection of ourselves and the creatures we know ourselves to be." *Salvation* is "the process that includes not only the redeeming action of God himself but also the faithful response to this action on the part of the individual sinner." And *emancipation* is "the fullest possible self-realization" of every creature.[30]

At the climax of this theological statement, Ogden moves beyond the person-centeredness that he finds in liberal, in neo-orthodox, and in many liberation theologies, to an insistence upon "the unity of history and nature and the intrinsic value of every creature."[31] Such a position, he believes, allows theology to function with integrity and to serve an essential interpretive function for modern secu-laristic society.

In *The Point of Christology* (1982) Ogden draws together major themes with unusual clarity and force as he moves to new positions in explicating his theology. This book contains one of the most significant and challenging statements on Christology in recent decades. Ogden attests that as the decisive re-presentation of the meaning of ultimate reality for people and for their authentic self-understanding as human beings, Jesus is the primal source of all authority. With careful argument, he claims that the earliest New Testament witness to Jesus is the apostolic norm by which all christological statements must be assessed in terms of their appropriateness; and that contemporary human search for freedom sets the context in which the credibility of Christology must be judged. Developing a "Christology of liberation," he argues for its appropriateness and credibility, moving beyond both traditional orthodoxy and recent revisionary Christologies. Ogden skilfully combines the diverse dimensions represented in the questions: Who am I? Who is Jesus? Who is God? But the point of Christology, he says, is the emphasis on the existential dimension of this dynamic complex. The conclusion of Ogden's argument establishes the uniqueness of the earliest Jesus-kerygma for Christian life and faith. This book, clear in conception and presentation, is an importat contribution to contemporary theology.[32]

An Overview

We have quickly surveyed recent and contemporary North American Methodist theology and have noticed one obvious fact: the diversity of theological expression—Michalson's exploration of existentialist themes, Oden's reaffirmation of traditional doctrines, Cone's and Jones' explication of black theology, and Cobb's and Ogden's constructive utilization of process philosophy. All these theologians, even in their diversity, are descendants in the Wesleyan tradition, but their awareness of that tradition and their methods of continuing it are as varied as their individual histories and intentions.

The fact that traditional Wesleyan theological categories and language are little used tends to exaggerate the seeming distance of these writers. In none of their developed work are such words as *grace, justification,* or *sanctification* given central consideration. The desire to speak to contemporary culture, to utilize current thought-forms, and to render the inherited faith intelligible to people for whom the inherited language is alien has stimulated use of a different vocabulary.

These circumstances make the task of identifying these theologians in terms of the Wesleyan tradition difficult. Yet the question of tradition is not answered by locating identical emphases or fine-tuned doctrinal agreements. Tradition may more logically be found in implicit assumptions, in characteristic attitudes, and in more subtly configured similarities. It is unrealistic to expect all these persons to be related to the tradition in the same way. Nevertheless, even with their differences, there are family resemblances. For instance, emphasis upon practical dimensions of applied theology is prominent in the work of Cone and Jones as well as in that of Cobb and Ogden. For these four men, social concern and action are the necessary companions of theological analysis and interpretation. Michalson also sought practical expression, initially in personal life, and later in service to the world; and Oden, one may assume, has not abandoned his earlier social interests upon his return to more traditional theological themes. Again, in the thought of all the persons discussed in this chapter, there is emphasis upon Christian experience and upon human responsibility for concurrence with God's will and activity. While social implications are more clearly drawn, there is also a residual emphasis upon personal religious conviction. Michalson, especially, was concerned with this dimension, but it is present in varying ways in the writing of all these thinkers.

There is also present in all these persons a strong ecumenical sensitivity. Openness to other Christian traditions and a generosity of spirit make them learners from and contributors to ecumenical Christianity. And Cobb has extended his horizon through interest in non-Christian religions, as well. The ecumenical context in which these writers live and their sensitive appropriation from the wider Christian community have reduced the awareness of their relation to the Wesleyan tradition. There is little explicit study of John Wesley or the Wesleyan tradition, and there is little explicit development of themes derived from that tradition. This fact does not lead to any lack of vigor or value in the constructive theology of these Methodist theologians; it does mean that the tradition in which they have been nurtured does not play as formative or corrective a role as it might, were it more directly assessed or engaged.

One area where the loss of a sense of tradition may be seen as having significant effect is in the decreased acknowledgment of the theological authority of Scripture. Ogden has struggled explicitly with the issue of biblical authority, but this dimension is not prominent as a foundational principle for the constructive efforts of most of these writers. Again, it must be acknowledged that implicit utilization is present, and this is evident especially in the work of Cone, Jones, and Oden. But to most of these writers, biblical thought is not as clearly authorizing as it has been through much of the tradition.

Of special importance, and from another angle, the contribution made to philosophical theology by North American Methodist theology must be noted. This interest, which has been present since the early nineteenth century, is reinforced by the developments just surveyed. Through its history, North American Methodism has been an especially fertile and productive ground for philosophical theological interests. From the time of Shinn and Bangs—who utilized Scottish common sense philosophy; through that of Whedon and Bledsoe—who explored prevenient grace with philosophical tools, this interest has been nurtured. In the work of Bowne—who developed a new metaphysical foundation for Christian interpretation of reality—it reached a nineteenth-century zenith; and in that of Brightman and Knudson, among numerous others, it was continued with concentrated effort. The writings of Cushman, Michalson, Cobb, and Ogden have, in singular ways, kept this interest alive.[33] Contribution to philosophical theology does constitute a distinctive characteristic of the Wesleyan tradition, but it also indicates a recharacterization of this tradition in the North American setting.

This diminished sense of tradition raises a fundamentally important question: Is the Wesleyan tradition now moving, or has it already moved beyond recognizable boundaries? And if so, has the tradition, in terms of giving special emphasis to themes within the larger Christian tradition, completed its contribution? Is Wesleyan theology now appropriately expanding into the wider community, its task basically defined not by its inheritance but by its present context? Or, exploring the situation in a reverse way, we might ask, Does the tendency to move beyond recognizable boundaries of the Wesleyan tradition constitute a loss for the larger Christian community? Is there still a significant role to play, for those who have come through the Wesleyan tradition as representatives of that tradition? Perhaps this is a question that can be reinforced by this survey, for it is a lively and critical issue, and it now faces Methodist theologians as they attempt to understand their theological responsibilities.

CHAPTER 11

UNITY IN DIVERSITY:
Indigenous Theologies

T HE EXPANSION of the Wesleyan influence in the nineteenth and twentieth centuries quickly outgrew the geographical limits of Great Britain and North America. The missionary impulse of the Wesleyan movement shared the general zeal of Protestant Christianity, beginning with the formation of missionary societies in both British and American Methodism in the second decade of the nineteenth century. This dynamic thrust gave rise to complementary emphases for the Wesleyan tradition: the indigenization of Wesleyan theology in different settings, and the enhancement of the Wesleyan ecumenical spirit. The growing diversity through various geographical and cultural settings and the developing unity within these areas have been dominant realities in the Wesleyan tradition as it has encompassed a world parish.

The possibility of diversity within unity was expressed by John Wesley himself, for the founding father understood Christian community to be built upon integrity-with-difference. He did not insist upon conformity in forms of

239

worship or in church polity. Catholicity, Wesley said, is a gracious quality of Christian life, which recognizes that although Christian expressions may vary, "there is a peculiar love we owe to those who love God."[1] With an open and enthusiastic spirit, he welcomed into common company all those who shared the Christian faith, and he endorsed participation in the widest range of Christian traditions and openness to ecumenical life. This spirit of unity in diversity has remained a dominant characteristic of the expanding Wesleyan movement.

Although Methodists quickly became fragmented after Wesley's death, the desire for cooperative effort remained strong throughout the nineteenth century. In 1820 the Wesleyan Methodist Conference in Great Britain welcomed John Emory, the first American church delegate to a British Methodist assembly, with this resolution: "That the Conference embraces with pleasure this opportunity of recognizing that great principle which it hopes will be permanently maintained . . . that the Wesleyan Methodists are one Body in every part of the world."[2] Methodism intended to be worldwide, even though it was predominantly a tradition within the English language culture, and it found its main courses along the trails of the British Empire. Methodism expanded around the world into a variety of different settings and the theological contributions that have come and are coming from these diverse contexts are significant.

German Methodism

We noted earlier the interaction of the Evangelical Association and the United Brethren Church with early Methodism in North America. These bodies were originally formed by German immigrants; and there were German-speaking converts in the Methodist Episcopal Church. By the 1820s some of these converts were returning to their

European homeland to spread the gospel, and for a century, an important segment of the Wesleyan movement utilized the German language in worship and theological expression. Illustrative of this movement were Christoph Gottlieb Müller, who traveled from London to southern Germany, and Ludwig Sigismund Jacoby, an immigrant to North America who returned in 1839 to Bremen in northern Germany. Through these and many other missionaries, German-speaking Methodism was established in Germany and was strengthened in North America.[3]

Theologically, there have been several significant leaders, and one periodical of special importance, *Der Christliche Apologet*. This journal was directed at German-speaking American Methodists and was published in Cincinnati from 1839 until 1940. In the first issue, editor William Nast set its theological stance; the themes were basic to evangelical Protestantism: the Incarnation, the penal satisfaction of the atonement of Christ, original sin, and depraved human nature. A stand was taken against any teaching that diluted the power of God's mercy or interfered with the manifestation of God's grace, which was sufficient for all human needs. The theme of regeneration was especially developed and projected into the moral qualities that are distinctive of Christian living. These emphases continued for the life of the periodical.

Among those who made significant theological contribution to the Methodist Church in Germany was Arnold Sulzberger (1832-1907), a professor in the Methodist seminary at Frankfurt and the author of a complete systematic theology, *Christliche Glaubenslehre (Christian Faith)*, published in 1886. That work represented an orthodox theology built upon the scriptural witness. Aware of both the philosophical and theological traditions, Sulzberger set forth his basic convictions, intending to present a truly Wesleyan theology. He understood Wesley's strength to be in his comprehensiveness, which holds together important elements of Pietism and mysticism, along with evangelistic fervor: the interaction of God and persons—rooted in the Holy Spirit; and the perfect love of God expressed in practical activity.[4] Sulzberger saw the normative position of the Bible for Christian theology as fundamental, especially as it communicates the saving knowledge of God as expressed in Jesus Christ. On this basis, he explored the witness of God in nature, history, and the human soul. The structure of the system began with the doctrine of God, then moved to anthropology, Christology, the Holy Spirit, and last things. The heart of the presentation is the discussion of the person and work of Jesus Christ. Throughout, Sulzberger's work was thoughtful, clear, and intense. Through his systematic theology, Wesleyan theology was carried into the German context.

Bishop John L. Nuelsen (1867–1946), of the Methodist Episcopal Church, wrote important German-language studies also—on Methodist history, ordination, and the relation of Methodism to the Reformation. Nuelsen was an early and courageous leader against National Socialism. More recently, Theophil Spörri (1887–1955), professor of systematic theology at the Methodist seminary in Frankfort; Vilém Schneeberger (born 1928) of Czechoslovakia; and Manfred Marquardt (born 1940), of the Methodist theological seminary in Reutlingen, West Germany, all have made significant contributions to Wesleyan theology.[5]

Theophil Spörri was a native of Switzerland and trained under Adolf Schlater and Karl Heim. From his teaching post and later from retirement in Switzerland, he was influential in European Methodist theology. Spörri's theological interpretation was presented in a number of pamphlets, and especially in a major systematic effort, *Der Mensch und die frohe Botschaft;* two volumes were published in 1939 and 1952, and a third, partially completed, in 1956 after his death.[6]

In constructing this major work (which was suggested by a Beethoven concert), he began with an analysis of human existence as a search for truth, justice, and ultimate authority. These questions are intensely existential and lead to a search for salvation. Soteriology, therefore, was the central organizing theme of Spörri's thought, and in this he was consciously Wesleyan. The search for genuine truth, justice, and sovereign power, whether expressed through religious or secular questing, is frustrated in human experience. That which people most want, they only partially find, and regularly misunderstand and misuse because of sin. Sin wrongly directs human searching, and people, in their questing, become lost, estranged from God and from one another. Sin distorts the meaning and hope of life.

This human condition sets the context into which the good news of God is spoken. Human beings, who exist in existential despair, are encountered by God in Jesus Christ, who comes as a redeemer; he conveys the love of the holy and righteous God to humankind. This truth for human existence appears as revelation, for the Word of God carries its own convincing power. Through God in Christ, human beings are presented with ultimate truth, justice, and sovereign purpose.

Spörri's theology was written against the background of German-language theology between the two world wars. There is, for him, a point of connection between all people and God, a connection grounded in the universal presence of the Holy Spirit. But this God-awareness is frustrated by the radical disorientation caused by willful sin. There is no pathway from humans to God; having misused God's original revelation, they are helpless to advance toward salvation. Only a new act of God can provide authentic existence. There is such action, for God in Jesus Christ comes to human beings, drawing those who respond into living community with God and extending the righteous community through relationship with the neighbor. For Spörri, the church as the community of believers is of crucial significance. The historical, embodied people of God witness to the message of God's revelation in Jesus Christ and express the worship of God and love of neighbor through the church's life in the world.

The theological work of Spörri is of importance since it reflects the way a self-conscious Wesleyan theologian attempts to utilize the soteriological concern of his tradition in interpreting the contemporary human condition and the expression of God's good news of salvation.

Both Schneeberger and Marquardt have carried on the exploration of Wesley's social ethics with theological thoroughness. Schneeberger sees Wesley's theology as the source of his social ethic. Coming from the mainline of the Reformation, Wesley grafted Catholic piety onto this root. For Wesley, therefore, theological proclamation and social responsibility formed an indivisible whole; his theology was always concrete as salvation becomes inclusive of personal and social dimensions. Consistently, Schneeberger emphasizes that faith and love stand in direct relation to God and neighbor; faith and life constitute a unity.

Marquardt moves from the other direction and derives Wesley's social ethic from his participation in attempts to alleviate social ills and economic deprivation; hence he explores the spheres of Wesley's social activity from his time at Oxford. As a result, Marquardt argues that Wesley's theology developed in dialectical relation to his work with those in poverty and in prison, and through his concern with slavery. Prevenient and renewing grace are refracted through and serve these social needs. Acknowledging weakness in Wesley's social ethics—his conservative understanding of the state and his failure to acknowledge the necessity of basic structural change in society—Marquardt believes that there is great strength in the positive relation that Wesley held between practice and theory, faith and works, love and reason, and individuals and community. In both Schneeberger and Marquardt, Methodist theology on the continent has continued its engagement with the study of Wesley as it also relates the received tradition to current life.

Other European Methodists have made important contributions. Several Scandinavian scholars have been especially significant (it is quite possible that Scandinavian Methodism has been the most theologically productive, in relation to its number of members, of any section of the Methodist connection). Harald Lindström (born 1905), now in retirement from a professorship, made a basic contribution in *Wesley and Sanctification;* Thorvald Källstad, presently dean of the theological faculty of Uppsala University, has written *John Wesley and the Bible.* Bishop Ole E. Borgen (born 1925) has produced a fine study of *John Wesley on the Sacraments,* and his brother Peder Borgen (born 1928), on the faculty of Trondheim University, is a New Testament scholar who has made excellent contributions, especially to the study of the Gospel of John. Thor Hall (born 1927), teaching at the University of Tennessee at Chattanooga, has published *A Framework for Faith* and *The Future Shape of Preaching.*[7] The Scandinavian church, through these theologians, has added to the interpretation of the Wesleyan tradition.

A World Movement

In the present century, the Wesleyan movement has decisively moved beyond the boundaries of Europe and North America. Methodism has shared in the missionary zeal and expansion of the last two centuries, and special notice must be given to several people.[8]

Frank Mason North (1850–1935) led the Methodist Episcopal Church's missionary enterprise and also became one of the founders of the Federal Council of Churches, serving as its executive chairman and as its president from 1916 until 1920. Always combining his missionary vision with concrete social service, it was said that North, "more than any other person . . . shaped the social policies of the Protestant Churches in this country between 1892 and 1912."[9] His convictions often found poetic expression, and he expressed his concerns in many of his hymns. One illustration carries his message.

> O master of the waking world,
> Who has the nations in Thy heart,—
> The heart that bled and broke to send
> God's love to earth's remotest part,—
> Show us anew in Calvary
> The wondrous power that makes men free. . . .
>
> We hear the throb of surging life,
> The clank of chains, the curse of greed,
> The moan of pain, the futile cries
> Of superstition's cruel creed;
> The peoples hunger for Thee, Lord,
> The isles are waiting for thy word.[10]

Two other men were also instrumental as Methodists and as world leaders: John R. Mott and E. Stanley Jones. John R. Mott (1865-1955) was a singular man, whose work in the expansion of the Christian faith through organizational genius and personal leadership was of crucial importance in Christian missions and in founding the World Council of Churches. Mott lived for ninety years, helping to shape the era and making a larger contribution than any other person of his time to the ecumenical movement.

The son of parents who moved from New York state to Postville, Iowa, Mott returned to New York, attended Cornell University, then followed Wesley's vision across the world. He professed sanctification and sought to implement holiness in terms of race relations, the ecumenical movement, and the social gospel. Mott moved rapidly into positions of prominence. As a layman, in 1889 at age twenty-three, he was named one of the two national secretaries of the YMCA. He believed his principal task was the enlistment of young people for missionary service, and he always retained great confidence in students and their capacity for changing the world. One of his greatest achievements was the founding of the World Student Christian Federation, and later, the Student Christian Movement—and all this while he also was leader of the Student Volunteer Movement. That movement's success may be judged by the conservative estimates which indicated that by 1945, at least twenty thousand students, many inspired by Mott and representing most major Protestant denominations, had served as missionaries under its banner. In 1946 Mott shared the Nobel Peace Prize.

Rooted in the Methodist tradition, a tradition that he believed nurtured his wider commitments, Mott was well aware of the need for united evangelistic effort and unity of fellowship as Christian churches confront the total world. In search of this unity, Mott provided leadership for the Edinburgh Missionary Conference in 1910, the most significant ecumenical meeting in modern times. He continued his formative role in ecumenical conferences at Jerusalem in 1928, at Tambaram in 1938, and at Amsterdam when the World Council of Churches was organized in 1948. Although he was always readily identified by his western confidence and desire to organize, it was even more true of Mott to say that he possessed a comprehensive vision of Christianity as a world religion.[11]

Methodism also provided strong leadership for the world missionary movement through E. Stanley Jones (1894–1973). Jones was to become an extraordinary evangelist and practicing missionary. India became his base of operations and the land he would call home. His reputation spread rapidly.

Elected to the episcopacy of his church in 1928, he declined; he was twice nominated for the Nobel Peace Prize; he wrote more than thirty books; he knew political leaders throughout the world—but he always remained a missionary evangelist.

An outline of Jones' theological affirmations parallels his life story. In his spiritual autobiography, *A Song of Ascents,* he presented his main assumptions and much of his developed thought.[12] His theology always remained simple and was riveted to the basic confession, Jesus is Lord. On this foundation he built his understanding of the kingdom of God, in which personal and social dimensions of the gospel were firmly joined. Rejecting all ideologies and viewing ecclesiastical structures as having only pragmatic importance, Jones refused identification with either fundamentalism or modernism and would not endorse either capitalism or communism. He also believed that the churches of the West had been corrupted by cultural ideologies and that the gospel of Jesus Christ must be disentangled from those alliances in order to remain authentic. The freedom of the gospel—in every culture and for every culture—was a theme that would influence the next generation of theologians.

North, Mott, and Jones set the path that led North American Methodism into a new world-sensitivity. These men helped to bring geographical regions with differing Christian traditions into intimate and challenging relationship, to engage non-Christian religions, and to encourage indigenous self-awareness. Others would follow them, and perhaps a signal illustration of this ecumenical commitment is Philip A. Potter (born 1921), a Caribbean Methodist who is presently general secretary of the World Council of Churches.

Daniel T. Niles

As a result of the missionary movement, theologians arose in diverse cultural settings. New voices began to speak to

248

particular contexts. The best known non-Western theologian of the mid-twentieth century, and an important transitional figure, was Daniel T. Niles (1908–1970) of Sri Lanka (Ceylon). Niles was of the Tamil culture. His sensibilities were formed by the Hindu heritage, amalgamated with the Methodist missionary presence, Charles Wesley's hymns, and E. Stanley Jones' theology and his Ashram movement. Niles' formal education took place after World War I and reflected strong Barthian and Eastern Orthodox coloration; he was also impressed by the work of Pierre Maury of France and John Baillie of Scotland. And all these rich resources were sifted through his Asian background.

By the age of thirty, Niles was a leading spokesman of the Asian churches. Soon afterward he became the evangelism secretary of the world YMCA, head of the National Christian Council of Ceylon, and preacher at the first session of the World Council of Churches (WCC) in 1948. He was appointed chairman of the Youth Department of the WCC, then served as secretary of its Evangelism Department from 1953 until 1958. He was also the first general secretary of the East Asian Christian Council, the author of more than a dozen books, and always an active preacher.

Niles' major contribution was the building of bridges between the traditional thought of the West and the new theologies of non-Western cultures, a contribution he made at an early stage and in tentative, exploratory ways. The possibility of such mediation was predicated upon his employment of the central doctrines of the Trinity, creation, and providence, and especially the work of the Holy Spirit.

Trinitarian emphasis is central in Niles' writings.[13] He found this theme congenial to the Asian idea of wholeness; and the two cultures were wedded as both the immanence and transcendence of God were stressed. Niles emphasized the event of Jesus Christ, in whom God moves downward to persons in Incarnation, suffering, and death, and through whom God carries persons upward in resurrection and ascension. Again, the Trinitarian theme finds special expression in Niles' understanding of the work of the Holy Spirit, through whom God graciously calls persons, and by whom persons are made responsive to God.[14]

Under the rubric of "wholeness," Niles was able to give special attention to the themes of prevenient grace and sanctification, of creation and providence—that is, to the comprehensive presence of God in human life. With his unusual range of awareness, Niles presented a theological interpretation with indigenous characteristics. Yet this was never his single intention. Rather, he was committed to drawing together, in synthetic manner, the insights of many traditions, so as to present the Christian gospel in its most comprehensive terms. His purpose was to convey a truly ecumenical theology.

José Míguez-Bonino

In Argentina, José Míguez-Bonino (born 1924) speaks as a contemporary Wesleyan theologian who comprehensively applies the gospel to his cultural setting. Míguez, although he does not define himself in narrow Methodist terms, is a legitimate heir of John Wesley, especially of Wesley's emphasis upon the Christian life as a response to the grace of God. Methodist theology in general, according to Míguez, has yielded to a radical individualism and has adopted the values of reigning cultural, economic, and political powers. This surrender has reduced the church's ability to speak the most crucial words. Míguez wants to see life whole, to understand people in their total setting, and to develop an evangelism that comprehends the full range of human existence.

Dean of postgraduate studies at the Protestant Theological Seminary in Buenos Aires, Míguez is deeply rooted in his own national and continental life. He is also an international leader, having served in many capacities, including as president of the World Council of Churches. His writing reflects this background and also utilizes his classical theological education, as he communicates traditional concerns with precision and understanding. Yet his perspective is distinctly that of a Latin American who speaks from within and to his society.

Miguez-Bonino understands himself as a Christian evangelist whose analysis of his society casts a fresh vision of Christian responsibility and a new theological interpretation. He rejects both the Roman Catholic colonial and the Protestant neocolonial Christianity that have condemned the majority of Latin Americans to poverty and impotence. His attack is sharp: The traditional church, with its themes of human autonomy and hope only beyond this world, has become an opiate, failing to offer genuine transformation or fundamental reconciliation. Miguez writes from this perspective in *Christians and Marxists: The Mutual Challenge to Revolution:*

> It is my thesis that as Christians, confronted by the inhuman condition of existence prevailing on the continent, they have tried to make their Christian faith historically relevant, they have been increasingly compelled to seek an analysis and historical program for their Christian obedience. At this point, the historical process, both in its objective conditions and its theological development, has led them, through the failure of several remedial and reformist alternatives, to discover the unsubstitutable relevance of Marxism.[15]

Miguez believes that his social situation demands a new theology, to convey new forms of piety, discipline, theological reflection, and above all, a new ethical sensitivity and commitment that will stand with the disadvantaged people. Esther and Mortimer Arias, Methodist leaders from South

America, state his position succinctly: "His theme is the Kingdom and his leitmotif is love, incarnate love, mediated in history through human solidarity and commitment to the oppressed."[16]

Using biblical models taken from Old Testament prophets, from the Gospel of John, and from the person and work of Jesus Christ, Míguez constructs a revolutionary theology founded upon the radical yet nonviolent discipleship of active engagement. History becomes the battleground of God's action, and Marxism provides the best available resource for interpreting South American society. This analysis helps to indicate the program Christians must use in their effort to serve the kingdom of God. Christian life is active work, not a reflective process, and Christian evangelism seeks the new possibility of free and meaningful life.

The gospel must be announced as a critique of all idols of society, as a participant in just struggles, and as a call for conversion of all life. With such a perspective, attempts to evangelize individuals without a radical change in social institutions is meaningless. But the goal is not revolution as such—the goal is the kingdom of God! Míguez turns theology around: Theological work must not be reserved for an academic elite; it must become a common effort expressed in conflict of the faithful with the powers of evil in society. The Latin American situation, Míguez believes, demands revolutionary consciousness that will reach beyond analysis to an actual achievement of freedom and salvation.

Emerito P. Nacpil

Among the most significant Wesleyan theologians in Asia is Emerito P. Nacpil (born 1932). Formerly professor of theology and president of Union Theological Seminary in Manila, dean of the federated faculty of the South East Asia Graduate School of Theology, executive director of the

Association of Theological Schools in South East Asia, and editor of *The South East Asia Journal of Theology,* Nacpil is now a bishop of the Philippines Central Conference. Although he received his doctorate at Drew and first came prominently to western attention as an interpreter of Reinhold Niebuhr, Nacpil has developed an indigenous awareness and has more recently been exploring the "critical Asian principle" of theology. He finds the elements of this principle to be: (1) an awareness of the variety and dynamics of the Asian social and cultural reality; (2) the gospel interpreted in its relation to the needs of that reality; and (3) Christian leadership as a guide for the changes that Asian experience is undergoing.[17] Nacpil further elaborates his position in a discussion of "A Gospel for the New Filipino." After analyzing the present theological situation and the social conditions of the Philippines, he calls for a theology of liberation that will free Filipinos from their inherited notion of eternally revolving cyclic time, from a cultural tendency to identify the universe with the divine, and from an overly restricted and ethically limiting kinship structure—all of which impede freedom. On the positive side, he seeks means to serve community development, and he hopes to discover responsible ethical imperatives that can enhance constructive change. He draws his conclusion: "It is in its social content and its power to heal human lives and to renew society and redirect world history toward the attainment of mankind's liberty and maturity, that the Kingdom of God is the horizon of hope."[18]

Nacpil has more recently come to see religion as being necessarily expressed in pluralistic cultural forms. Religion is the substance of culture, and culture is the form of faith. The church must now decide whether it is prepared to say that it is a faith only, or to claim that it is also a culture—whether it is only a way of believing, or a way of organizing and shaping life. Both multiplicity of cultural expressions and a need to create multiple forms of Christian culture are necessary in the

253

present world. With these more recent emphases, Nacpil is developing an indigenous theological expression. But it is not quite the same as that of the liberation theologians we have been discussing, for in Nacpil's thought, participation in culture takes primacy over critique of social conditions.

The struggle to achieve this goal is part of the Christian's identification with the crucified Christ; and hope beyond the battle comes from identification with the resurrection. With these understandings, Nacpil has placed liberation theology, with its ethical mandates, upon a traditional theological foundation, with its sustaining roots.

Other International Voices

In Africa there are diverse representatives of Wesleyan thought such as Kwesi A. Dickson of Ghana, who pursues Old Testament studies with an eye to their implications for African consciousness, and Canaan Banana, who is the first president of Zimbabwe.[19] Dickson is aligned with western styles of biblical study, but he is exploring means of relating this study to the present situation on his continent. Banana has opted for a more direct liberation approach, moving theological statement directly into ethical action.

In Australia, Norman J. Young (born 1930) has been the major theological writer in the Wesleyan tradition. A native of that continent, he received his Ph.D. from Drew University. Young has had two books published. The first, *History and Existential Theology,* is a study of Rudolf Bultmann and reflects an interest developed under the tutelage of Carl Michalson. This work provides a careful analysis of the role of history in Bultmann's thought and calls for both a more thorough and a more flexible use of Bultmann's hermeneutical method. The study concentrates on the point in Bultmann's theology where the transition from inauthentic to authentic existence occurs. This is the moment of new life, the inaugurating experience of salvation. Young stresses the grace of God, which enables free decision on the part of humans. Wesleyan themes of prevenient grace, salvation, and hope are implicit in Young's interpretation.[20]

In his second book, *Creator, Creation, and Faith*, Young reviews biblical notions of creation, the Fall, and new creation, and then surveys the thought of Barth, Tillich, Bultmann, and Jürgen Moltmann in regard to these issues. The point of the discussion is that different ways of viewing God as creator make for differences in the way people relate to the created order. The interaction of theology and ethics, of interpretation and application, is central. Young emphasizes a liberation theme as he concludes, asserting the need for responsible ethical action—both innovative and revolutionary—on the part of participants in the new creation.[21]

An Overview

A vision of world mission compelled the ministry of John Wesley, yet he was specifically attentive to his immediate context. The world was his parish, but his parish responsibilities began with the neighbor next encountered. Realization of a comprehensive Wesleyan movement that would surround the globe was achieved by the twentieth century. The first move was mission outreach; the second was acknowledgement of distinctive specific contexts. Expansion led the way to indigenization, and ultimately, concern for concrete location must yield again to an enriched sense of world community.

The character of the Wesleyan movement, as it has become world inclusive and taken incarnate form in different situations, has been renewed in its sense of practical divinity. The theme of grace underwrites theological effort as theory and application, theology and ethics, are held together. There are no simple agreements as to interpretation or strategy, but concern with social ethics and with the practical implementation of Christian moral responsibility, in the concreteness of specific situations, has been close to the center of international Wesleyan theological interests. As the gospel has found footing in diverse cultures, there has been an increased consciousness of the meaning of that gospel for people in their own settings. While there have been a variety of efforts to relate theory to practice, for most of the writers we have discussed, the dominant theme has become liberation, the freeing of life in a holistic manner. The awareness of the need for liberation has led to new analyses of the actual situations in which Christians find themselves, and these assessments have lifted up the reality of oppressive structures that negate the possibility of meaningful life for people and societies. These studies also have led to political and economic awareness and the sense that social, cultural, and political structures have a direct bearing upon the development of true, God-intended humanness. The Christian message is recognized as a challenge to demeaning conditions.

Theology, in these situations, has looked again to its biblical roots and has found that the understanding of God as active in history has taken on new significance. God has a stake in the conditions in which people live, and therefore this active God of history is involved in the struggle for freedom. Realization of God's involvement in human history has also placed a new emphasis upon God's historical presence in the person of Jesus Christ, who, through suffering, has brought the actual conditions of salvation.

The kingdom of God becomes a central theme, for the kingdom is the context and the final hope of Christian activity. That kingdom is seen as a present reality; the rule of God has to do with the actual conditions and possibilties of all people. The achievement of the kingdom carries immediate responsibilities for struggle against evil, oppressive persons, and repressive systems. The hope of the kingdom is both this worldly and ultimate; it begins in the concrete conditions of everyday life and reaches ahead to God's final reign. The expectation of the kingdom of God reinforces people in their engagement with their social settings, and it conveys the assurance that God is now present in conflict and in ultimate reconciliation.

Liberation theologians represent a significant emphasis in the Wesleyan tradition. There is, among them, a continuing sense of the fallen condition of people and of the distorted social order that is brought about by sin. There also continues a strong sense of the importance of personal relationship with God and the need for renewal of life. Recipients of Wesley's energy, which reached to make the world his parish, they have been alive to their specific environments and have attempted to speak relevantly to the condition of their people. They have gone beyond much inherited Methodist theology in their strong sense of the corporate bonding of life and the systemic character of sin. They have, with persistent effort, made theology practical; they have tied theory to practice and have insisted upon the ethical import of theological interpretation. There is variety in their approaches and conclusions, but there is also a sense of continuity with a tradition that has understood itself as being practical, as seeking to speak a word of redemption to all of life, and as finding in the grace of God the strength to confront life and to hope for its redemption.

And so we return to the beginning. There is one holy, catholic, apostolic Church. The Wesleyan tradition is a part of that Body. It rejoices in its inheritance, prays for faithfulness in present life, and looks forward to the fulfillment of God's will in the coming kingdom. Charles Wesley again provides a hymn:

Build us in one body up.
Called in one high calling's hope;
One the Spirit whom we claim,
One the pure baptismal flame,
One the faith and common Lord,
One the Father lives adored,
Over, through, and in us all,
God incomprehensible.

CHAPTER 12

THE CHARACTER OF
WESLEYAN THEOLOGY

THE WESLEYAN stream of Christianity grew out of a spirit of revival that preceded the Wesleys and was broader than their influence. But it was in those revivals of eighteenth-century England that the tradition had its origin. John Wesley was the dominant figure. He was a leader and, as though expected by right, he exercised leadership over much of the revival with his assured sense of purpose, extraordinary energy, selfless drive of mission, effective preaching, and care for the whole life of people.

At the founding of City Road Chapel in London on May 21, 1777, Wesley attempted to describe his movement:

> You will naturally ask, "What is Methodism? What does this new word mean? Is it not a new religion?" . . . Nothing can be more remote from the truth. . . . Methodism, so called, is the old religion, the religion of the Bible, the religion of the primitive Church, the religion of the Church of England. This old religion . . . is no other than love, the love of God and all mankind.[1]

Wesley believed that Methodism was a renewed expression of Christian faith. Consequently, he did not actually present a new interpretation of Christian truth, but placed increased emphasis upon special elements in the Christian tradition. Wesley was indebted to a wide range of Christian history; rooted in Scripture, he read—and recommended for reading—the writings of the church Fathers, both East and West, the Roman Catholic spiritual tradition, the Reformation traditions, and Anglican divines. In this spirit the Wesleyan tradition began. Wesley's comprehensive, richly textured theology represented an altered perspective, which provided a new frame of reference for theological construction. The centering theme of Wesley's thought was grace, expressed in Jesus Christ and conveyed to individuals by the Holy Spirit: Christian life is rooted and fulfilled in grace. Wesley explicated this theme—from prevenience to justification, to assurance, to sanctification, to final glorification—and this theology possessed the power to inaugurate and nourish a tradition.

Granted this role of the founder, what may be said of the relation of the Wesleyan movement to John Wesley himself? There is both continuity and discontinuity. John Wesley's theological interests were fundamental to the genesis of the movement and have continued to instruct the tradition. The tradition, however, cannot be understood by exclusive appeal to Wesley. Although Methodism cannot be understood apart from John Wesley, it also cannot be understood except as it has moved beyond Wesley.

Wesleyan theology, as it advanced beyond Wesley, has exhibited characteristic qualities of his thought more than it has adhered to distinctive doctrines. Consequently, John Wesley has been a guide to theological reflection more than a definitive doctrinal source. None of the theologians we have reviewed has merely repeated what was received. Each has participated in the tradition in his or her own time and place, and each has made selections, reshaped, and added to it. Today the Wesleyan tradition is the result of its inclusive history; it has flourished because it has been vital; it has grown because it has allowed diversity; it has been enhanced by the continual infusion of new streams, both compatible and challenging. Beginning with Wesley, it did not stop with Wesley—this is one important mark of this tradition.

A tradition cannot be identified simply with what is traditional, with what has been and is now immutably set. Tradition is alive; it lives out of the past and toward the future. Tradition is not only a conveyance of the past; it is also, given its character, a turning to what is new in history. The ethos of a particular historical stream is projected from the past, but it is kept vital by the pull of the Spirit, which stands beyond and draws the movement toward a providential end. The Wesleyan tradition is most true to its character when it is open and responsive to both its past and its future. Always there is struggle for the conservation of value and for the creation of new meaning; and it is through the tautness of this tension that the past is honored and the future welcomed.

The eminent New Testament scholar Englishman C. K. Barrett has put the essence of this truth in a striking way. He mentions the work of Helmut Flender, who claims "that just as Paul, in faithfulness, not unfaithfulness, to Jesus, had in a new generation to say things that Jesus had not said, so Luke in a third generation, had, in faithfulness to Paul, to say things Paul had not said."[2] New interpretation for a new generation may be an act of faithfulness to be viewed positively. The input of John Wesley into this tradition has acted not so much to force a return to himself as to be a constant re-presenting of his spirit and a continued movement outward in missional fidelity.

The fact that Methodist theological distinctiveness is elusive may itself be an important characteristic. For the

261

Wesleyan tradition, from the beginning, has been ecumeni-
cally open and generously inclusive. The developing
movement continually escaped neat categorization and
simple identification; it has been known by its process of
change and development. But within this broad stream, can
enduring characteristics be identified?

Center and Circumference

Methodism, as a historical community of faith, is
consciously aware of itself as a part of the larger Christian
tradition. This ecumenical consciousness became prominent
in Wesley's later years, and it has continued to be
characteristic of Methodist self-understanding. A sense of
broad inheritance has been more prominent than a desire for
narrow self-definition.

In every tradition, however, there are commitments that
stand at the center of corporate awareness, and others that,
although important, are peripheral. Focal and peripheral
commitments need one another and live only in relation to
one another. There is dynamic interaction as peripheral
awareness is utilized to attend to focal interests, and as focal
interest organizes peripheral areas.

If our reading of the tradition is correct, then the theology
of the Wesleyan movement has been an extended consideration of the grace of God as expressed in Jesus Christ. This
theme has constituted the pivot point of this theological
tradition and, over time, has functioned as a creative center.
The tradition has been formed, not by continuous conformity, but by acknowledgment of grace as the criterion for
judging theological value. There have been, as our survey
reveals, distortions as well as faithful emphases, but all these
may be judged and interpreted as they relate to the normative
fact of God's gracious love in Jesus Christ. Sir Herbert
Butterfield, a distinguished British Methodist historian,

captured the unique status of this affirmation in his tradition as he concluded his study of *Christianity and History.*

> I have nothing to say at the finish except that if one wants a permanent rock in life and goes deep enough for it, it is difficult for historical events to shake it. There are times when we can never meet the future with sufficient elasticity of mind, especially if we are locked in the contemporary systems of thought. We can do worse than remember a principle which both gives us a firm Rock and leaves us the maximum elasticity for our minds: the principle: Hold to Christ, and for the rest be totally uncommitted.[3]

Around this point—the grace of God in Jesus Christ—several attendant commitments form a tight nexus: biblical witness to Jesus Christ, vital experience of God in Christ as Savior and Sanctifier, commitment to human freedom and ethical discipleship, and the shaping of church life around missional responsibility. Together these themes constitute the nucleus of the Wesleyan tradition, and around these determinate marks of character, the more extended life of the tradition has taken shape and has been contoured into its distinctive forms. On the periphery are particular historical, cultural, intellectual, or social formations of this essential core. There have been a number of variations on these themes, at times almost overwhelming or distorting, and at other times sustaining, reinforcing, and creatively restating the themes.

For instance, grace may be taken as an open notion, subject to a variety of interpretations. Hence, while Wesley consistently explained its meaning in christological terms, the tradition has given expression to a range of alternatives. For some (Whedon and Bledsoe), grace is focally expressed in the constitution of human personhood; for others (Knudson and Tillett), it is grounded in God's immanental presence. For some (Cobb and Ogden), grace refers to God's creation;

for others (Outler and Cushman), it retains specificity of reference to Jesus Christ. But in all the options, grace must be attended to and explicated. Through commitment to this central theme, the tradition becomes self-critical and provides a common point for exchange as to the adequacy of variant interpretations.

Biblical Witness to Jesus Christ

Wesleyan theology has understood itself as to be built upon a biblical base. Hence John Wesley's sermons and his *Notes on the New Testament* constitute the theological foundation of the movement. Wesley set the pattern for such commitment. He was acquisitive in his use of the best available resources for interpreting the New Testament and drew from a wide range of perspectives to aid his exposition. Wesley's own interpretation, however, was never assumed to be final. In this, as in other areas, his work mediates more ultimate reality; he continuously pointed beyond himself to that which is primary. And Wesleyan theology has characteristically adopted this attitude. With Wesley, it has assumed that the meaning of Scripture is not entirely self-evident or the text completely self-interpreting; Scripture must be interpreted, and therefore it stands in relation to tradition, reason, and experience, and to the ever-shifting perspectives of the interpreters themselves. Underlying all valid interpretations of Scripture is the guidance of the Holy Spirit. The internal witness of the Holy Spirit is the foundation upon which the authority of the Bible is built. Commitment to the biblical witness is basic, but the best resources must be utilized in the interpretive process, so that individual interpretation, while encouraged, remains subject to correction and enhancement by the inclusive and ongoing Christian community.

Acknowledgment of biblical authority has remained a

prominent characteristic of Wesleyan thought. This is not to be taken in the negative sense of an authority externally imposed, an arbitrary governor. Rather, Scripture is authoritative as a vital power that organizes, shapes, and releases life. In a strict sense, only God in Christ is authoritative for Christian community and Christian life, but the Bible is important as the mediator of Christ to the community of faith, and as the bearer of the correcting and projecting power of God within that community. Adequate exposition always requires the internal witness of the Holy Spirit, and this emphasis has prevented bibliolatry. The dialectical relation between the central mystery of God in Christ and its various legitimate theological interpretations is acknowledged and affirmed in the Wesleyan tradition. This understanding of biblical authority has kept the variety of interpretations, which has expanded over more than two centuries, open to change, new understandings, and fresh expressions of its authoritative norm.

To say that the Wesleyan tradition has been scripturally oriented is not to indicate a static condition; rather, precisely because it is biblically based, the tradition has been affected as biblical interpretation has changed. Commitment to the biblical message has varied as presuppositions about and exposition of that message have shifted. There is no single or final interpretation of the Bible; what has held firm for most theologians has been the awareness of the primacy of the biblical message as it has witnessed to Jesus Christ. And this commitment has characterized the Wesleyan tradition.

Vital Experience of God

Participation in the life of God is a vital reality, and it has been characteristic of the Wesleyan tradition to place emphasis upon Christian experience. Being "in Christ" is primary; theological explication consists of reflection upon this reality, its source, its meaning, and its implications. Both the experience and its interpretations are guided by the witness of the Holy Spirit. Consequently, Wesleyan theology has maintained both a fixed point of reference and an openness to new understanding.

John Wesley believed that evangelical experience is crucial as evidence of actualized relationship with God. For Wesley, experience was a medium, not a source of faith. Christian experience is experience of Jesus Christ, and Jesus Christ is made alive by the Holy Spirit's vitalizing of the Word of God. Hence, the theological task is to interpret actual experience of God against the biblical background, and in light of the long historical company of witnesses who have interpreted their experience against this same Scripture.

In the developing tradition, the role of experience has been variously regarded. As the issue of personhood moved to center stage in late nineteenth-century North America, experience came to be the subject of primary interpretation and was viewed as a source of theological knowledge. This was true of Bowne and the personalist tradition. Predicated upon the immanental presence of God, religious experience, as the general and immediate awareness of God, became the source of the knowledge of God; and to this natural experience were added distinctive Christian motifs. Interpretation of religious experience depended upon prior assumptions about human nature and its possibility for a positive relationship with God. Even when these understandings were challenged—for instance, by Edwin Lewis and Robert E. Cushman—the issue of experience remained the focus of philosophical and theological interest.

The role of experience continues to be emphasized in the Wesleyan tradition; but it has recently taken on more corporate and ethical dimensions. Many contemporary theologians believe experience not to be adequately interpreted in exclusively individualistic ways or in terms of emotional intensity. Christian experience of God projects into community with the neighbor. Hence Geoffrey Wainwright takes worship as the foundation for his systematic theology, and liberation theologians insist upon a more corporate sense of personhood. Tradition itself is a corporate transmission and emphasizes the inclusive character of the mediation of God and continuing faithfulness.

Ethical Expression

Another enduring characteristic of Wesleyan theology has been ethical commitment: Holy living carried moral responsibility. John Wesley, represented this type of discipleship. He insisted that salvation is ethical throughout and that redemption is a present reality as well as a future hope; that salvation involves the whole life of people and that redemption is realized in community.

Several themes have persisted since Wesley's time. There has been a general sensitivity to the corporate bonding of life and an increased awareness of the systemic character of sin. Practical religious activity has served the kingdom of God, a kingdom envisioned as being significantly realized in the concrete conditions of life. Wesleyanism has not thought of the kingdom in exclusively spiritual terms or as being realized only within the Church. The kingdom is found within the actual life of the world, and it is to be served in the arena of concrete history.

To say that ethical expression has been characteristic of this movement is not to imply that the Wesleyan tradition has maintained a single understanding of ethical application. Both conservative and radical social stances have been expressed in different cultures and also within the same culture. Variety and even conflict were typical of nineteenth-century Wesleyans; and in the twentieth century the same differences continue, although there has been an increased sense of the practical application of Christian faith to the economic, political, and social conditions of life.

Indeed, it may be claimed that so much emphasis has been given to the ethical mandates of new life in Christ that it has been difficult to keep these interests in dialogue with theological underpinnings. In the twentieth century, the Wesleyan tradition has been, on the whole, more concerned with changing the world than with interpreting it, or even with interpreting the reasons for the changes it has sought. But a tension has remained—moral commitment and theological critique move in and out of relationship with each other. Theology can become speculative, and ethics merely pragmatic; yet at times, each does meet and challenge the other. The development of liberation theology as a major thrust of the Wesleyan tradition is a concrete indication of positive interaction between theory and practice, expressing an important commitment of this tradition.

Church as Mission

A prime purpose of Wesleyan theology has been to share the good news and the new life to which the Christian tradition witnesses. The tradition, therefore, must be interpreted in these terms, also. Methodism finds Christian unity in mission, and its theology has underwritten this missional activity. John Wesley was clear—there is no one organizational pattern for the church, no single prescription in the New Testament for structuring Christian community. For Wesley, structure was dictated by mission—form followed function. Martin Schmidt has argued that John Wesley was the first theologian in church history to understand that the Church must be interpreted as mission.[4] The Church is in mission, and as it fulfills its apostolic responsibility to preach the gospel—through word and life—it finds its mode of being in the world.

As related to mission, church polity is subordinate, but crucial; the structure of a church enhances the fulfillment of its mission. "Polity is the form of our obedience."[5] A particular polity is not essential, but organization does contribute to the well-being of a church. To be uncritical of polity is to misunderstand its subordinate role to mission; to treat polity lightly is to misunderstand its critical importance for mission.

Mission implies a theological base. Mission for what? To whom? To share what message? Here the theme of grace once again becomes central, for theology and ethics reflect the source and motivation for mission. It is the impartation of the grace of God that is the task of Wesleyan preaching and service, and this sense of mission has kept the tradition vital and developing.

The Wesleyan tradition has been aware of itself as a witness, pointing to an ecumenical past and an ecumenical future. At its best, it has known that "heritages are for sharing."[6] Wesleyan Christianity embodies a charitable spirit that acknowledges the validity of other Christian expressions and the authenticity of other Christian communities. The task of mission draws Christians together for worship and service. Wesley's "Catholic Spirit" not only named a sermon but indicated an embracing intention.

A Living Tradition

This survey of the Wesleyan theological tradition has described distinctive characteristics of the movement. Yet the future of the tradition is not clear. As witnessed by the theological movements in the last several decades, there has been an evident tension between the increased interest in the Wesleyan tradition among some theologians and a concurrently diminished consciousness of identification among others. As a consequence, basic questions have been raised:

Has the Wesleyan tradition already made its contribution? Has the time come for the tradition to be dispersed into the broader Christian stream? Or in contrast: Is there significant reason for the tradition to continue? Is there a role within Christian ecumenism for a continuing Wesleyan tradition?

The tradition may be viewed as having already made the contribution of which it is capable. This might be said with appropriate pride in the rich deposit left by the tradition: emphasis upon the grace of God and biblical authority, moral understanding of God and human beings, enhancement of Christian experience as conversion and growth, and ecumenical commitment. These are characteristics of positive value and have been adequately fulfilled. The tradition, it may be argued, has made its mark, has achieved its possibilities, and it should now, with gratitude and dignity, set aside its special interests and thoroughly identify with ecumenical Christianity.

Further, it may be argued, there is no value in continuing a tradition only to perpetuate its life. Indeed, there is a pernicious idolatry in sustaining an organizational form only in the interest of self-preservation. As the vitality of purpose within a movement declines, there is often an aggressive effort to reinforce the organizational structure that earlier served its dynamic life. A developed church order may be confused with the initiating and ultimate cause it was intended to serve; and by subtle shift, structure may be perpetuated in the name of the cause. If the Wesleyan tradition no longer possesses a distinctive contribution and no longer enriches total Christian witness and life, then this tradition and its ecclesiastical structures have no reason to continue.

These arguments represent a possible response, even as it is recognized that the Wesleyan tradition, because of its geographical diversity and varying historical developments, its ecclesiastical formations are at such differing junctures that decisions about continuance are difficult. Contexts vary, and what may be appropriate for one Methodist body may not be appropriate for others. In different settings, answers to continued distinctive contribution may differ. But on the whole, the issue must be pressed: Is there a role within catholic Christianity for a continuing Wesleyan tradition?

It is possible to draw a positive conclusion. The Wesleyan tradition remains vital. It possesses sufficient life to continue in its own right and it also possesses life to contribute to creative ecumenical witness and structures. The present situation of the Wesleyan tradition—and perhaps of every authentic tradition within Christendom—is one that calls for a dual affirmation of both its specific history and the inclusive history of the Christian Church. This dialectical interaction requires both a yes and a no to its particular history and a yes and a no to catholic history. Each of these histories—the more narrow and the broader—should stand as contributor to and critic of the other. In conscious and critical ways, the Wesleyan tradition needs to value itself properly while also appropriately evaluating other Christian traditions.

The Wesleyan tradition is false to itself when it becomes parochial, and it is false to itself when it does not allow its own history to function as a critical guide for self-evaluation and for assessment of its contribution to inclusive Christianity. Only clarity about who it is can adequately inform what it ought to be. There must be both commitment and openness, an appreciation of life received and of life to be given. Either to forget its heritage or to hold narrowly to its own distinctiveness may contribute to a diminution in the life of ecumenical Christianity.

The Wesleyan tradition now stands at a critical juncture as its past meets its future. Those within this tradition need to understand and honor its history; and they need to be aware that Wesleyanism constantly reaches beyond itself in shared Christian life and mission. Such an attitude promises practical implications for worship, mission, and ecclesiastical structure. And these implications must be decided upon by those who know themselves to be both Wesleyan and members of the total Body of Christ.

Living streams continuously flow over the terrain of history, sometimes as meandering flat-water, at other times gushing rapidly through newfound downfalls, usually to merge with larger bodies of water. So do living traditions, and so does the Wesleyan theological stream.

With persistent conveyance of original gift, with an adventurous spirit of exploration, and with an open embrace of new additions, this tradition continues alive and life-giving. Its past has left its mark in personal life and social structure. Its present is achieving new configurations. Its promise is in creative response to new challenge. Faithfulness and openness have been and must be the sinews of its strength.

NOTES

Chapter 1—A Living Tradition

1. John Wesley, *The Journal of the Reverend John Wesley*, ed. Nehemiah Curnock, 8 vols. (London: R. Cully, 1909-1916), vol. 1, pp. 475-76 (hereafter cited as *Journal*, with date).
2. Quoted in M. R. Brailsford, *The Tale of Two Brothers* (New York: Oxford University Press, 1954), p. 48.
3. S. Baring-Gould, *The Evangelical Revival* (London: Methuen & Co., 1920), p. 114.
4. Frank Baker, *A Charge to Keep* (London: Epworth Press, 1947), p. 26.
5. David Thomson, *England in the Nineteenth Century, 1815–1914* (Middlesex, England: Penguin Books, 1950), p. 12.
6. Butterfield, "England in the Eighteenth Century," in *A History of the Methodist Church in Great Britain*, ed. Rupert E. Davies and Gordon Rupp (London: Epworth Press, 1965), vol. 1, p. 29.
7. The relation of the Methodist movement to the changing social order has been sharply debated. Historians have, at times, argued that Wesley and his followers were basically conservatives, and even reactionary, and that they resisted the imposed changes. From this perspective the Wesleyans helped to maintain the status quo and prevented a more radical social transformation, see esp. E. P. Thompson, *Making of the English Working Class* (New York: Pantheon Books, 1964) and H. E. Hobshawm, *Labouring Men: Studies in the History of Labour* (New York: Basic Books, 1964). Other historians, taking a contrary point of view, have stressed that Wesley and those who joined him were effective in bringing about a significant revolution in British social order, see Elie Halévy, *England in 1815* (London: E. Benn, 1949) and Bernard Semmel,

The Methodist Revolution (New York: Basic Books, 1973). The most focused discussion of this issue is found in Semmel's introductory ch. to Halévy, *The Birth of Methodism in England* (Chicago: University of Chicago Press, 1971). See also Howard A. Snyder, *The Radical Wesley and Patterns for Church Renewal* (Downers Grove, Ill.: Intervarsity Press, 1981).

8. Cell, *The Rediscovery of John Wesley* (New York: Henry Holt & Co., 1935), p. 1.

9. Reprinted as an appendix in Thomas Jackson, *The Life of the Reverend Charles Wesley* (London: John Mason, 1841), vol. 2, pp. 500-34.

10. Outler, "The Place of Wesley in the Christian Tradition," in *The Place of John Wesley in the Christian Tradition*, ed. Kenneth E. Rowe (Metuchen, N.J.: Scarecrow Press, 1976), p. 22.

11. *Ibid.*, p. 27.

12. *Ibid.* See also Jean Orcibal, "The Originality of John Wesley and Continental Spirituality," in *History of the Methodist Church in Great Britain*, ed. Davies and Rupp, vol. 1.

13. The most recent and helpful survey of Wesley scholarship is Frank Baker, "Unfolding John Wesley: A Survey of Twenty Years' Studies in Wesley's Thought," *Quarterly Review* 1/1 (Fall 1980): 44-58. To move beyond Wesley in an attempt to survey his ensuing tradition involves risk. John Henry Newman, *An Essay on the Development of Christian Doctrine* (London: James Toovey, 1845), p. 39, provides a sober word of caution: "I conclude with an example: No one but will allow that Wesleyanism represents an idea, a doctrine, system, and polity; no one but will connect it with the well-known divine and preacher whose name it bears. Yet, when we look back upon its course during the hundred years since it commenced, how many are the changes and vicissitudes through which the man is connected with his work! So much so that it is a most difficult task, and one which perhaps must be reserved for a later age, duly to review its history—to say what really belongs and what is foreign to it, to find a key for the whole and a clue for the succession of its parts. The event alone still future, which will bring its completion, will also bring its interpretation."

Chapter 2—Scriptural Christianity

1. *Journal*, May 11, 1739. On scriptural inspiration, Wesley wrote: "The Spirit of God not only once inspired those who wrote, but continually inspires, supernaturally assists, those that read it with earnest prayer" (*Explanatory Notes upon the New Testament*, II Timothy 3:16).

2. George Croft Cell, in his study *The Rediscovery of John Wesley* (New York: Henry Holt & Co., 1935), considers experience the central category of Wesley's theology, even asserting that biblical witness must be judged by experience, see esp. pp. 5-6, 72, 87, 135, 168. Cell enriches the study of Wesley and releases him from some of his previous interpreters. But Cell is unaware of the manner in which his own interpretation is controlled by the issue that was paramount at his time. In the final analysis, Cell overstates the role of experience, which was a medium for, not a source of theology for Wesley.

3. John Wesley, *The Works of John Wesley*, ed. Thomas Jackson, Vols. 5, 6, 7 (London: Wesleyan Methodist Book Room, 1879), "Justification by Faith," "Righteousness of Faith" (hereafter cited as *Sermons*, with sermon title); also see Gerald R. Cragg, ed., *The Appeals to Men of Reason and Religion* (New York: Oxford University Press, 1978), p. 107.

4. *Sermons*, "Salvation by Faith," part iii.

5. *Ibid*. "Our Church," of course refers to the Church of England, and the words in italics are taken from that church's Homilies, see next note.

6. *Journal*, November 12, 1738. The work he "printed for the use of others" is *The Doctrine of Salvation, Faith, and Good Works, Extracted from the Homilies of the Church of England*, 1736.

7. *Sermons*, "Salvation by Faith," part ii, sec. 7.

8. *Sermons*, "Justification by Faith," part ii, sec. 5.

9. Wesley, "Genesis 2:27," sermon, holograph manuscript, The Methodist Archives and Research Centre, London.

10. He expresses this understanding in his prayers in a direct manner, see "Forms of Prayer," in Wesley, *Works*, vol. 11, pp. 208, 219 (hereafter cited as *Works*, with vol. and p.). See also *Sermons*, "The New Birth," part i, sec. 1-4.

11. *Sermons*, "Justification by Faith," part iv, sec. 5.

12. *Ibid*. See also Cragg, *Appeals to Men of Reason*, p. 46.

13. *Sermons*, "Justification by Faith," part iv, sec. 2.

14. John Deschner makes this point in *Wesley's Christology* (Dallas: Southern Methodist University Press, 1960), p. 185.

15. *Sermons*, "Working Out Our Own Salvation," part iii, sec. 4.

16. *Works*, "On Predestination Calmly Considered," vol. 10, pp. 229-30.

17. See Rupert E. Davies, "The People Called Methodist: 'Our Doctrines,' " in *History of Methodist Church in Great Britain*, ed. Davies and Rupp, p. 158. For the most direct statement of this position, see Umphrey Lee, *John Wesley and Modern Religion* (Nashville/New York: Cokesbury Press, 1936), p. 110.

18. See William R. Cannon, *The Theology of John Wesley* (New York: Abingdon Press, 1946), p. 113; Harald Lindström, *Wesley and Sanctifiation* (Stockholm: Nya Bokförlags Aktiebolaget/London:Epworth Press, 1946), p. 46; Colin Williams, *John Wesley's Theology Today* (Nashville/New York: Abingdon Press, 1960), pp. 42-43.

19. See Robert E. Cushman, "Salvation for All," in *Methodism*, ed. William Anderson (Nashville/New York: Abingdon/Cokesbury Press, 1947), esp. pp. 105-11.

20. *Works*, "Minutes of Some Late Conversations," vol. 8, p. 276. Wesley mentions other passages to corroborate this teaching: Ephesians 4:32; II Corinthians 8:5; Hebrews 8:10; I John 4:10.

21. *Works*, "Letters to His Brother Samuel," vol. 12, pp. 30, 36.

22. *Sermons*, "On Faith," part i, sec. 11.

23. *Works*, "Letter to Mr. Richard Thompson," vol. 12, p. 468.

24. *Works*, "Letters to Mr. John Smith," vol. 12, pp. 67, 97.

25. *Works*, "Minutes of Some Late Conversations," vol. 8, p. 290.

26. *Works*, "Letter to Mr. Richard Thompson," vol. 12, p. 468.

27. Wesley, *The Letters of the Reverend John Wesley*, ed. John Telford, 8 vols. (London: Epworth Press, 1931), vol. 3, pp. 120-21.

28. On Christian perfection, see *Sermons*, "The Circumcision of the Heart";
Works, "A Plain Account of Christian Perfection," vol. 11, pp. 366-446.
29. *Sermons*, "Justification by Faith," part. ii.
30. Cell, *Rediscovery of Wesley*, p. 361.
31. Albert C. Outler, *Theology in the Wesleyan Spirit* (Nashville: Tidings, 1975), pp. 81–88.
32. Cragg, *Appeals to Men of Reason*, pp. 77-78.
33. On Wesley's understanding of the church, see Williams, *Wesley's Theology Today*, pp. 152-53.
34. He also makes this distinction in his sermon "The Ministerial Office."
35. See Williams, *Wesley's Theology Today*, pp. 147-48.
36. *Sermons*, "The New Birth," part. ii, sec. 5. See also *Sermons*, "On Working Out Our Own Salvation."
37. *Works*, "Treatise on Baptism," vol. 10, pp. 190, 191, 193, 198.
38. *Sermons*, "Marks of the New Birth," part. iv, sec. 2. See also Lindström, *Wesley and Sanctification*, p. 107. Ole E. Borgen notes that "Wesley, in the *Treatise on Baptism*, changes Samuel Wesley's 'damning guilt,' to plain 'guilt.' He omits from his version of the Articles the whole section where it is affirmed that 'in every person born into this world, it deserveth God's wrath and damnation.' Instead he writes, 'and none ever was or can be a loser but *by his own choice*' " (*John Wesley on the Sacraments* [Nashville/New York: Abingdon Press, 1972], p. 124).
39. See G. Osborn, ed., *The Poetical Works of John and Charles Wesley* (London: Wesleyan Methodist Conference Office, 1896), vol. 1, p. 186.

Chapter 3—Interpreters and Successors

1. Pope, *The Wesley Memorial Volume*, ed. J. O. A. Clarke (New York: Phillips & Hunt, 1881), p. 171.
2. These comments on Fletcher are taken from W. A. Sangster, "Called to be Saints," *Proceedings of the Ninth World Methodist Conference* (Nashville: Methodist Publishing House, 1956), p. 363.
3. Cf. respectively J. A. Dorner, *History of Protestant Theology* (Edinburgh: T. & T. Clark, 1871), vol. 2, p. 92; C. A. Briggs, *Theological Symbolics* (New York: Charles Scribner's Sons, 1914), p. 327; both quoted in David C. Shipley, "Methodist Arminianism in the Theology of John Fletcher" (Ph.D. diss., Yale University, 1942).
4. See esp. John A. Knight, "John William Fletcher and the Early Methodist Tradition" (Ph.D. diss., Vanderbilt University, 1966). The idea of dispensations also is important for the Holiness movement that developed in the second half of the nineteenth century—esp. Fletcher's reference to Pentecost and his use of the phrase "baptism by the Holy Spirit."
5. Shipley, "Methodist Arminianism," p. 372.
6. Fletcher, "On Reconciliation," *Checks to Antinomianism* (New York: J. Collard, 1837), vol. 2, pp. 333-34.
7. Adam Clarke et al., *An Account of the Infancy, Religious and Literary Life of Adam Clarke, LL.D., F.A.S.*, 3 vols. (New York: B. Waugh & T. Mason, 1833), bk. 1, p. 126.
8. *Ibid.*, bk. 3, p. 61.

9. Clarke, *Discourses on Various Subjects Related to the Being and Attributes of God* (New York: B. Waugh & T. Mason), sermon 21, vol. 3, p. 51.
10. *Ibid.*, sermon 27, vol. 2, p. 252.
11. Clarke et al., *Account of Infancy*, bk. 2, p. 51. The most direct discussion of this issue may be found in his *Commentary*, Luke 1:35.
12. Pope, *Wesley Memorial Volume*, p. 176.
13. Watson, in his *Observations on Southey's Life of Wesley* (Nashville: Publishing House, Methodist Episcopal Church, South, 1820, 1918) defends John Wesley against Southey, but speaks also to other opponents—Bishops Lavington and Warburton, E. B. Pusey, and Isaac Taylor. Of Wesley and John Fletcher's discussions with opponents, he writes, "The doctrines of Justification by faith, assurance of pardon, regeneration, and divine influence, which had been considered by many as necessarily connected with the Calvinistic scheme, were now seen in harmony with the doctrines of God's universal love, the unrestricted extent of Christ's death, and the fullness of Divine grace. Men were no longer compelled into a choice between two extremes, Calvinism and Pelagianism, into which last error most of our English divines had fallen in opposing the doctrine of decrees" (pp. 132-33). Again, the mediating position of the Wesleyan tradition is apparent.
14. Richard Watson, *The Life of The Reverend John Wesley, A.M.* (Nashville: Publishing House of the Methodist Episcopal Church, South, 1831, 1918), p. 185.
15. Watson, *Theological Institutes* (New York: G. Lane & P. P. Sandford, 1843), vol. 1, pp. 44-45; vol. 2, pp. 448, 492.
16. *Ibid.*, vol. 1, p. 335; for "infallible truth," see p. 263.
17. Thomas Jackson, *Memoirs of the Life and Writings of the Reverend Richard Watson* (New York: T. Mason & G. Lane, 1836), p. 474.
18. Watson, *Theological Institutes*, vol. 1, pp. 474, 209, 211.
19. *Ibid.*, vol. 2, pp. 245-46, 248, 497.
20. *Ibid.*, p. 307.
21. *Ibid.*, p. 284.
22. Cf. Robert E. Chiles, *Theological Transition in American Methodism* (Nashville/New York: Abingdon Press, 1965); E. Dale Dunlap, "Methodist Theology in Great Britain in the Nineteenth Century" (Ph.D. diss., Yale University, 1956). Both these interpreters have presented exceptionally good studies but tend to see a falling away from original Wesleyan emphases among his successors, beginning with Watson. I find Watson to be generally faithful in his continuation of Wesley's thought.
23. R. W. Moss, *The Reverend W. B. Pope, D.D.* (London: Robert Culley, n.d.), p. 70.
24. *Ibid.*, p. 38.
25. *Ibid.*, pp. 29-32.
26. Pope, *Wesley Memorial Volume*, pp. 168–90.
27. Pope, *Peculiarities of Methodist Doctrine* (London: Wesleyan Conference Office, 1873), p. 7.
28. Pope, *Wesley Memorial Volume*, p. 171.
29. Moss, *Reverend Pope*, pp. 58-59.

30. *A Compendium of Christian Theology*, 2nd ed., 3 vols. (New York: Phillips & Hunt, n.d.), vol. 1, p. 20.
31. *Ibid.*, vol. 1, p. 3.
32. *Ibid.*, pp. 36, 27, 38, 41, 214.
33. J. G. Mantle, *Hugh Price Hughes* (London: S. W. Partridge & Co., 1902), p. 85.
34. *Ibid.*, pp. 94, 116.
35. Hughes, *Essential Christianity* (New York: Fleming H. Revell Co., 1894), p. 41.
36. Mantle, *Hugh Price Hughes*, p. 154.
37. Hughes, *Ethical Christianity* (London: Simpson Low, Marston & Co., 1892), p. 14.
38. Hughes, *Essential Christianity*, p. 57.
39. *Ibid.*, p. 15.
40. *The Arminian Magazine* (1790), pp. 553-54; also see *Works*, vol. 11, p. 365.
41. Clarke, *Account of Infancy*, vol. 3, pp. 59-60.
42. Jackson, *Memoirs of Richard Watson*, p. 466.
43. I have only recently discovered William Arthur (1819–1901), a significant theologian in the second half of the nineteenth century. A native of Ireland, Arthur was a missionary, a minister in England, missionary secretary, principal of the Methodist College in Belfast, and an author of unusual power. Arthur came upon the scene with his *Tongue of Fire* (1856) which witnessed to the power of the Holy Spirit in Christian life and thought. The book continued to be reprinted for a century and was widely influential in ecumenical circles, especially among Holiness theologians. Written as a tract for the times, the book possessed continuing life because of its comprehensive coverage of the work of the Holy Spirit and its engaging style. For our study, Arthur should be recognized as a Methodist theologian who did engage the intellectual issues of his day. In *God Without Religion* (1886) he challenged the deism of Fitzjames Stephen, and in *Religion Without God* (1888) he challenged the positivism of Frederick Harrison and the agnosticism of Herbert Spencer. These volumes, also written in an energetic style, explore the positions of those antagonists and respond with careful, extended argument. Their direct engagement of the changing intellectual environment reveals a side of Methodist theology different from that of Arthur's contemporary W. B. Pope. For this reason, Arthur's contribution merits extended and appropriate treatment. I am disappointed that I have discovered him too late to set him into the general context and explore the particulars of his argument. It should be noted that Arthur also wrote a number of popular travel books and, in opposition to Roman Catholicism, *The Pope, the Kings, and the People* (1877). For a short biography, see T. Bowman Stephenson, *William Arthur* (New York/Cincinnati: Methodist Book Concern, n.d.).

Chapter 4—Americanization

1. Perry Miller, *The Life of the Mind in America* (New York: Harcourt, Brace, & World, 1965), p. 88 and esp. pp. 12-13.
2. J. Bruce Behney and Paul H. Eller, *The History of the Evangelical United*

Brethren (Nashville: Abingdon Press, 1979), pp. 55, 84, 109, 201. For Otterbein's sermons, see Arthur C. Core, *Philip William Otterbein: Pastor, Ecumenist* (Dayton, Ohio: Board of Publication, EUB Church, 1968), pp. 77-91. Relationship to the Methodist Episcopal Church, especially that of the United Brethren, is taken for granted and described well in Abel Stevens, *A Compendious History of American Methodism* (New York: Nelson & Phillips, 1867). Stevens writes with a fine literary style and remains a source of great value.

3. Sydney E. Ahlstrom, *A Religious History of the American People* (New York: Yale University Press, 1972), vol. 1, p. 532.

4. Shinn, *An Essay on The Plan of Salvation*, 2nd ed. (Cincinnati: J. H. Wood, ca. 1813, 1831), p. 230.

5. *Ibid.*, p. 251.

6. See Leland H. Scott, "The Message of Early American Methodism," in *The History of American Methodism*, ed. Emory S. Burke, 3 vols. (Nashville/New York: Abingdon Press, 1964), vol. 1, p. 341. Also see E. Brooks Holifield, *The Gentlemen Theologians* (Durham, N.C.: Duke University Press, 1978), pp. 193-94.

7. Perry Miller, *The New England Mind* (Cambridge: Harvard University Press, 1939), vol. 1, pp. 365-97.

8. Hopkins, *The System of Doctrines* (Boston: Thomas & Andrews, 1973), vol. 1, pp. 367, 531. On the development from Edwards through Hopkins and into the next century, see Frank Hugh Foster, *A Genetic History of the New England Theology* (New York: Russell & Russell, 1907, 1963).

9. Nathaniel Taylor, *The Christian Spectator* 7 (March 1835): 76-89; (December 1835):591-97. On Taylor, see H. Shelton Smith, *Changing Conceptions of Original Sin* (New York: Charles Scribner's Sons, 1955), pp. 86-87.

10. It is important to note, remembering Shinn, that in 1822 Bangs reprinted for sale the complete works of Thomas Reid, the father of Scottish common-sense philosophy. This philosophy constituted a common ground for nineteenth-century North American theology.

11. Bangs, *The Errors of Hopkinsianism* (New York: Privately published, 1815), pp. vii, 78-79, quoted in Scott, "Message of Methodism," p. 348.

12. Scott, "Message of Methodism," p. 351, gives this synopsis.

13. Wilbur Fisk, *Calvinistic Controversy* (New York: Mason & Lane, 1835), p. 95.

14. See Scott, "Message of Methodism," p. 354.

15. *Ibid.*; cf. esp. Fisk, *Calvinistic Controversy*, pp. 159-60.

16. Fisk, *Calvinistic Controversy*, p. 206. Fisk especially sees the range of Calvinistic positions as setting different challenges. On this issue, see also R. S. Foster, *Objections to Calvinism* (Cincinnati: Privately published, 1849; Swormstedt & Poe, 1856).

17. In 1839 Amos Binney's *Theological Compend*, intended for the instruction of youth, quickly struck its mark. In the ensuing 35 years, 35,000 copies were printed, and it was translated into German, Swedish, Arabic, Chinese, and other languages. The intention of the book was to counter false doctrines. The *Compend* was revised in 1874 by Binney's son-in-law Daniel Steele (New York: Easton & Mains) and in 1885 by Thomas O.

Summers (Nashville: Southern Methodist Publishing House). The book begins with a declaration of the unique revelation of God, then fills out its content with the natural and moral attributes of God, Christology, and pneumatology. Binney also discusses angels, the devil, humankind, atonement, justification, regeneration, sanctification, and last things. His final sections are on moral duties and the institutions of Christianity. The book is in outline form, with short statements and biblical texts.

Daniel Steele (1824–1914) was to become a professor of theology at Boston University and the first president of Syracuse University. He continued his father-in-law's basic position; in 1870 he experienced sanctification and thereafter taught Christian perfection as a central and vital doctrine. The work of Binney and Steele became influential in the Holiness movement, see Steele's *Mile-Stone Papers: Doctrinal, Ethical, and Experimental on Christian Progress* (New York: Phillips & Hunt, 1881).

18. Hudson, "The Methodist Age in America," *Methodist History* 12/3 (April 1974): 3-15, see esp. pp. 4, 13-15.

19. H. Shelton Smith, *In His Image, But . . .* (Durham, N.C.: Duke University Press, 1972), pp. 46, 94. On the issue of slavery and its role in American Christianity see H. Shelton Smith, Robert T. Handy, and Lefferts A. Loetscher, eds., *American Christianity: An Historical Interpretation with Representative Documents*, Vol. 2, *1820–1960* (New York: Charles Scribner's Sons, 1963), pp. 167-79.

20. Grant Shockley, "The AME and the AMEZion Churches," in *History of American Methodism*, ed. Bucke, vol. 2, p. 526.

21. *Zion's Herald* (Boston), extra ed., February 4, 1935. Sunderland wrote the document. For a full account, see Ira Ford McLeister and Roy Stephen Nicholson, *Conscience and Commitment: The History of the Wesleyan Methodist Church in America*, ed. Lee M. Haines, Jr., and Melvin E. Dieter, 4th rev. ed. (Marion, Ind.: Wesley Press, 1976), esp. chs. 4, 5.

22. Smith, *In His Image, But . . .* , p. 107.

23. Walter W. Benjamin, "The Methodist Episcopal Church in the Postwar Era," in *History of American Methodism*, ed. Bucke, vol. 2, pp. 355-56.

24. Charles R. Thrift, Jr., "Rebuilding the Southern Church," in *History of American Methodism*, ed. Bucke, vol. 2, p. 280.

25. Cf. Timothy L. Smith, *Revivalism and Social Reform* (Nashville/New York: Abingdon Press, 1957), p. 115.

26. Phoebe Palmer, *The Way of Holiness and Notes by the Way* (New York: Lane & Scott, 1851).

27. *Ibid.*, pp. 20, 34, 37.

28. *Ibid.*, p. 65.

29. Nathan Bangs, *The Present State and Prospects, and Responsibilities of the Methodist Episcopal Church* (New York: Lane & Scott, 1850), pp. 58–59.

30. Cf. Abel Stevens, *Life and Times of Nathan Bangs, D. D.* (New York: Carlton & Foster, 1863), pp. 395-402.

31. Foster, *Christian Purity*, 2nd ed. (New York: Eaton & Mains, 1869, 1897), pp. 11-12, 54-56.

32. *Ibid.*, p. 206.

33. For biographies, see Stevens, *Life of Bangs, D. D.*, and A. H. Tuttle,

Nathan Bangs (New York: Eaton & Mains/Cincinnati: Jennings & Graham, 1909).

Chapter 5—Dimensions of Being Human

1. The broader context of the era is significant for understanding this development in episcopal Methodism. These writers were reacting against a prevailing intellectual conviction expressed by José Ortega y Gasset, the Spanish philosopher: "Life is reduced to mere matter, physiology to mechanics. The human organism, which seemed an independent unit, capable of acting by itself, is placed in its physical environment like a figure in a tapestry. It is no longer the organism that moves but the environment that is moving through it. Our actions are no more than reactions. There is no freedom, no originality *(Meditations on Quixote,* trans. Evelyn Rugg and Diego Marín [New York: W. W. Norton & Co., 1961], p. 51). On Bledsoe, see E. Brooks Holifield, *The Gentlemen Theologians* (Durham, N.C.: Duke University Press, 1978), pp. 199-202. The development of the discussion of freedom of the will in eighteenth- and nineteenth-century North American theology is thoroughly discussed by Frank Hugh Foster, *A Genetic History of the New England Theology* (New York: Russell & Russell, 1907, 1963), ch. 9. For a response to Bledsoe, see J.S.R. Clarke, *Methodist Quarterly Review* 9 (1855).
2. Whedon, *The Freedom of the Will* (New York: Carlton & Porter, 1864), p. 4.
3. Whedon, *Essays, Reviews and Discourses* (New York: Phillips & Hunt, 1887), p. 110.
4. *Ibid.*
5. *Ibid.*, pp. 109-46.
6. Curry, "A New Orthodoxy," *Methodist Quarterly Review* 68 (1886): 445-54.
7. On this topic and the era in general, see Holifield, *Gentlemen Theologians,* esp. ch. 4; George M. Marsden, *Fundamentalism and American Culture* (New York: Oxford University Press, 1980); William R. Hutchison, *The Modernist Impulse in American Protestantism* (Cambridge: Harvard University Press, 1976).
8. Summers, *Systematic Theology,* ed. J. J. Tigert, 2 vols. (Nashville: Methodist Episcopal Church, South, Publishing House, 1888).
9. Miley, *Systematic Theology,* 2 vols. (New York: Hunt & Easton, 1893). On Miley, see Robert E. Chiles, *Theological Transition in American Methodism 1790–1935* (Nashville/New York: Abingdon Press, 1965); Conrad Cherry, "The Theology of John Miley," *The Drew Gateway* 33/2 (Winter 1963): 71-81.
10. Miley, *Systematic Theology,* vol. 2, pp. 481-89, append. 1.
11. Chiles, *Theological Transition,* p. 60.
12. James W. Hood, *Sketch of the Early History of the African Methodist Episcopal Zion Church* (Charlotte, N.C.: AMEZ Publishing House, 1914), p. 61.
13. See David Henry Bradley, *A History of the A.M.E. Zion Church,* Part II (Nashville/New York: Abingdon Press, 1970), pp. 475-79.
14. Daniel Alexander Payne, *Recollections of Seventy Years* (New York: Arno Press & The New York Times, 1968), intro., p. 1.
15. *Ibid.*, pp. 34, 355.

16. Payne, *Sermons and Addresses 1853–1891* (New York: Arno Press, 1972); see also Charles Denmore Killian, "Bishop Daniel A. Payne: Black Spokesman for Reform" (Ph.D. diss., University of Indiana, 1971).
17. Payne, *Recollections*, p. 174.
18. Payne, "Document: Bishop Daniel Alexander Payne's Protestation of American Slavery," *Journal of Negro History* 3 (January 1967): 60.
19. Cf. Payne, "God," in *Religion in America*, ed. Charles Killian (New York: Arno Press, 1972), p. 3; see also Henry J. Young, *Major Black Religious Leaders, 1755–1940* (Nashville: Abingdon Press, 1977), pp. 61-72.
20. Payne, "Document," p. 60.
21. Payne, *Recollections*, p. 28, quoted in Young, *Major Leaders 1755–1940*, p. 143.
22. Bowne, *The Immanence of God* (New York: Houghton Mifflin Co., 1905), preface.
23. McConnell, *Borden Parker Bowne* (Nashville/New York: Cokesbury Press, 1929), pp. 13-14. In interpreting Bowne, it is of value to follow his own utilization of his philosophical position for the construction of theological interpretation. Of special importance is Bowne's *Atonement* (Cincinnati: Jennings & Pye/New York: Eaton & Mains, 1900). In this clear and succinct statement, Bowne evidences his understanding of theological language as metaphorical and relative, rather than exact, in speaking of divine reality (which always transcends human ability to comprehend or express its mystery) (pp. 6-11); the primacy of grace (pp. 124-25); and moral and developmental themes of God's action and human maturation (pp. 73-74). A further explication of Bowne's thought may be found in his sermons, *The Essence of Religion* (Boston/New York: Houghton Mifflin Co., 1910), see esp. pp. 187-208.
24. A. C.Knudson, *The Philosophy of Personalism* (Boston: Boston University Press, 1927), pp. 433-34.
25. *Ibid.*, p. 87.
26. Paul M. Bassett, "The Fundamentalist Leavening of the Holiness Movement (1914–1940), The Church of the Nazarene: A Case Study," *Wesleyan Theological Journal* 13 (Spring 1978): 67, comments that the principle of the internal witness of the Holy Spirit in biblical interpretation continued as a strong emphasis in Wesleyan theology and served to differentiate between biblical hermeneutics in this tradition and late nineteenth-century Calvinism.
27. Terry, *Biblical Hermeneutics* (New York: Hunt & Eaton, 1893), p. 143. An important document in the history of Methodist biblical interpretation in the United States is William Nast, *The Gospel Records: Their Genuineness, Authenticity, Historic Variety and Inspiration* (Cincinnati: Cranston & Stowe, 1866).
28. Munhall, pamphlet (Chicago: Winona Publishing Co., n.d.), review of Terry, *Methodism and Biblical Criticism* (New York: Eaton & Mains/Cincinnati: Jennings & Graham, 1905), see pp. 5-7, 18.
29. *Ibid.*, p. 1.
30. Sheldon, *Unbelief in the Nineteenth Century* (New York: Eaton & Main, 1907), p. 6.
31. The development of theology in North America was not limited to the United States. One significant leader in Canada also deserves

recognition. Nathaniel Burwash (1839–1918) was a leader in the Methodist Church in Canada, served as president of Victoria Theological College, Toronto, and authored a number of theological works. Sensitive to the rising scientific ethos, he attempted to maintain central ligaments of the Wesleyan tradition and present them to his era. A selection of his works indicates the range of his interest: *John Wesley: Doctrinal Standards*, with intro., analysis, notes (Toronto: W. Briggs, 1881); *A Handbook on the Inductive Studies in Theology* (Toronto: W. Briggs, 1896); *Manual of Christian Theology* (London: Horace Marshall & Sons, 1900). In his introduction to *John Wesley: Doctrinal Standards*, Burwash makes a perceptive comment on Methodist doctrine: The first fifty-two sermons, he says, constitute the standard of preaching; *Notes on the New Testament* constitutes the standard of interpretation; and *Twenty-five Articles* constitutes the standard of unity with the churches of the Reformation (p. xi).

32. Two theologians from the EUB tradition spanned the turn of the century: S. J. Gamertsfelder, professor at the Evangelical Theological Seminary in Napersville, Illinois, and Jonathan Turner Weaver, a bishop of the UB Church. Both identified with the Wesleyan tradition and were open in spirit, ecumenical in awareness, and irenic in temper. Both wrote systematic theologies which were distillations of contemporary theological discussion and intended for the general reader. Gamertsfelder's *Systematic Theology* (Cleveland, Ohio: C. Hauser, 1913) was built upon three themes: "The absolute sovereignty of God, the saviorhood of the Trinity, and the undeniable, yet limited freedom of man" (p. vii). His intention was to present a theology which underwrote the "plan of salvation in the gospel of Jesus Christ" (vii). Weaver edited *Christian Doctrine* (Dayton, Ohio: UB Publishing House, 1889) to fill the gap created by his church's lack of published theology. In 1900 his *Christian Theology* (Dayton, Ohio: UB Publishing House) was published. The subtitle is explanatory: *A Concise and Practical View of the Cardinal Doctrines and Institutions of Christianity*. Weaver's biographer called this "a Gospel for Common People" (H. A. Thompson, *Biography of Jonathan Turner Weaver, D.D.* [Dayton, Ohio: United Brethren Publishing House, 1901], p. 362). Weaver was typical of nineteenth-century rational orthodoxy. He began with a natural theology, supplemented and completed by revelation. He was especially indebted to Miley but gives evidence of eclectic use of sources. He, like Gamertsfelder, was consciously continuing nineteenth-century Methodist theology.

Chapter 6—Holiness Theology

1. Charles Edwin Jones, *A Guide to the Study of the Holiness Movement* (Metuchen, N.J.: Scarecrow Press, 1974), p. xix.
2. For the general movement, see Donald W. Dayton, *Discovering An Evangelical Heritage* (New York: Harper & Row, 1976); Vinson Synan, *The Holiness-Pentecostal Movement in the United States* (Grand Rapids, Mich.: Wm. B. Eerdmans Publishing Co., 1971); Charles Edwin Jones, *Perfectionist Persuasion* (Metuchen, N.J.: Scarecrow Press, 1974). On

Church of the Nazarene, see Timothy L. Smith, *Called Unto Holiness* (Kansas City, Mo.: Nazarene Publishing House, 1962); Charles W. Carter, *The Person and Ministry of the Holy Spirit: A Wesleyan Perspective* (Grand Rapids: Baker Book House, 1974), esp. biblio.

3. Dunlap, "Tuesday Meetings, Camp Meetings, and Cabinet Meetings: A Perspective on the Holiness Movement in the Methodist Church in the United States in the Nineteenth Century," *Methodist History* 13/3 (April 1975): 92-93.

4. *Ibid.*, pp. 98-100. The founding and history of Asbury College and Asbury Theological Seminary illustrate the developing interest and strength of the Holiness movement within episcopal Methodism. In 1890 John Wesley Hughes, a Methodist Episcopal Church, South, minister, established the college as a distinctively Christian institution, with particular emphasis on "free salvation for all and full salvation from all sin" (Howard F. Shipps, *A Short History of Asbury Theological Seminary* [Berne, Ind.: Herald Press, 1963], p. 15). The most distinguished leader of the school and founder of the theological seminary was Henry Clay Morrison (1857–1942). Morrison, in spite of stormy relations with the Methodist Episcopal Church, South, was one of the most representative and influential leaders of the Holiness movement among Methodists. In 1910 he became president of the college, and in 1926 the theological seminary was officially established. The need, he believed, was for a theological school "which could maintain the faith against the inroads of modern liberalism" (p. 23). The charter of the seminary stressed the divine inspiration of the holy Scriptures, the virgin birth, and the mediatorial death and bodily resurrection of Jesus Christ, "placing special emphasis upon the necessity of the regeneration of the individual and entire sanctification subsequent to regeneration" (Percival A. Wesche, *Henry Clay Morrison: Crusader Saint* [Berne, Ind.: Herald Press, 1963], p. 139). These schools, although never official institutions of the church, represent Holiness interests within Methodism. See also Henry Clay Morrison, *Some Chapters of My Life Story* (Louisville, Ky.: Pentecostal Publishing Co., 1941).

5. On Finney, see Timothy L. Smith, "The Doctrine of the Baptism of the Sanctifying Spirit: Charles G. Finney's Synthesis of Wesleyan and Covenant Theology," *Wesleyan Theological Journal* 9 (Spring 1978). On Asa Mahan, see Donald W. Dayton, "Asa Mahan and the Development of American Holiness Theology," *Wesleyan Theological Journal* 9 (Spring 1974).

6. Jones, *Guide to Holiness Movement*, p. xvii, states, "The foundation of the holiness movement is theological." See also Walter W. Benjamin, "The Methodist Episcopal Church in the Postwar Era," in *The History of American Methodism*, ed. Emory S. Bucke, 3 vols. (Nashville/New York: Abingdon Press, 1964), vol. 2, p. 342, for a general statement of causes of separation.

7. Donald W. Dayton, "The Doctrine of the Baptism of the Holy Spirit: Its Emergence and Significance," *Wesleyan Theological Journal* 13 (Spring 1978): 118, 114.

8. *Ibid.*, pp. 116, 119.

9. *Ibid.*, pp. 121-22. There is some uncertainty about the origins of

empowerment language. It may originate in Keswick writing in the late nineteenth century. Grant Wacker has called this to my attention.

10. Dunlap, "Tuesday Meetings," p. 89.

11. See Timothy L. Smith, *Revivalism and Social Reform* (Nashville/New York:Abingdon Press, 1957).

12. Ellyson, *Theological Compend* (Chicago: Christian Witness, 1908).

13. Bassett, "A Study of the Theology of the Early Holiness Movement," *Methodist History* 13/3 (April 1975): 62-63.

14. *Ibid.*, p. 65.

15. A. M. Hills, *Fundamental Christian Theology: A Systematic Theology* (Pasadena, Calif.: C. J. Kinne, 1931), vol. 2, pp. 179-80.

16. Bassett, "Study of Holiness Movement," sets Hills position in contrast to classical Wesleyan thought (pp. 65-71); also see Bassett, "The Interplay of Christology and Ecclesiology in the Theology of the Holiness Movement," *Wesleyan Theological Journal* 16/2 (Fall 1981): 79-94.

17. Bassett, "Study of Holiness Movement," p. 68.

18. H. Orton Wiley, *Christian Theology*, 3 vols. (Kansas City, Mo.: Nazarene Publishing House, 1940), vol. 1, pp. 38, 58. Initially, Wiley was read as being in agreement with Hills. Only recently have the differences—of which Wiley was clearly aware, but which he muted—been recognized. Wiley presents a more thoroughly Wesleyan theology in regard to method and sources. Bassett made this evident in "Interplay of Christology" (p. 81).

19. *Ibid.*, vol. 1, p. 224.

20. *Ibid.*, vol. 2, pp. 47, 137, 138.

21. *Ibid.*, pp. 303, 322-25.

22. *Ibid.*, vol. 3, p. 75.

23. *Ibid.*, p. 127.

24. *Ibid.*, p. 391.

25. Smith, "The Doctrine of the Sanctifying Spirit in John Wesley and John Fletcher," *The Preacher's Magazine* 55/1 (September/October/November 1979): 58.

26. Staples, "The Current Wesleyan Debate on the Baptism with the Holy Spirit," privately circulated paper (March 1979), pp. 10, 16-17. We are following Staples' delineation of the debate. Also see McGonigle, "Pneumatological Nomenclature in Early Methodism," *Wesleyan Theological Journal* (Spring 1973): 61-72.

27. Staples, "Current Wesleyan Debate," p. 19.

28. Bassett has commented that some Methodist theologians such as George Peck, Asbury, Lowry, and J. A. Wood did use this language, although "standard" Methodist theologians such as Pope and Miley did not.

29. Staples, "Current Wesleyan Debate," p. 20.

30. *Ibid.*, p. 27.

31. Wynkoop, *Foundations of Wesleyan–Arminian Theology* (Kansas City, Mo.: Beacon Hill Press, 1967), p. 69.

32. Wynkoop, *A Theology of Love* (Kansas City, Mo.: Beacon Hill Press, 1972), pp. 15, 100, 199-200.

33. *Ibid.*, p. 208. Another Nazarene theologian, John A. Knight, has supported the inclusive notion of holiness: "A theology of holiness must be judged by how it handles this crisis-process issue. A theology of

holiness which is biblical must hold together both these aspects—continuing sanctification and realized sanctification—and reflect this tension in its fundamental doctrines" (*The Holiness Pilgrimage* [Kansas City, Mo.: Beacon Hill Press, 1973], p. 59).

34. Wynkoop, *Theology of Love*, p. 347.
35. From Mildred Bangs Wynkoop, *A Theology of Love* (Kansas City, Mo.: Beacon Hill Press of Kansas City, 1972). Used by permission. A recent study of biblical theology by three Holiness theologians also emphasizes the theme of love as the center of the experience of sanctification: "In summary, purity as a present quality may be sound and firm, while the love that is thereby set free is open-ended. It can keep on deepening and expanding as long as we continue to grow in our experience and capacity as persons (cf. Col. 3:12-14)" (W. T. Purkiser, Richard S. Taylor, and Willard H. Taylor, *God, Man, & Salvation* [Kansas City, Mo.: Beacon Hill Press, 1977], p. 472, also see ch. 26). See also John E. Hartley and R. Larry Shelton, eds., *An Inquiry Into Soteriology* (Anderson, Ind.: Warner Press, 1981), a collection of essays on biblical theology from Wesleyan perspectives. There is no distinguishing Wesleyan emphases in most of the essays, the major exceptions being the contributions of R. L. Shelton, Bert H. Hall, and Gilbert W. Stafford (the latter two tend to move from Wesleyan convictions to the text). Most of the essays represent general conservative Protestant biblical theology.
36. Snyder, "The Church as Holy and Charismatic," *Wesleyan Theological Journal* 15/2 (Fall 1980): 20, 21.
37. This is evidenced by the recent book *Cry Justice: The Bible on Hunger and Poverty*, ed. Sider (Downers Grove, Ill.: Intervarsity Press, 1980). See also Sider, *Rich Christians in an Age of Hunger* (Downers Grove, Ill.: Intervarsity Press, 1977); *Living More Simply* (Downers Grove, Ill.: Intervarsity Press, 1980).

Chapter 7—British Methodism

1. For an extended discussion of this period, see Thomas A. Langford, *In Search of Foundations: English Theology 1900–1920* (Nashville/New York: Abingdon Press, 1969).
2. John Scott Lidgett, *My Guided Life* (London: Methuen & Co., 1936), pp. 21-22. Lidgett had written a previous autobiography, *Reminiscences* (London: Epworth Press, 1928).
3. *Ibid.*, pp. 72-73.
4. Lidgett, *God and the World* (London: Epworth Press, 1943), p. 9.
5. Lidgett, *Guided Life*, pp. 146-48, 153. In Lidgett, *The Victorian Tradition of Theology* (London: Epworth Press, 1934), which contains the Maurice lectures, he makes his indebtedness to Maurice clear.
6. Lidgett, *The Fatherhood of God in Christian Life and Thought* (Edinburgh: T & T Clark, 1902), p. 292, 287.
7. Quoted in Rupert Davies, ed., *John Scott Lidgett: A Symposium* (London: Epworth Press, 1957), p. 103. In this volume, the essay in this volume by E. Gordon Rupp (pp. 79-106) is the best survey of Lidgett's theology.
8. Lidgett, *Guided Life*, pp. 156-57. That Lidgett was representative of British Methodist thought in this period is reinforced by the work of John

NOTES FOR PAGES 152-164

S. Banks, *A Manual of Christian Doctrine* (London: Charles H. Kelly, 1902). Banks develops a scientific theology that is sensitive to the issues of his day and retains inherited doctrinal categories, but is open to the results of biblical criticism, the tradition of interpretation, and new areas of learning, such as non-Christian religions. The volume is more a survey of alternative positions than a constructive presentation of Banks' own position. The spirit and the range of awareness of theological possibilities, however, are congenial to Lidgett's persuasions.

9. John T. Wilkinson, *Arthur Samuel Peake* (London: Epworth Press, 1971), p. 41.
10. Peake, *The Nature of Scripture* (London: Hodder & Stoughton, 1922), pp. 264-47. For Peake's theological perspective, see *Christianity: Its Nature and Its Truth* (London: Duckworth & Co., 1908).
11. In a lecture on the 75th anniversary of the establishment of the Rylands Chair of Biblical Exegesis, Manchester University, 1979, Professor Morna Hooker commented on Peake's continuing strength.
12. Cf. W. Fiddian Moulton, *William F. Moulton* (London: Isbister, 1899); H. K. Moulton, ed., *James Hope Moulton* (London: Epworth Press, 1963); W. F. Lofthouse et al., *Wilbert F. Howard* (London: Epworth Press, 1954).
13. Cf. Gordon Wakefield, *Robert Newton Flew, 1886–1962* (London: Epworth Press, 1971). Wakefield's discussion of these two major books is particularly helpful. *Nature of the Christian Church* was published by The Methodist Publishing House in 1937.
14. For Taylor's own emphases, see *Jesus and His Sacrifice* (London: Macmillan & Co., 1951), pp. 207-9; *The Atonement in New Testament Teaching* (London: Epworth Press, 1940), pp. 171-72; *Forgiveness and Reconciliation* (London: Macmillan & Co., 1948), pp. 201-202. In a series of public lectures at Drew University, Taylor drew his studies together in *The Cross of Christ (London: Macmillan & Co., 1956), pp. 86-104.*
15. *Howard, Methodism: Its Message for Today* (London: Epworth Press, 1931), p. 41.
16. Baker, *Faith of a Methodist* (Nashville/New York: Abingdon Press, 1958).
17. Davies, *What Methodists Believe* (London: Mowbray & Co., 1976), pp. 105-9.
18. Davies, *Methodism* (Hammondsworth, Middlesex: Penguin Books, 1963, rev. ed. 1976). Of special note is Rupert E. Davies and Gordon Rupp, eds., *History of the Methodist Church in Great Britain*, Vol. 1 (London: Epworth Press, 1965). Davies includes a chapter on Wesley and the entire volume is valuable.
19. On these men, see Paul Sangster, *Doctor Sangster* (London: Epworth Press, 1962); William Purcell, *Portrait of Soper* (London: Mowbray & Co., 1972); A. Kingsley Weatherhead, *Leslie Weatherhead: A Personal Portrait* (Nashville/New York: Abingdon Press, 1975).
20. Vincent, *Christ and Methodism* (London: Epworth Press, 1955), p. 1.
21. *Ibid.*, pp. 65, 70.
22. *Ibid.*, p. 50.
23. Wainwright, *Eucharist and Eschatology* (London: Epworth Press, 1971), p. 6.

24. Wainwright, *Doxology* (London: Epworth Press/New York: Oxford University Press, 1980), pp. 463 (n. 4), 1.
25. Wainwright, "Is Christianity Credible?" *Epworth Review* 7/1 (January 1980):57.
26. Wainwright, *Doxology*, pp. 293, 3, 217.
27. *Ibid.*, pp. 16, 350-51.
28. *Ibid.*, pp. 62, 107.
29. *Ibid.*, pp. 218-19, 252, 250.
30. *Ibid.*, pp. 62, 69, 181, 360. For p. 62, see also "Towards God," *Union Seminary Quarterly Review* 36 (suppl. issue 1981):16.

Chapter 8—Theology of Experience

1. The fact that in 1916 the *Outline of Christian Theology* (New York: Charles Scribner's Sons, 1898) by William Newton Clarke, a Baptist, was adopted as the chief text for the course of study in the church illustrates the open and ecumenical character of Methodist Episcopal theological commitments.
2. Knudson, "Henry Clay Sheldon—Theologian," *Methodist Review* 41 (March 1925):175-92. In 1906 Lynn Harold Hough had indicated the characteristics of the new theological situation: (1) confidence in modern science; (2) critical biblical scholarship; (3) Christian experience; (4) an intensified ethical sense; (5) utilization of psychology in theological interpretation; and (6) an enlarged social vision. Hough advised that each of these characteristics, which was also a part of the general cultural sensibility, must be carefully assessed from a Christian perspective. Interestingly, he speaks against Ritschlianism because it differentiated between Christian and cultural values and consequently failed to challenge the cultural assumptions ("The Present Theological Situation Regarding the Atonement," *Methodist Review* 22 [November 1906]: 929-32).
3. *Ibid.*, p. 179.
4. "Experience" is not understood by twentieth-century American theologians in the classical or British sense (of which David Hulme is a chief representative), which stresses immediate reception of sense data from some "object" that has created a mental or private content in contrast to the external or public world known to science. Rather, Americans utilize a broader notion of experience (deriving from James and Dewey), a notion that is wider and more inclusive and emphasizes experience as a reciprocal affair in organic togetherness. Experience, in this sense, involves an interpretation by an experiencing subject who is not merely receptive; there is a fluidity and continuity of experience which involves a holistic sense of the environment and an intensive reaction of the conscious subject to the experienced world, cf. John E. Smith, *Experience and God* (New York: Oxford University Press, 1968), pp. 173-83.

   In Methodism, James W. Lee, *The Religion of Science* (New York: Fleming H. Revell Co., 1912) expressed the primacy of experience in a singularly clear manner: "To find the meaning of Christianity, therefore, it is not necessary to look outside the confines of human life. Christ introduced and acted in accordance with no principle foreign to man" (p. 283). "As in the first centuries of Christian history, the Church today is being thrown back upon experience as the source of the spiritual life. The final test of Christianity as the religion of science, is the experience of those who amid all the trials and temptations of life have tried it and objectified it in character" (p. 65).

5. Curtis, *The Christian Faith* (New York: Methodist Book Concern, 1905), p. 185. See also Curtis, "The Catechism of Sir Oliver Lodge," *Methodist Review* 24 (September 1907): esp. 681-82. On Curtis, see Charles B. Dalton, "The Theology of Olin Alfred Curtis," *Methodist Review* 37 (November 1921): 891-903; Michael D. Ryan, "The Theology of Olin Curtis," *The Drew Gateway* 33/2 (Winter 1963): 82-90.

6. Curtis, *Christian Faith*, p. 421.

7. George Albert Coe was representative of a different and significant movement within personalistic idealism. Trained at the University of Rochester and Boston University, he was initially influenced by Bowne. As a professor of philosophy at Northwestern University, and of religious education and psychology of religion at Union Theological Seminary and at Teachers College of Columbia University, he became less congenial to the apologetic interest of Bowne's epistemology and metaphysics, and to Bowne's rational as opposed to an empirical psychology. Coe moved toward a more radically liberal position. McMurry S. Richey has insightfuly traced Coe's thought "From Personal Idealism to Personalistic Naturalism," in "Concepts of Man in the Thought of George Albert Coe and William Clayton Bower" (Ph.D. diss., Duke University, 1954). Coe moved from an understanding of God as a presupposition of the cognitive and moral life to God as a postulate, a practical help in living a moral life; to God as an hypothesis, an outcome of moral and religious living (pp. 338-65). He continued to have a personalistic interest, in opposition to John Dewey's antipersonalistic interest: "For me," Coe said, "the spiritual life is identical with life as a person, and fulfillment of the demands of personality is religious" (Ernest J. Chave, "Contributions to Religious Education," *Religious Education* 47 [1952]:74, quoted in Richey, p. 339).

8. Brightman, *An Introduction to Philosophy* (New York: Henry Holt & Co., 1925), p. 385.

9. *Ibid.*, p. 126.

10. *Ibid.*, p. 330.

11. *Ibid.*, p. 329.

12. Brightman, *The Finding of God* (Nashville: Cokesbury Press, 1932), pp. 33, 38, 82.

13. Brightman, *Introduction to Philosophy*, p. 363.

14. Brightman, *Finding of God*, pp. 115, 117-18, 119.

15. Knudson, *The Validity of Religious Experience* (Nashville:Cokesbury Press, 1937), p. 186. Knudson understands this perspective to be characteristic of Wesleyan theology and its chief contribution to Christian theology (p. 212). See also "Methodism," in *An Encyclopedia of Religion*, ed. Ferm Vergilius (New York: Philosophical Library, 1945). Knudson says that the explicit theology of Methodism is centered in the idea of human freedom (and he notes D. D. Whedon as typical of the tradition) and that

the implicit theology of Methodism is to be found in its emphasis upon religious experience.

16. Knudson, *Validity of Religious Experience*, p. 220.
17. *Ibid.*, p. 223.
18. Knudson, *The Doctrine of God* (Nashville: Cokesbury Press, 1930), *The Doctrine of Redemption* (Nashville: Cokesbury Press, 1933). Francis J. McConnell should also be mentioned as an early participant in personalistic theology. McConnell explored the implications of this theological position earlier and was influential upon Knudson. McConnell was a rare combination of preacher, church statesman, and theologian. He was modest about the theological dimension of his work, and in his autobiography does not discuss his theological development, his books, or the maturation of his ideas. His mentor was Bowne, and in *The Divine Immanence*, published the year after Bowne's *The Immanence of God*, McConnell presents the presence of God in nature and in human nature, in Christ, the church, and individuals. But he goes further than Bowne in stressing the centrality and unique status of Jesus Christ. This was a nuanced emphasis, but its impact may be seen in his *Christlike God* (Nashville: Cokesbury Press, 1927) and in the concluding chapters of *Is God Limited?* (Nashville: Cokesbury Press, 1924). McConnell also wrote biographies of Bowne (1929) and Wesley (1939). He influenced other personalistic theologians; at crucial junctures, Knudson quotes McConnell as decisive.
19. Knudson, *Doctrine of God*, pp. 24, 19, cf. also 64.
20. *Ibid.*, pp. 62-63, 65; 174; 187; 186, cf. also 185; 196.
21. *Ibid.*, pp. 204, 370, 426-27.
22. Knudson, *Doctrine of Redemption*, p. 319. This is a consistent emphasis; see also *Doctrine of God*, p. 117, *Validity of Religious Experience*, p. 198.
23. Two other personal idealists need to be recognized. George John Blewett (1873–1912), a Canadian Methodist whose Nathaniel Taylor Lectures of 1910-1911 were published as *The Christian View of the World* (New Haven: Yale University Press, 1912) and reveal a finely trained philosophical mind built especially upon the base of British idealism. Christian consciousness, he argued, provides the foundation for exploring reality as a spiritual society of persons (pp. 11-14). The central chapter contains a discussion of human experience and the Absolute Spirit and concludes with an affirmation of the unity of religion and reason, of the relation of human life to an Absolute Spirit who seeks in persons a fulfillment of himself (pp. 149-65). Unfortunately, Blewett died the same year the book was published.

Among those who took personalism to thoroughgoing conclusions was Ralph Tyler Flewelling, who taught at the University of Southern California and at Claremont. For almost forty years, Flewelling wrote on themes that centered around the nature and possibility of personhood. Possessed of a sensitivity to general literature and a desire to communicate in nontraditional theological style, he explicated an understanding of people that emphasized innate goodness and actualizable goals of self-realization. In *The Reason in Faith* (Nashville: Cokesbury Press, 1924), Flewelling stated a persistent thesis: "The incarnation, then, does not degrade God, but it does lift man to his feet and sets him forth as the crown of evolution. The one creature capable of voluntary oneness with God. The Fatherhood of God is witnessed by the deity of Jesus, of whom man is but the younger brother" (p. 101). This perspective continued throughout his writing. He repeated its essence almost thirty years later in *The Person* ([Los Angeles: W. Ritchie Press, 1952], pp. 312-13).

24. Cf. Rall, "Theology, Empirical and Critical," in *Contemporary American Theology*, 2nd series, ed. Vergilius Ferm (New York: Round Table Press, 1933), pp. 245-76.
25. Rall's comments on Ritschl are found primarily in unpublished notes, used here as presented in W. K. McCutcheon, *Essay in American Theology: The Life and Thought of Harris Franklin Rall* (New York: Philosophical Library, 1973), pp. 21-22.
26. Rall, "The Attitude of the Church Toward New Truth," *The Mid-Year Assembly of the New York East Annual Conference* (Mamaroneck, N.Y.: New York East Conference, October 1902).
27. Rall, *The Christian Faith and Way* (Nashville/New York: Abingdon/Cokesbury Press, 1947), pp. 16-17.
28. Rall, *A Faith for Today* (Nashville:Cokesbury Press, 1936), p. 30.
29. *Ibid.*, p. 48.
30. Rall, *Religion as Salvation* (Nashville/New York: Abingdon/Cokesbury Press, 1953), p. 8.
31. Rall, *Faith for Today*, chs. 6, 7.
32. *Ibid.*, p. 48.
33. McCutcheon, "American Methodist Thought and Theology, 1919-1960," in *The History of American Methodism*, ed. Emory S. Bucke, 3 vols. (Nashville/New York: Abingdon Press, 1964), vol. 3, p. 263. There were others whom Robert E. Chiles mentions in *Theological Transition in American Methodism: 1790-1935*, (Nashville/New York: Abingdon Press, 1965), pp. 69-70, but Faulkner was the significant voice.
34. John Alfred Faulkner, *Modernism and the Christian Faith* (New York: The Methodist Book Concern, 1921).
35. *Ibid.*, pp. 26-27, 53-55.
36. *Ibid.*, pp. 59, 74.
37. *Ibid.*, p. 114.
38. *Ibid.*, p. 160.
39. *Ibid.*, pp. 208-9, 226, 229, 234, 233.
40. *Ibid.*, p. 236.
41. Tillett, *The Paths That Lead to God* (New York: George H. Doran, 1924), p. viii.
42. Tillett, *Personal Salvation* (Nashville: Publishing House, Methodist Episcopal Church, South, 1902).
43. *Ibid.*, pp. 6-7, 10-15, 229, 21-36, 45.
44. *Ibid.*, pp. 105, 117, 134-35.
45. *Ibid.*, pp. 261, 277-87.
46. Tillett, *Paths That Lead to God*, pp. 30, 32-33.
47. *Ibid.*, p. 395.
48. Tillett, *Providence, Prayer, and Power* (Nashville: Cokesbury Press, 1926), p. 60.
49. Tillett, *Paths That Lead to God*, p. 566.

50. Tillett, *The Hand of God in American History* (Nashville: Cokesbury Press, 1923).
51. Rowe, *The Meaning of Methodism* (Nashville: Cokesbury Press, 1930), pp. 13-27.
52. *Ibid.*, p. 112.
53. *Ibid.*, p. 123.
54. Rowe, *Reality In Religion* (Nashville: Cokesbury Press, 1927), p. 189.
55. *Ibid.*, pp. 169, 301.
56. Some of the important work of these men can be briefly indicated: William F. Albright: *The Archeology of Palestine and the Bible* (New York: Fleming H. Revell Co., 1933), *From Stone Age to Christianity* (Baltimore: Johns Hopkins Press, 1940), *New Horizons in Biblical Research* (New York: Oxford University Press, 1966); B. Harvey Branscomb: *The Gospel of Mark* (New York: Harper & Brothers, 1937), *The Teachings of Jesus* (Nashville/New York: Abingdon Cokesbury Press, 1931); Clarence T. Craig: *The Beginning of Christianity* (Nashville: Cokesbury Press, 1943), *Jesus in Our Teaching* (Nashville: Cokesbury Press, 1931); Ernest W. Saunders: *John Celebrates the Gospel* (Nashville/New York: Abingdon Press, 1968), *Jesus in the Gospels* (Englewood Cliffs, N.J.: Prentice-Hall, 1967); Bernard W. Anderson: *Rediscovering the Bible* (New York: Associated Press, 1951), *Understanding the Old Testament* (Englewood Cliffs, N.J.: Prentice-Hall, 1957); D. Moody Smith, *The Composition and Order of the Fourth Gospel* (New Haven: Yale University Press, 1965), with R. A. Spivey, *Anatomy of the New Testament* (New York: Macmillan Publishing Co., 1969, 1974, 1981); Victor Paul Furnish: *Theology and Ethics in Paul* (Nashville/New York: Abingdon Press, 1968), *The Love Commandment in the New Testament* (Nashville/New York: Abingdon Press, 1972). John Knox and Howard Clark Kee might also be mentioned as Methodist scholars, although they later joined other churches.

Chapter 9—Continuity and Change

1. Harkness, *Understanding the Christian Faith* (Nashville/New York: Abingdon/Cokesbury Press, 1947), p. 83.
2. DeWolf, *A Theology of the Living Church* (New York: Harper & Brothers, 1960), p. 13.
3. DeWolf, *Responsible Freedom* (New York: Harper & Row, 1971).
4. Michalson, "The Edwin Lewis Myth," *The Drew Gateway* 30/2 (Winter 1960): 102.
5. Lewis, *A Christian Manifesto* (Nashville: Cokesbury Press, 1934), p. 16. The force of this change can be seen when contrasted to the Christian humanism espoused by Lewis' colleague Lynn Harold Hough.
6. *Ibid.*, pp. 229-41.
7. Ramsdell, *The Christian Perspective* (Nashville/New York: Abingdon Cokesbury Press, 1950), p. 12.
8. *Ibid.*, pp. 9, 10, 33.
9. *Ibid.*, p. 57.
10. *Ibid.*, p. 111, see also 79, 81-93.
11. *Ibid.*, pp. 127, 150-51, see also 142-43.
12. *Ibid.*, p. 194.

13. A perusal of the notes in this volume as well as this short list of recent studies will illustrate the range of interpretation currently active: Franz Hildebrandt, *From Luther to Wesley* (London: Lutterworth Press, 1951); Albert C. Outler, ed., *John Wesley* (New York: Oxford University Press, 1970); Martin Schmidt, *John Wesley: A Theological Biography*, trans. Denis Inman, 3 vols. (Nashville/New York: Abingdon Press, 1962-66).

14. Frank Baker has greatly enriched study of the Wesleys and his work may be found in a number of publications: *Charles Wesley, As Revealed by His Letters* (London: Epworth Press, 1948), *Charles Wesley's Verse, An Introduction* (London: Epworth Press,1964), *John Wesley and the Church of England* (Nashville/New York: Abingdon Press, 1970), *From Wesley to Asbury* (Durham, N.C.: Duke University Press, 1976).

15. A complete bibliography of Outler's writings is found in the *Perkins Journal* 27/3 (Spring, 1974): 42-51.

16. Outler, *Psychotherapy and the Christian Message* (New York: Harper & Brothers, 1954), pp. 45-46.

17. Outler, *Theology in the Wesleyan Spirit* (Nashville: Tidings, 1975), p. 18.

18. *Ibid.*, pp. 84-85.

19. See esp. Outler, *That the World May Believe* (New York: Joint Commission on Education and Cultivation, Board of Missions of The Methodist Church, 1966), pp. xi-96. This book reveals Outler's ecumenical concern and program as do *The Christian Tradition and the Unity We Seek* (New York: Oxford University Press, 1957); *Who Trusts in God* (New York: Oxford University Press, 1968), Outler's most thorough discussion of God's providence; "Scripture, Tradition, and Ecumenism," in *Scripture and Ecumenism*, ed. Leonard J. Swidler (Pittsburgh: Duquesne University Press, 1965).

20. J. Robert Nelson (born 1920) has contributed to interpretation of the nature and meaning of the church and has been active in the ecumenical movement. In *The Realm of Redemption* (London: Lutterworth Press, 1951), he worked through recent biblical and theological studies on the relation of the church to the Holy Spirit, to Christ, and to the Bible; explored the sacramental life of the church and the church as the realm of salvation; and climaxed with an ecumenical and eschatological vision.

21. Here it is necessary to mention David C. Shipley (1907–1977), who, although he wrote little, other than his dissertation on John Fletcher, was a major influence in neo-Wesleyan theology and is remembered by students at Garrett, at Perkins, and at the Methodist Theological School in Ohio as a truly remarkable teacher. A student of the development of Methodist theology, he systematically utilized his historical knowledge, his acuteness for biblical study, and the resources of neo-orthodox theology for constructive purposes. Through his teaching and personal influence he was an important contributor to mid-century Methodist theology. For an appraisal, see Robert E. Cushman, "Theological Reflections on Occasion of the Forthcoming Retirement of a Master Theologian and Teacher—David C. Shipley," *Journal, Methodist Theological School in Ohio* 10/1 (Fall 1971): 2-12; a bibliography of Shipley's works is found on pp. 26-27.

22. Cushman, "The Shape of Christian Faith—A Platform," *The Iliff Review* 13/1 (Winter 1956): 33-34; see also Cushman, *Faith Seeking Understanding* (Durham, N.C.: Duke University Press, 1981), pp. 181-97.

23. Cushman, "Shape of Christian Faith," p. 37.
24. *Ibid.*, p. 36.
25. Cf. Cushman, "A Study of Freedom and Grace," *The Journal of Religion* 25/3 (July 1945):205; also in Cushman, *Faith Seeking Understanding*, pp. 75-102.
26. Cushman, *Therapeia* (Chapel Hill: University of North Carolina, 1958).
27. Cushman, "The Socratic-Platonic Conception of Philosophy as Therapy," *The Duke Divinity School Review* 43/3 (Fall 1978): 160.
28. *Ibid.*, pp. 161-62
29. *Ibid.*, pp. 164, 166, 167.
30. Cushman, "Study of Freedom and Grace," p. 210.
31. For Augustine, see Cushman, *Faith Seeking Understanding*, pp. 3-21.
32. Cushman argues that these theologians have mislocated the miracle of the Incarnation—Bultmann through emphasis upon the eschatological or existential moment of faith; Knox by domiciling the Christ-event in the corporate experience of the believing community; and Tillich by *ecstasis*, see chs. in Cushman, *Faith Seeking Understanding*.
33. *Ibid.*, p. 197.
34. Runyon, ed., *Sanctification and Liberation: Liberation Theologies in Light of the Wesleyan Tradition* (Nashville: Abingdon Press, 1981), pp. 9-48.

Chapter 10—Contemporary Directions

1. Carl Michalson, in *The Drew Gateway* 36/5 (Spring/Summer 1966): 65-69.
2. Godsey, "Thinking the Faith Historically: The Legacy of Carl Michalson," *The Drew Gateway* 36/5 (Spring/Summer 1966): 82.
3. See esp. Michalson, *The Hinge of History: An Existential Approach to the Christian Faith* (New York: Charles Scribner's Sons, 1959); *The Rationality of Faith: An Historical Critique of Theological Reason* (New York: Charles Scribner's Sons, 1963); *Worldly Theology: The Hermeneutical Focus of Theology as History* (New York: Charles Scribner's Sons, 1967). The best introduction to Michalson's work is found in Godsey, "Thinking the Faith Historically," pp. 76-88. See also Charles Courtney, Olin M. Ivey, and Gordon E. Michalson, eds., *Hermeneutics and the Worldliness of Faith*, special edition of *The Drew Gateway* 40/1, 2, 3 (1974-75).
4. Michalson, *Worldly Theology*, chs. 8, 11.
5. Runyon, "Carl Michalson, As a Wesleyan Theologian," *The Drew Gateway* 51, 2 (1980): 2.
6. It is important to mention John D. Godsey (born 1922) as a contributor to theological study in this period. Godsey has taught theology at Drew University and at Wesley Theological Seminary. As an interpreter of contemporary theology, he has made a fine contribution through perceptive and careful study of theologians and of issues that are both basic to and on the cutting edge of present theological activity. See *The Promise of H. Richard Niebuhr* (1970), *The Theology of Dietrich Bonhoeffer* (1960) and *Preface* (Bonhoeffer) (1965), *Karl Barth's Table Talk* (1963).
7. Thomas C. Oden, *Agenda for Theology* (San Francisco: Harper & Row, 1979), pp. 21-24.
8. *Ibid.*, p. 117.
9. *Ibid.*, p. 164, 168, 127-28. In relation to new construction, Theodore

Jennings, Jr. (born 1942), *Introduction to Theology* (Philadelphia: Fortress Press, 1976) is a suggestive interpretation of Christian faith, structured around the themes of imagination and mythos. Locating theological reflection in the human capacity for creating symbols, in actual living faith, and in the context of humanistic studies, Jennings presents Christian theology with a promise for elucidation of the content of the Christian vision.

10. Among other distinctive positions, that of Julian Norris Hartt (born 1922) must be mentioned because of his contribution to philosophical theology. Through his career, which culminated with his teaching at Yale and at the University of Virginia, Hartt has moved between an analysis of American culture in *The Lost Image of Man* (1963) and *A Christian Critique of American Culture* (1967), to philosophical theological themes in *Humanism Versus Theism* (1951) and *Theological Method and Imagination* (1977), to practical implications of theology in *Toward A Theology of Evangelism* (1955). Hartt has explored the foundation and context of theological activity and has been the mentor of several others who continue to contribute to this work.

11. Cone, *Black Theology and Black Power* (New York: Seabury Press, 1969), p. 1.

12. Cone, *A Black Theology of Liberation* (Philadelphia: J. B. Lippincott Co., 1970), p. 17.

13. *Ibid.*, p. 174.

14. Cone, *Black Theology and Black Power*, p. 2.

15. Cone, *Black Theology of Liberation*, p. 181.

16. Cone, *Black Theology and Black Power*, p. 147. See also Cone, "Black Theology and the Black Church: Where Do We Go from Here?" in *Mission Trends, No. 4,* ed. Gerald H. Anderson and Thomas F. Stransky, C.S.F. (New York: Paulist Press/Grand Rapids, Mich.: Wm. B. Eerdmans Publishing Co., 1979), pp. 131-32; *God of the Oppressed* (New York: Seabury Press, 1975).

17. Jones, *Black Awareness: A Theology of Hope* (Nashville/New York: Abingdon Press, 1971), see esp. pp. 63-64.

18. *Ibid.*, pp. 116, 105.

19. *Ibid.*, p. 120.

20. *Ibid.*, p. 129.

21. *Ibid.*, pp. 132, 40.

22. Jones, *Christian Ethics for Black Theology* (New York: Abingdon Press, 1974), pp. 8, 106.

23. See Hartshorne, *Creative Synthesis and Philosophical Method* (LaSalle, Ill.: Open Court Publishing Co., 1970), p. 276.

24. Cobb, *God and the World* (Philadelphia: Westminster Press, 1969), p. 9. In an insightful account of the modern sundering of nature from history and the effort of each alternative (positivism or historicism) to consume the other, ending in dogmatism or nihilism, Cobb speaks for a reuniting of these two realms in a more comprehensive perspective: "The only God we can worship will be the God of *this* world in which nature and history are indissolubly united" ("Towards a Displacement of Historhicism and Positivism," in *Church History in Future Perspective*, ed. Robert Aubert [New York: Herder & Herder, 1970], p. 38). His most systematic

presentation is found in *A Christian Natural Theology: Based on the Thought of* . . . *Whitehead* (Philadelphia: Westminster Press, 1965).

25. Cobb, "A Critical View of Inherited Theology," *The Christian Century* 97/6 (February 20, 1980): 194-97.
26. Ogden, *The Reality of God* (New York: Harper & Row, 1966), pp. 8, 20, see also 9-12.
27. *Ibid.*, p. 37.
28. *Ibid.*, p. 48. It should be noted that Ogden sees his interpretation of God as congenial with Wesley's central understanding, see "Love Unbounded: The Doctrine of God," *The Perkins School of Theology Journal* 19 (Spring 1966): 5-1.
29. Ogden, *Reality of God*, pp. 57-61, 69. See also his statement of his own position in "Faith and Freedom," *The Christian Century* 97/41 (December 17, 1980): 1241-44.
30. Ogden, *Faith and Freedom* (Nashville: Abingdon Press, 1979), pp. 83, 86, 87, 90.
31. *Ibid.*, p. 112.
32. Ogden, *The Point of Christology* (New York: Harper & Row, 1982).
33. See also note 10, Julian N. Hartt.

Chapter 11—Unity in Diversity

1. Wesley, *Sermons*, "On the Catholic Spirit," part ii.
2. Quoted in Frank Baker, *A Charge to Keep* (London: Epworth Press, 1947), p. 95.
3. On early developments, see Paul F. Douglass, *German Methodism* (Cincinnati: Methodist Book Concern, 1939); Carl Witke, *William Nast: Patriarch of German Methodism* (Detroit: Wayne State University Press, 1959). For the history of the Central Conference of central and southern Europe, see Wilhelm Nausner, Vilém Schneeberger, and Edith Varner, *Be Eager to Maintain the Unity of the Spirit Through the Bond of Peace* (Zurich: CVB Buch, 1981); Rolf Knierim, *Entwurf eines Methodistischen Selvstverstandnisses* (Zurich: Christliche Vereinsbuchhandlung, 1960).
4. Sulzberger, *Christliche Glaubenslehre* (Bremen: Verlag des Traktathauses, J. Staiger, 1898), p. 28.
5. See Nuelsen, *Geschichte des Methodismus*, 2 vols. (Bremen: Buchhandlung and Verlag des Traktathauses, 1920), *John William Fletcher, der erste Schweizerische Methodist* (Zurich: Kartoniert, 1929), *Reformation und Methodismus* (Bremen: Verlagshaus der Methodisten Kirche, 1935); Schneeberger, *Theologische Wurzeln des sozialen Akzents bei John Wesley* (Zurich/Stuttgart: Gotthelf Verlag, 1972); Marquardt, *Praxis und Principien der Sozialethik John Wesleys* (Gottingen: Vandenhoeck & Ruprecht, 1977). See also Theophil Funk, *Die Anfange der Laienmitarbeit im Methodismus* (Bremen: Anker-Verlag und Druckerei, 1941); Wilhelm Thomas, *Heiligung im Neuen Testament und bei John Wesley* (Zurich: Christliche Vereinsbuchhandlung, 1965); Jürgen Weissbach, *Der Neue Mensch im theologischen Denken John Wesleys* (Stuttgart: Christliche Verlagshaus, 1970).
6. Theophil Spörri's bibliography is quote long and his work deserves careful and extended study, see *Der Mensch und die frohe Botschaft*, 3 vols.

(Zurich: Christliche Vereinsbuchhandlung, 1939, 1952, 1956); *Masse und Gemeinchaft* (Berlin: Im Furche-Verlag, 1928); *Wir Glauben bekennen Lehren* (Zurich: Verlag Christliche Vereinsbuchhandlung, n.d.); *In der Schule des Leides* (sermons) (Zurich: Gotthelf-Verlag, 1941); *Not und Hilfe* (sermons) (Zurich: Gotthelf-Verlag, 1944); *Alles in Dienste Christi* (studies in II Cor.) (Zurich: Gotthelf-Verlag, 1945); *Die Lehre von der Kirche* (Zurich: Christliche Vereinsbuchhandlung, 1947); *Das Basis des oekumenischen Rates und unser Bekenntnis zur Gottheit Jesus Christi* (Zurich: Christliche Vereinsbuchhandlung, 1949); *Was Bedeutet uns die Christliche Taufe?* (Zurich: Christliche Vereinsbuchhandlung, 1950); *Das Wesentliche Methodistischer* (Zurich: Christliche Vereinsbuchhandlung, 1954).

7. See Lindström, *Wesley and Sanctification* (London: Epworth Press/Stockholm: Nya Bokförlags Aktiebolaget, 1946); Källstad, *John Wesley and the Bible* (Stockholm: Nya Bokförlags Aktiebolaget, 1974); Ole E. Borgen, *John Wesley on the Sacraments* (Nashville/New York: Abingdon Press, 1972); Thor Hall, *The Framework of Faith* (Leiden: E. J. Brill, 1970), *The Future Shape of Preaching* (Philadelphia: Fortress Press, 1971), *The Evolution of Christology* (Nashville: Abingdon Press, 1981). For general coverage, see Bishop Odd Hagen, *Preludes to Methodism in Northern Europe* (Oslo: Norsk Forlagsselskap, 1961).

8. Walter Russell Lambuth (1854–1927) should also be mentioned for his leadership in missions for the Methodist Episcopal Church (MEC), South, during this period. Born in China of missionary parents, Lambeth became a physician, a medical missionary, and in 1894, general secretary of the Board of Missions of the MEC, South. His vision and energy gave impetus to the missionary movement, and he was the author of three books on medical missions.

9. Quoted in Creighton Lacy, *Frank Mason North* (Nashville/New York: Abingdon Press, 1967), p. 69.

10. *Ibid.*, p. 213.

11. The two best sources on Mott are Robert C. Mackie, *Layman Extraordinary: John R. Mott, 1865–1955* (London: Hodder & Stoughton, 1965); C. Howard Hopkins, *John R. Mott, 1865–1955: A Biography* (New York: Oxford University Press, 1979).

12. Among Jones' books which present his theology are *Conversion* (Nashville/New York: Abingdon Press, 1956), *A Song of Ascents* (Nashville/New York: Abingdon Press, 1968), *The Reconstruction of the Church on What Pattern?* (Nashville/New York: Abingdon Press, 1970).

13. Daylan Niles (son of D. T. Niles), "Search for Community: A Preliminary Exploration of the Theology of Daniel T. Niles," privately circulated paper (1977), p. 5.

14. Among Daniel Niles' books which present his thought are *Eternal Life Now: A Presentation of the Christian Faith as an Evangelist Would Present It to a Non-Christian* (Calcutta: YMCA Publishing House, 1946), *The Preacher's Task and the Stone of Stumbling* (London: Lutterworth Press, 1958), *Who Is This Jesus?* (Nashville/New York: Abingdon Press, 1968). Also see Daylan Niles, compiler, *A Testament of Faith* (London: Epworth Press, 1972).

15. Míguez-Bonino, *Christians and Marxists: The Mutual Challenge to Revolution* (Grand Rapids: Wm. B. Eerdmans Publishing Co., 1976). See also Míguez-Bonino, *Doing Theology in a Revolutionary Situation* (Philadelphia: Fortress Press, 1975).
16. Esther Arias and Mortimer Arias, *The Cry of My People* (New York: Friendship Press, 1980), p. 131. These authors deserve to be noted for this clearly written and engaging short history of the development of Latin American liberation theology in the last two decades. Mortimer Arias is a former bishop of the Methodist Church in Bolivia and executive secretary of the Latin American Council of Methodist Churches, in 1979 was a political prisoner of the military rulers of Bolivia, and is now on the faculty of the School of Theology at Claremont. Esther Arias has led a service program for children and is a writer of ability. They represent a direct Methodist involvement in Latin American Christian witness.
17. Nacpil, "The Question of the New Filipino," in *Mission Trends, No. 3*, ed. Gerald H. Anderson and Thomas F. Stransky, C.S.P. (New York: Paulist Press/Grand Rapids: Wm. B. Eerdmans Publishing Co., 1974), p. 28.
18. Nacpil, "A Gospel for the New Filipino," in *Asian Voices in Christian Theology*, ed. Gerald H. Anderson (New York: Orbis Books, 1976), p. 143, also see entire article. Nacpil's work on Niebuhr may be found in Charles Kegley, ed., *Politics, Religion, and Modern Man* (Quezon City: University of Philippines Press, 1969). A New Testament scholar from the Philippines, Daniel C. Arichea (born 1934) has also made significant contributions in the field of biblical translation and as an interpreter of theological issues, see "The Holy Spirit and Ordained Ministry," in *The Holy Spirit*, ed. Dow Kirkpatrick (Nashville: Tidings, 1974).
19. See Dickson, "Continuity and Discontinuity Between the Old Testament and African Life and Thought," in *African Theology En Route*, ed. Kofi Appiah-Kubi and Sergio Torres (New York: Orbis Books, 1979), pp. 95-108.
20. Young, *History and Existential Theology* (Philadelphia: Westminster Press, 1969).
21. Young, *Creator, Creation, and Faith* (Philadelphia: Westminster Press, 1976), pp. 185-86.

Chapter 12—Wesleyan Theology

1. Wesley, *Works*, "At the Foundation of City-Road Chapel," vol. 7, p. 423.
2. Quoted in C. K. Barrett, *The Signs of an Apostle* (London: Epworth Press, 1970), p. 50.
3. Butterfield, *Christianity and History* (London: G. Bell & Sons, 1950), pp. 145-46.
4. Schmidt, "Wesley's Place in Church History," in *The Place of Wesley in the Christian Tradition*, ed. Kenneth E. Rowe (Metuchen, N.J.: Scarecrow Press, 1976), pp. 81, 91.
5. Bishop Wayne E. Clymer, private conversation, October 23, 1978.
6. Albert C. Outler, "Methodism in the World Christian Community," in *Dig or Die*, ed. James S. Udy and Eric G. Clancy (Sydney, Australia: World Methodist Historical Society, Australasian Section, 1981), p. 28.

INDEX

OF NAMES CITED

INDEX

INDEX